The Shade

K.L. Denman

Orca currents

ORCA BOOK PUBLISHERS

Library and Archives Canada Cataloguing in Publication

Denman, K. L., 1957-
The shade / K.L. Denman.
(Orca currents)

ISBN 978-1-55143-933-4 (bound).--ISBN 978-1-55143-931-0 (pbk.)

I. Title. II. Series.
PS8607.E64S53 2008   JC813'.6   C2008-900400-0

First published in the United States, 2008
Library of Congress Control Number: 2008920733

Summary: As if her sister's wedding wasn't enough, now Safira has a ghost to worry about.

Orca Book Publishers is dedicated to preserving the environment and has printed this book on paper certified by the Forest Stewardship Council®.

Orca Book Publishers gratefully acknowledges the support for its publishing programs provided by the following agencies: the Government of Canada through the Canada Book Fund and the Canada Council for the Arts, and the Province of British Columbia through the BC Arts Council and the Book Publishing Tax Credit.

Cover photograph by Getty Images
Author photo by Jasmine Kovac

ORCA BOOK PUBLISHERS
PO Box 5626, Stn. B
Victoria, BC Canada
V8R 6S4

ORCA BOOK PUBLISHERS
PO Box 468
Custer, WA USA
98240-0468

www.orcabook.com
Printed and bound in Canada.

15 14 13 12 • 6 5 4 3

For my sisters, Kendra and Tanya.
Remember Champ and the Ouija?

Life is a mystery,
not a problem to be solved.
—Albert Einstein

Chapter One

I'm wakened by a clanking rattle. It seems to be coming from the washstand. I squint across the dark room, past the other girls snoozing in their bunks. From my upper bunk I have a clear view, but I don't see anything unusual.

And then there's this tingling sense that someone is behind me. I turn slowly and meet the hollow stare of...who?

I've never seen her before. She isn't one of the campers. She isn't a counsellor. She's wearing striped clothing, maybe blue and white. It's too dim to be certain. Her eyes are huge, but they're deeply set and reflect no glimmer of light. Or maybe the fall of jagged dark hair across her forehead shadows them? She looks so sad. So unbearably sad. She's standing near the foot of my bed, her face level with mine, and we gaze at each other. Neither of us speaks.

An instant later, my mind registers this certainty: She is not of this world. My throat constricts, strangling my scream. The choking sound I manage is no more than a whimper. I yank my sleeping bag over my head and hold it tight. Maybe I pant a little in the utter black of my cocoon. What is she doing? The sweat oozing from every pore on my rigid body itches. Has she come closer? I'm suffocating. Has she gone?

I strain to hear something, anything, over the roar of my blood. I wait for a very long time.

When I can no longer bear the swelter of blind sweat and silence, the not knowing, I peek. Carefully. My fingers climb to the edge of the sleeping bag and inch it down past my eyes. I don't see her. I tug the cover down further and suck in a breath of cool air. I lift my head, turn it this way and that. Nothing. I stay like this, wide-eyed and tense, until the rising sun brings light and I can sit up. Everything is perfectly normal. I guess I doze a bit, because the next thing I'm aware of is the bell sounding to wake us. I watch the others get up, yawning and moaning. Who wears striped pyjamas? No one does.

I don't tell anyone at swim camp about her. I'm not exactly close to the other girls. Sure, I've had fun with them, but my dislike of the water has put a fence between us. They are so into it, so focused on improving their strokes. Me? Not.

Eight months ago, I begged my parents to send me to this camp. Swimming was my world. I used to dream about being a dolphin. But a lot can change in eight months. No, that's wrong. A lot can change in a moment. Especially if that moment was devastating. The sort of thing that yanks away your identity.

Back then, my parents came up with the money to pay for camp. When I changed my mind, it turned out they couldn't get a full refund. My dad really wanted me to go, no matter what. He seemed quite sure it would fix things. I couldn't get out of it.

For the first few days, the counsellors were determined to get me to participate. One of them sat with me and talked. "Come on, Safira. If you get in the water and just float, I'll be happy."

I said, "No, thanks. I'm working on my tan."

She asked if I was sick, did I need to talk to the nurse. She asked if there was a problem with the other kids. She asked if I was afraid. I answered no, every time.

I told her, "I just don't feel like it. I hate swimming. It's boring. The smell of chlorine is gross, and it wrecks my hair. I really wish I could have gone to a horse camp, but my parents sent me here."

"Hmm," she said. "I know people who ride horses. They say the best thing to do if you fall off is get right back on. Conquer your fear."

"I'm not afraid, okay? And isn't summer camp supposed to be fun?" I smiled at her. "Don't worry about me.

I'm totally fine just watching and reading a book."

She finally backed off. I guess since I participated in all the other activities, she figured I was all right. Maybe she thought I was a brat, but at least she left me alone.

Anyway. Today is the last day, and everyone is racing around, trying to find their stuff. There's a lot of fake gagging as filthy clothes are dropped into suitcases. By the time my things are packed, the sad girl seems hazy crazy. Nothing more than a bad dream.

When my parents arrive to pick me up, I see an eager light in Dad's eyes. He's smiling so hard his face looks deformed. He hugs me and says, "So? So, how did it go?"

"Good," I say.

"Oh, that's wonderful, honey. Great news! What was your time for the backstroke? Better?"

I don't want to take that light out of his eyes. That light is hope. He's hoping everything is back to the way it was.

Mom cuts in and says, "Do I get a moment here?" She steps close and hugs me. "I missed you, Safira."

Dad keeps grinning. "Yeah, me too. You look good, kid. Let's get your bags into the car and then you can tell us all about it on the drive home."

"Dad, there's nothing to tell. I didn't swim. I had fun doing lots of other stuff. Campfires, games, crafts. But I told you I wouldn't swim. And I didn't."

The light disappears. He looks away. "Oh," he says. And that's it. Oh.

We don't drive home in silence. Mom comes up with nonstop chatter about The Wedding. My sister, Mya, is getting married soon, and it sounds like things are intense. Mom's voice keeps rising as she runs through the list of preparations. "The cake has been ordered.

Mya finally decided on blue for the church decorations. The hair appointments are booked. I've had no luck finding shoes to go with my dress."

On and on she goes. Ribbons, music, flowers, menus…I really don't want to hear it, but it's better than the dead quiet surrounding my father.

Ten minutes after I'm home, I call my best friend. "Hey, Trinity."

"Safira!" she screeches. "You're back! Can you come over? Now?"

"For sure," I say. "At least I think so. I'll ask."

"Tell your mom I have a crisis and I need you."

I have to smile. Trinity is always having a crisis. "Okay, I'll be right there. I've got something to tell you too."

"Yeah? Is it about swimming?"

"As if. I'll tell you when I get there, okay?"

Mom starts to give me guilt about taking off so soon, but Mya saves me. She doesn't do the saving on purpose. It's more like an accidental rescue. We hear her before we see her. She slams through the back door, yelling, "I can't believe we're getting fruitcake! I've realized that fruitcake is just wrong!"

She's clearly having one of her "Mya Mia Moments." She bursts into the kitchen and notices my presence. Sort of. She says, "Hey, Safira. You're back. Was camp fun?"

She doesn't wait for me to answer. She never does. She looks at Mom and says, "So like I was saying, I don't want fruitcake. No way. I want carrot cake."

Dad rolls his eyes. Mom frowns and starts defending fruitcake.

I go to Trinity's.

Chapter Two

Trinity drags me into her room the moment I arrive and closes the door. "Let me look at you," she says. "Hmmm. Yep. You've changed in the past two weeks."

I raise an eyebrow. "It's probably just my tan." I do have an excellent tan.

"Nope," Trinity says, "it's not your tan. It's something else." She tilts her head to one side and taps her cheek with a dainty finger as she studies me. Trinity is a tiny person, though not as short as her Filipino mother. Her personality is not tiny. She reminds me of a hummingbird, a bright lively creature but hardly delicate. She vibrates with energy. That sound hummingbirds make, like the light sabres in *Star Wars* movies, reminds me of Trinity too. She whirs with ideas, sometimes talking so fast everything blurs together.

"Darn it," she says. "I can't put my finger on it. What happened to you, Safira?"

I shake my head. "You first. What's the crisis?"

Trinity's eyes widen. Her voice drops to a whisper. "I got into trouble. Really freaky trouble."

"With who?"

"Not who," she says. "What."

"What?"

"Right. What." Trinity grabs a book from her nightstand and hands it to me. "Look at this."

The book's cover is plain black, no title, no picture. "What is it?" With Trinity, it could be anything.

"I picked it up in the secondhand bookstore. It's sort of occultish."

"Occultish? As in magic or something?" No surprise there. Trinity loves that stuff.

"Not exactly. It tells you how to leave your body."

A shiver snakes through me. I hand the book back. "Are you kidding me?"

"No." She shakes her head. "Trust me, it's for real. I know because I did it."

"You *what*?"

"I did it. And it was terrible, Safira. I went through all the steps, meditating with a candle and stuff, and then...whoosh! There I was, floating around on the ceiling, looking down at myself sitting there."

"No way!"

"Way! But the worst part was that I wanted to get back into my body and I couldn't. I felt like I was going to drift into space or something. I was so scared, you wouldn't believe it."

"Uh, yeah, I believe it. That was a crazy thing to do. So what happened? How did you get back?"

She shrugs. "I don't know. One minute I was panicking, totally desperate, and the next, I was just back. Snap. Thank God."

"Wow. Trinity, I don't think you should do that again."

"Too right I'm not doing it again." She shudders. "I'm going to stick to Tarot cards and spells. And ESP."

I stifle the impulse to roll my eyes. This is one of the things I do and don't like about Trinity. It's fun sometimes to hear her nutty ideas, but other times, I just wish she'd get over it. I am so *not* into that stuff. Except, well, there is that little episode from camp, and I do want Trinity's take on it.

"So what about you?" she asks. "I know something happened. Did you swim?"

I give her a look. "What do you think?"

She sighs. "Sorry. I just thought the camp might have…inspired you."

"It didn't."

"Okay," Trinity says. "So tell me."

"Right." I take a deep breath and I tell her about the striped girl. Trinity listens straight through, her dark eyes widening and narrowing. She makes little gasping sounds here and there.

When I'm done, she wraps her arms around herself and says, "Too cool."

"What? Cool? It wasn't cool, Trinity. It was freakin' scary."

"Yeah, of course. But it's still cool." She gets this wistful look on her face. "I sure wish I could see a ghost."

"Trinity?"

"Yeah?"

"Trust me," I say, "you don't want to see a ghost. If it even *was* a ghost."

"Oh," she says, "it was a ghost all right."

"How do you know?" I ask.

"Because it was classic. See, the thing is, Safira, you handled it all wrong. If *I* had been there, I would have asked her what she wanted."

I raise an eyebrow. "Excuse me? Ask her what she wanted?"

Trinity nods. "Yes. I've researched ghosts. And when they're hanging around like that, it's because they have unfinished business."

"Unfinished business?" I ask. "She didn't have any business with me. I don't even know who she was."

"I didn't say you did. But since you were able to see her manifest, you should have helped her. Find out what she had to say. Maybe she was murdered or something and she wants the murderer caught."

"Jeez," I moan. "Trinity. I was scared, okay? I thought she was going to murder *me*."

Trinity waves a hand. "Don't be silly. How could she do that? Ghosts don't have any substance."

"No? Then how did she make the clanking noise?"

It takes Trinity a minute to answer that one. "Hmm. You don't know for sure *she* made the sound, but if she did, maybe it was through telekinesis?"

"Yeah," I say sarcastically. "Maybe. Look, the other big problem I have with this whole thing is, I don't even believe in life after death."

Trinity gives me a pitying look. "I know," she says. "Maybe that's why you saw her? So you could believe."

I sigh. "Don't you have any other explanation? I mean, even though it didn't feel like a dream, that's probably all it was. We were telling ghost stories at camp—I bet I just imagined it."

More pity from Trinity. "Yeah. And on Tuesdays I'm a tall troll. C'mon, Safira. You wouldn't be so freaked if it was a dream. It happened."

Chapter Three

"You bought *another* dress?" Mom's face has paled to white. Only her nose is bright pink and quivering. This is a face a smart person would run from. Lucky for me she's looking at Mya.

"Mom, please, just chill." Mya rolls her eyes and sighs. "It's no big deal. How am I supposed to know what I'll feel like wearing that day? It's the biggest day of my life. I can't predict my mood ahead of time."

"*Two* wedding dresses?" Mom actually spits when she says "two."

"I don't get your problem. I can return the one I don't wear. It makes perfect sense. One of the dresses is extremely elegant, all smooth and sleek, right? The other one is lacy, with satin and a touch of pink—it's the romantic look." Mya ponders. "Really, I wouldn't mind having a third one, maybe that one with the sheer sleeves, in case it's a bit chilly…"

Mom cuts her off. "A third one? Unbelievable. Mya, are you telling me these dresses fit you perfectly, right off the rack? They don't require any alterations? And you don't feel the slightest degree of guilt for taking advantage of the bridal shop like this?"

"Oh." Mya waves a hand. "I went to a different shop for the second one.

And one of the dresses does fit a bit bigger than the other. But see, that's another factor to consider. What if I gain or lose a few pounds before the wedding? If I only have one dress, it might not fit." Her voice rises. "And then what will I do?"

"Gee," Mom says, "I don't know. Why don't you order doubles of everything? Two bouquets, two limos. Then of course the groom will need two tuxedos, and I'm certain there ought to be at least two reception halls to choose from…"

"Mom." Mya squeezes her eyes shut. "Please. I can't take this stress."

"The problem with you, young lady, is you aren't ready for this. You're only twenty years old. You don't even know who you are. And you're getting married? What a joke!" Mom's hand flies up and covers her mouth. It's like she can't believe she said that. And then her hand falls down and she shrugs. She's not taking it back.

Tears well in Mya's blue eyes, but for once, she doesn't start yelling. Quietly, she says, "Look who's talking. At least I'm not pregnant. And I know who I am all right. I'm the person who can't wait to get out of this joke of a family."

She glares at Mom who glares right back, and I say, "I'm going over to Trinity's."

I don't even know if Mom heard me. There are tears in her eyes now too.

Trinity is happy to see me. "Do you want to go to the beach?" she asks.

"The beach?" I shake my head. "As in, swimming?"

"Okay." She sighs. "Forget I mentioned it. We've got something important to work on anyway. I've been doing some ghost research and

I'm wondering—were there any antiques in your cabin?"

I say, "Huh?"

"You know, old furniture. Like old dressers or mirrors or paintings."

"All that stuff looked old to me." I shrug. "Why do you want to know?"

Trinity frowns. "*All* of it was old? Hmm. See, sometimes the spirit of a person gets attached to a piece of furniture."

I raise my eyebrows. "Really?"

"Yes, really. It could be something the person owned. They stick close to it because it's familiar. Or," she adds, "the item in question had something to do with their death."

"Oh, right." I giggle. "Like a painting fell on their head and killed them?"

Trinity puts her hands on her hips. "It's not funny, Safira! If you would just concentrate for one minute and try to remember any unusual items, we might be able to figure this out."

"Figure what out?" I ask.

She stamps a foot. "Who your ghost is, of course!"

I'm surrounded by crazy people. Everywhere I go, there they are. Trinity is waiting for me to say something. I tell her, "Now that I think about it, the washstand looked totally ancient."

Her eyes light up. "Omigod! That makes perfect sense. She came out of the washstand."

I blink. "Yes, of course. That must be it. She lives in the washstand." Sometimes, it's just easier to go with the flow.

"Excellent." Trinity flits over to her desk and grabs a pen and paper. "Now, describe it."

"Describe what?"

"The washstand, you idiot. What did it look like?"

"Now I'm an idiot?" I ask.

Trinity waves her pen. "Sorry. But please, just try to get into this, will you?"

"Fine. Whatever. It was shaped sort of like a block. It was probably painted white at one time, but it's all dinged up and yellowish now. It has an old sink set in the top and…Jeez, I don't know. It could be in one of the pictures I took. Why don't I check that out?"

Trinity's eyes go round. "For sure," she breathes. "There might even be an aura around it."

"An aura around the washstand?" I can't keep the sarcasm out of my voice.

Trinity's mom chooses that moment to call from the kitchen, "Triniteee! I've made *lumpia*."

"Coming, Mamang," Trinity calls back. She looks at me. "Do you want some *lumpia*?"

When Trinity first asked me that question, about five years ago when we started hanging out, I said no thanks. I mean, *lumpia*? It sounded disgusting. But it turned out Trinity's mom makes fabulous Filipino food, and *lumpia* are yummy deep-fried spring rolls.

"Are you kidding?" I ask.

Her eyes narrow. "Then you're going to show me the picture of the washstand?"

"What is this, blackmail for *lumpia*?"

She tosses down her pen and stands up. "You got it."

I follow Trinity to the kitchen where Mrs. Turner greets me with a hug around my waist. "Ah, Sapira!" Mrs. Turner does not do the letter *F*. "I'm glad you're here. Now hurry up, sit down."

She shoos me to the table, and I grab a chair next to Trinity's five-year-old brother, Kipp. "Hey, cupcake," I say.

He sticks out his tongue and says, "You better watch it. I know Kung Fu."

"No way," I say.

"Wanna bet?" he asks. "I'll show you." He leaps from his chair and strikes a pose. Then his arms fly about like he's fighting off a mad bee attack and he starts throwing out kicks. All the while he yells stuff like, "Hu! Ha! Ga!"

Mrs. Turner watches the performance in silence for about ten seconds. Then she calmly picks him up by the back of his pants and sets him down in his chair. "We do not Kung Pu in the kitchen," she tells him.

Trinity snorts. "No poo of any kind, I hope."

Kipp makes a face at her and then grins fiercely at me. "See?"

"Amazing," I say. I take a bite of *lumpia* and glance at Trinity. She's smiling at her little brother and the smile says it all: she loves him to bits. My sister has never looked at me that way. Never. The lump in my throat has nothing to do with the food.

Chapter Four

When Trinity finds out I have my camp pictures on film that hasn't been developed, she starts moaning. "Film? Why didn't your mom let you take her digital camera?"

"I don't think she trusted me with it. Didn't want to take any chances on it getting broken before the wedding, right? That would be the end of the world."

Trinity snorts. "That bad, eh?"

"Oh, yeah. She also wanted me to test one of those disposable cameras. Mya plans to hand them out to guests at the wedding and have them take candid shots."

"Well then," Trinity says. "How about we get the camera and take it to that one-hour photo place at the drugstore?"

"I guess. I'll have to ask my mom for some money too."

"All right then." Trinity waves a hand. "Let's go."

On the way to my house Trinity starts talking about auras and how she's been trying to see them. "It would be so cool. You can tell how someone is feeling, just by reading their aura."

"Is that right?" I ask.

"Yeah. The book I read says everyone sees auras when they're little. Then for some reason, we grow out of it."

"Uh-huh," I say.

"I think it's true." She gives me a sideways look. "Growing up makes us sort of…dull."

"No way. I can't wait to grow up. Look at Mya. She gets to do whatever she wants."

We've reached my front door and stop there. Trinity says, "Yeah. But is she happy?"

I shrug. "How would I know?"

Trinity narrows her eyes. "You don't know if your sister is happy?"

"Aren't people supposed to be happy when they're getting married?"

Trinity sighs. "I guess. But you should be able to tell."

"Oh, come on," I say. "You know what she's like. She barely notices I'm alive. She hardly ever says two words to me. She's way older than me, right?"

"True." Trinity studies me closely. "But she's still your sister. And she's around."

I shake my head. "She's not around me. She's always been this super-smart, busy person. Always knows what she wants and goes for it. She doesn't have time for me. And when she got engaged last year, I knew that was it for us. We'll never be close."

Trinity pats my arm. "You're like a sister to me, Safira."

I grin and give her a hug. "Thanks. You too. Come on, let's get the film, and I'll see if Mom's around to give me some cash."

We didn't notice the car pulling up to the curb on the street, but the male voice that mocks us is hard to miss. "Aw, isn't that cute. Don't stop on my account, girls."

It's Lino, Mya's jerk of a fiancé. We turn and stare at him. He swaggers up the driveway, his eyes hidden behind a pair of dark shades. His mouth is set in the sneer that is his version of a smile.

And he's wearing his uniform—low-riding black jeans and a white T-shirt.

"What?" he says. "No hug for your new big bro, Safira?" He looks at Trinity. "And you can give some love too, little chickie."

Trinity wrinkles her nose. "I don't think so. Little chickie? Are you for real?"

Lino's sneer is gone, replaced by a blank mask. "Oh, yeah," he says softly. "I'm real all right. Now if you kids don't mind, I'm here to get my *woman*." He shoves past us and opens the door. "Mya?" he yells. "Come on, move it. We got things to do."

And Mya's there in a flash, wrapping her arms around Lino, saying, "Hey, Hon, I'm here. Right where you want me."

"I'd rather you were waiting outside, like your snotty little sister," he growls. He takes hold of Mya's long ponytail and gives it a tug.

Mya startles and says, "Hey!"

Before she can say anything else, he plasters an arm around her. It's an arm that says he's taking what's his. "Come on, Babe," he says. "I'm just playing around. Don't be so touchy." Then he propels her toward his car.

Mya glances back at us, eyes narrowed, one side of her mouth pulled up into something that isn't a smile. I can't read her expression. It's like she's embarrassed, yet she's daring us to notice.

I blurt, "Bye, Mya."

Her smile is real this time. She gives a tiny wave. Then they climb into the car and with the usual squeal of tires, they're gone.

"What a creep." Trinity says.

"Yeah," I agree. And even though it's a warm afternoon, I shiver. "Blech," I add.

"What does she see in him, anyway?"

"You've got me." I walk through the open door and head upstairs to my room. "I'll just grab the film, Trin. Be right back."

The truth is, I need a minute alone. Maybe it's the way I've been raised, in a family that keeps quiet about feelings. Right now my feelings are messed up, and I need a quick review. What happened in the past few minutes? We talked about growing up. I thought about losing Mya. Trinity made me feel better. We were trashed by Lino. There was that thing he did to Mya's hair. What else? The shiver. What *is* that? I've been getting shivers off and on ever since that time in the pool…

"Safira? Is that you?" There's Mom, actually aware of my existence for a change. Okay, so she always was, up until the weird wedding world took hold.

"Yeah, just a minute." I pick up the film, go back downstairs and find Trinity hovering by the front door. "Hey," I say, "come in."

She gives me a faint smile and follows me into the kitchen. Mom is sitting at the table, frowning, as she sorts through a stack of paper. It takes a minute before she looks up. "There you are. And you too, Trinity. How are you?"

"I'm good," Trinity answers. "How are you, Mrs. Nelson?"

Mom shakes her head. "I'm muddled. I'd forgotten how much work a wedding can be. Not that I ever really knew. Mine wasn't exactly a big splash…" Her voice trails away.

Mom doesn't tell the whole story now, but I've heard it many times. Mya had her first "Mia Moment" before Mom and Dad got married. Mom was only twenty, and their wedding was a small celebration. Just family and a few close friends. She says it meant a lot to their parents. She often sighs when she adds that she doesn't regret it, she'd do it again because her and Dad are still in love. There's always the final sigh when she tells us they were very young.

"At least it'll be over soon," Trinity says. "Weekend after next?"

"Oh my Lord," Mom replies, "don't say it like that. Is it so soon? It is, isn't it?"

"Yes, Mom," I say, "it really is. So I should get my camp film developed and make sure it worked, right?"

"Camp film?" You can actually see her mind shifting gears. "Oh, yes, it would be great to see your pictures." She pauses. "Let me see if I have some money."

She digs into her purse, and her brow wrinkles. "Maybe I'll have to go with you so I can put it on my credit card. Ah! Here's a ten. Will that be enough?"

"I don't know," I say. I hate this. It seems like my parents have been broke ever since Mya got engaged.

Mom scrounges in her purse again and pulls out a five. "There. This ought to do it."

Chapter Five

Once we're outside and on our way, I mutter, "Wow. It sure seems like weddings cost a lot."

"I guess." Trinity shrugs. "But if I ever get married, it won't be a big waste."

"As in, you won't marry a loser?" I ask.

"No. Well, yes, that too. But I meant I'd have a green wedding. It's way cooler.

I'd get a previously loved gown. *Everything* would be secondhand. Okay, not the food, of course. And if we got diamonds, I'd make sure they weren't mined by slaves."

Her face goes dreamy. "I'd get married in a woodland garden. Everyone would wear costumes. They'd dress up as fairies or birds or elves. And I'd ask them for gifts like donkeys and goats to be sent to third world families."

"Right," I scoff. "How do you send a donkey halfway around the world?"

Trinity rolls her eyes. "You don't send the actual donkey. You send money to a charity and *they* buy the donkey."

"Oh." I think about this for a minute. "I'd really like to give Mya and Lino an actual donkey."

Trinity bursts out laughing. "That would be hilarious! Do it."

"How about a chicken?"

"Yeah, a chicken too." Trinity starts clucking and I join in.

It's really bad timing for clucking, because we've reached the mall parking lot and suddenly there are people everywhere—including a group of the ultra-popular girls. They look at us with disgust and one of them says, "Wow. You are sooo immature."

I feel my face go red, but Trinity giggles and says, "Lighten up, Nat. Haven't you heard? This is the latest in voice training. It builds vocal range."

Now Nat's face turns red. Everyone knows she's a wannabe famous singer. "You are so full of it, Trinity."

Trinity looks dead serious. I don't know how she does it. "Fine. Don't believe me then. But if I were you, I'd at least check it out." And she flits past them without a second glance.

I follow, hoping my fake show of cool is good enough. I hate getting caught acting like a kid. It's fine when it's just me and Trin, but around those girls…I don't know. Sometimes, I want to *be* those girls.

Once we're safely inside Trinity emits a final cluck, and I'm giggling again. I ask, "Do you think she'll try to find lessons on clucking for voice?"

"Maybe," she says. "For all I know, it's true. Makes sense, don't you think?"

"Absolutely," I say.

We turn in the roll of film and then spend an hour checking out makeup and jewellery. There's a really cute pair of earrings I'd like to get, but there's only enough money left over for a bag of chips. Hopefully, Mom didn't want the change back.

And then we pick up the pictures. Trinity insists we open the envelope as soon as we leave the store. When she finds one with the washstand in the background, she actually stops breathing.

"Look at it!" she gasps. "Omigod! Look!"

Chapter Six

I'm afraid to look at the picture. There will be a ghoul face in the mirror above the washstand. Or a grinning skeleton with its bony finger pointing. Or the sad girl will be standing next to the camp girls, crying.

None of these things are in the picture. There are my pals, showing off their crazy hairstyles, and the washstand behind them. And that's it.

"What?" I ask Trinity. "It was just a hair contest the counsellors put on when it rained one day. Trust me, those girls don't always look like freaks."

"I'm not worried about their hair, Safira. Look at the light behind them. See? It's an aura."

I squint at the picture. There *is* a rather strange glow around the wash-stand. I don't remember noticing it when I was at camp. And then it clicks. "There's a light bulb above the stand. That's all it is."

"You think?" She asks. "Then why is the light brightest down low, instead of over their heads?"

"Then it's the flash from my camera, reflected in the mirror. Come on, Trin, there's a simple explanation for this."

Trinity shakes her head. "I wouldn't be so sure about that. This light doesn't look right. It looks sort of greenish."

"It does?" Again, I examine the picture. She's right; there is a tinge of green in the light. Still. "Look, you can see a bit of the wall there, by the mirror. It's sort of green. That would explain it."

Trinity squints at the strip of wall behind the girls and then plants her hands on her hips. "That is not green. That's more like vomit yellow. Why are you so determined to ignore the evidence?"

Before I can answer, she goes on. "I'll tell you why. You had an experience you can't explain. Since you can't explain it, you want to pretend it didn't happen. It's like what happened to you in the pool. You're not being logical, Safira."

"Oh, really?" I say. "Maybe *you're* the one who's not logical. The pool thing has *nothing* to do with this. And if you showed this picture to anyone who didn't know about the...whatever she was, they wouldn't notice anything funny."

"See?" Trinity says. "You're in denial. You can't even admit you saw a ghost. Hmm. I wonder. You *are* under a fair bit of stress. Tell me, do things around your house go missing? Or do objects go flying around?"

We've reached a bus stop with a bench, and I sit down. I glare at her. "What?"

Trinity sits beside me. "You can tell me the truth. You know you can."

I sigh. "No, Trinity. Objects do not go missing or fly around."

"Good. I had to ask because it occurred to me that you could be dealing with a poltergeist. They cause those sorts of things."

"Jeez, Trinity. Why can't you leave this alone?"

"Why can't you see that you need to do something?" Trinity is practically vibrating. "It's like this. If this girl has been murdered or whatever, and she's come to you for help, how can you turn your back on her?"

I jump to my feet. "Because I don't know what to do about it, that's how. She shouldn't have asked me, okay? Besides, she didn't ask me anything. She just stood there."

"So?" Trinity says. "You can't expect her to talk. I have an idea for that, though. We'll try to contact her with the Ouija Board. And we'll contact the camp and ask them if they know the history of the washstand."

Right. She is so darn loopy, if she wasn't like the sister I wish I had, I'd ditch her so fast..."Whatever. Fine. Can we go home now?"

"Do you want to sleep over tonight so we can try the Ouija?" she asks.

I get that shiver again. "I don't know. I'll have to ask."

Trinity grins. "All right! This is going to be so cool."

I decide I won't ask and tell her my parents said no. Maybe I should start clucking again, because the truth is, I'm scared of Ouija boards. It's not that I believe in them or anything, but why take a chance on something like that?

It turns out that my house is even scarier than the Ouija. When I get home, Mom and Mya are at it again in the kitchen. I take refuge in the living room with Dad.

"How are you doing, Safira?" he asks. But he looks tired, not really interested.

I tell him I'm fine and switch on the TV.

I guess I misjudged him. He switches the TV off and looks at me closely. "No, really. How are you?"

"Really," I say, "I'm fine."

"Good. That's good. And, uh, what about the swim team? Any chance you've changed your mind?"

"No chance," I say.

"Aw, Safira. Are you sure? I know last year was tough for you, but…"

"No, Dad. It's history."

"But…" He doesn't get any further. The volume of the fight in the kitchen just went up about ten decibels.

Mom yells, "First you don't want any children at your wedding. No children, for heaven's sake. A wedding is not a stage production. It's a community celebration, the community of your near and dear ones. Your cousin is so hurt that she can't bring her baby. Worse, you didn't even ask your sister to be a bridesmaid!"

I bite hard on my lower lip and keep listening.

"Mom. You know why I couldn't ask Safira. She would be a junior bridesmaid, and Lino didn't have anyone to be a junior groomsman. End of story."

"Oh, I'm sure you could have found someone, if you'd bothered to try. And now. Now you're saying your best friend is a loser and you don't want her for a bridesmaid either? Think about that, Mya."

Mya screeches back, "Jill doesn't care about me anymore, Mom! She's hardly helping at all. And every time I try to talk to her about the wedding, she changes the subject."

I mutter, "Maybe she's sick to death of it."

Dad gives me a look.

Mya continues. "I asked her to go with me and Lino to check on the guys' suits and she said no. She didn't even have a reason. So when I bugged her some more, she almost started crying and finally said she can't stand Lino. Can you believe that? How can she be my best friend and hate my man?"

"She's not the only one," I say. I catch Dad's eye and see his look is keener now. Thoughtful.

We listen on and hear Mom saying, "Jill's entitled to her opinion, Mya. Just because she doesn't like Lino doesn't mean she doesn't care about you. Please, think about this. Are you really willing to cut her out of your life? She's been a good friend to you for years."

"Some friend," Mya hisses.

Mom's voice softens, but I can still hear her. "Why don't you and Jill go out for coffee? Just the two of you. Try to work it out."

"Lino doesn't want me to see her. I told him what she said and he said to forget her. He said no real friend would hurt my feelings like that."

"Oh," says Mom, "I don't know. Real friends are sometimes the only ones who can tell it like it is. She's never let you down before."

I tune them out and ask Dad, "Would it be okay if I slept over at Trinity's?"

He doesn't answer right away. When he finally does, he says, "So you don't like Lino either?"

I shake my head. And then the *way* he asked this question strikes me as interesting. Is he saying he dislikes Lino? I don't usually ask my parents about their feelings, but this seems like a breakthrough moment. "Dad, how do *you* feel about Lino?"

His mouth presses into a hard line, and I see a tiny muscle twitching in his jaw. But he only says, "Seems like your sister loves him and she's made up her mind. We can accept that or make her a stranger."

"What do you mean?" I ask.

He sighs. "If we refused to go along with this, she might shut us out of her life."

I don't think this would be anything new, at least for me. But before I can ask another question, he adds, "Parents and children don't always agree on what's best. You should understand that, Safira. You know how I feel about your swimming, and yet—"

I cut him off. "Dad. Stop."

His gaze is full of sorrow. "You're such a natural. I know you had that incident, but if you kept trying, you'd get over it."

I turn away from him and mutter, "I don't want to try."

"But, honey…"

"Can we just forget about this? And can I sleep over at Trinity's?"

He rubs his eyes and says, "Fine with me. Go ahead."

Chapter Seven

The only light in Trinity's room comes from the flickering candles. The major smell in the room comes from the incense. "It's all about creating the right atmosphere," she says.

We sit cross-legged on the floor with the Ouija board between us. We poise our fingers on the pointer dealie. Nothing happens. We wait. Nothing happens.

"Trinity?" I whisper.

"Shhh!" she whispers back. "Keep concentrating. Hold the image of the girl in your mind."

My legs are starting to cramp, and I'm trying very hard to *not* think about the girl.

"Picture her hair," Trinity says, "her eyes. Her stripes. Bring all the details back into your mind, Safira."

As she says this stuff, I do see the girl again. My scalp tingles. The hair on the back of my neck quivers. The incense tickles my nose. I sneeze, and the pointer goes flying.

"Jeez, Safira," Trinity grumbles. "Now we'll have to start over."

"Maybe we should take a little break," I say.

"No. We were getting somewhere. I could feel it. Come on, Safira, it's important."

"Fine," I mutter.

"I think we should try asking a question," Trinity says. "Let's see. I know!" She closes her eyes, and in a low voice she asks, "Is the spirit of the girl we seek present?"

The pointer starts to move. Slowly.

"Are you pushing it?" I hiss. "Stop pushing it!"

"I'm not doing anything. Look, I'm barely touching it."

It's true. Her fingers are hardly contacting the pointer. My fingers are almost off it too. The pointer picks up speed and slides directly to the word *YES*.

"Omigod," I breathe.

"She's here." Trinity breathes.

"Now what?" I ask.

Again, Trinity closes her eyes and deepens her voice. "Do you need help?"

The pointer remains in place.

"That must mean yes," Trinity whispers. She's vibrating with excitement as she asks, "Who are you?"

For a second, nothing happens. And then the pointer starts sliding again. It goes to the letter *S*. It pauses, then moves to *I*. Then back to *S*. It takes a short trip to *T*, zips over to *E*, slides to *R*, then back to *S*. And that's it. It has spelled out the word *SISTERS*.

"Wow!" Trinity says. "I've tried this so many times and it never worked."

"It never worked?" I ask.

"Nope. You see how important this must be? And now we know she was likely murdered by her sister!"

I blink at her. "How do we know that? You just asked her who she is, and it spelled sisters. Which, if you ask me, doesn't tell us anything."

"Safira, the Ouija never gives a straight answer. We have to interpret."

"What if we can't?" I ask.

"Please, just be patient. And quiet. You're spoiling the atmosphere. We need to ask more questions." Again with the closed eyes. "Did your sister kill you?"

Nothing happens.

Trinity sighs. "Okay. Wrong question. Let's see. Where did you live?"

Nothing.

"Do you want us to help you?" she asks.

The slider gives a slight jerk and then shuffles to *YES*.

I am totally creeped out. But I ask the next question. "How?" I croak.

The slider trembles, as if it's going to go somewhere, then stops.

"What should we do?" Trinity asks.

Again, nothing.

She tries more questions, but it's obvious the Ouija is done.

Chapter Eight

I never should have gone along with the Ouija idea. I'm having a crisis. I can't explain the appearance of the girl or the actions of a cheap plastic thing sliding around on cardboard. Last year, even before I quit swimming, I decided I didn't believe in anything that couldn't be properly explained. I felt comfortable with this. It made things simple. I'm not a little kid anymore and I figured if there wasn't *proof* for something, then it was no more than a fairy tale.

I dislike having a crisis. Trinity should keep them to herself. Now, she's being freakier than ever. She says, "There's no such thing as proof, Safira. You can't even prove that you're here."

I say, "Get real. Of course I can."

"How?" she says.

I reach over and smack her arm. "There you go. You felt that, didn't you?"

"Hmm," she says. "You think I felt it. Maybe even *I* think I felt it. But the fact is, we could be nothing more than brains in a bottle somewhere. Scientists could be poking these brains with little probes. The probes make the brains believe they have bodies and are walking around doing things. Can you prove you're not a brain in a bottle that's part of some sick experiment?"

"I'm not a brain in a bottle."

"Prove it," she says.

I open my mouth. I close it. I think of lots of things to say, like how I have parents who will swear my mom gave birth to me. But what if I've been programmed to believe that? I smell things. I taste things. I feel and hear and see. But if all of that comes out of my brain, then what? I say, "You are so depressing, you know?"

She grins. "Nope. I don't think I'm a brain in a bottle. I think I'm a soul in a body, creating my life. And my soul will go on from here. It's way better to keep proof in its place. Proof is highly overrated."

"How did you get like this?" I ask.

"Like what?"

I don't know exactly what I mean, but say, "You feel so sure about having a soul."

"I've told you before," she says. "When my Mama was pregnant with me, she visited the Philippines and she touched a faith healer, an *Albularyo*. That made some of the healer's traits rub off on me. It helps me be sure."

She *did* tell me this before. I thought it was so dumb. "Okay," I moan. "Let's say you're right. I did see a ghost. And she needs help." I wave my arms around. "I still don't know how to help her."

"Sisters," Trinity murmurs.

"I know. You think her sister killed her. But what if the Ouija was just messing around with us? What if it heard us talking earlier about being like sisters?"

"Hmm." Trinity's brow wrinkles. "I *guess* that could be it. Or it could be that her sister was murdered too? What we need to find out is if there's a case of death involving sisters."

"How do we do that?"

"Let's start with the washstand," she says. "We'll call the summer camp tomorrow and ask about it. They could pretend to know nothing, so we're going to have to be clever."

"Right," I say. "Clever. Maybe nothing is what it seems. What if we're missing the point of the washstand? What if it's symbolic of, oh, I don't know. Water?"

Trinity stares at me, her brows puckered. "Wow. I never thought of that. Water is so elemental, isn't it? Safira, I think you're going to be really good at this stuff, now that you're allowing yourself to be free."

Enough already. I say, "You know what? I'm starving. Do you think your mom made *lumpia* today?"

"If she did, she probably took it to my Auntie's house. They were going to have a Karaoke night over there."

I feel a little pang of envy. I would never admit this to anyone other than Trinity, but when they do Karaoke here, I love joining in. It's way more fun than the Ouija. "Ice cream?" I ask hopefully.

"Let's check it out," Trinity says.

And after we've polished off a bowl of chocolate ice cream in the kitchen, I feel much better. I even manage to sleep.

First thing in the morning, Trinity starts nagging me to call the camp. Okay, so it isn't first thing in the morning, because we slept until eleven, but it's the first thing we do. She comes up with a plan for being clever about my questions. And then I'm on the phone with the camp director.

"Hello, this is Safira Nelson calling. I was at camp there last week, remember? What? No, I didn't lose anything. I'm just wondering about your, um, washstand."

Trinity is hovering beside me, watching like a beady-eyed hummingbird.

"Yes," I say. "That's right. The washstand in the girl's cabin. Can you tell me anything about it?"

Trinity puts her ear to the phone beside mine, and I miss the camp director's reply.

"Pardon? Did you say you don't know anything about it?"

The camp director asks why I want to know about a darn old washstand.

"Careful!" Trinity hisses.

"Well, you see," I say, "I sort of liked that washstand and I was wondering if I might be able to buy it. But I need to know more details, so I can explain it to my parents."

The director laughs.

"No, seriously," I stammer. "It's really cool. Do you know how old it is, or where it came from?"

The director stops laughing long enough to gasp, "You kids these days!"

I feel offended. I mean, why wouldn't someone want to buy a washstand? It isn't that strange. People are always finding old stuff at yard sales that might seem trashy, but really isn't. "Honest," I say, "I want to explore the history of the washstand."

Right, so maybe that did sound silly. The director goes off in another fit of laughter then finally chokes out, "Thanks for the laugh, dear. Tell you what. If you want that old thing, you just find me a replacement and you can have it." Then she hangs up.

"Hmph!" says Trinity. "She's either very good at hiding what she knows, or she doesn't know a thing."

"My guess is she doesn't know a thing," I say glumly.

"I wonder who owns that camp," Trinity says.

"Oh, no. Uh-uh. Forget it, Trin. I am not going any further with this. Not."

She eyes me. "Fine. I'll take care of the research on that. You focus on staying open to the spirit world. I think that's best. The spirit contacted you, and now that you're finally starting to see past your nose, chances are she'll visit you again."

Isn't that a lovely thought? I can't wait.

Chapter Nine

The days drag on. I've never had such a boring summer and I actually start thinking it would be a good thing to go back to school. That is so not like me. Maybe it's another sign of growing up? Must be a sign of something.

Trinity continues to do research on ghosts, washstands and cases of murder involving sisters. I don't tell her that I now sleep with a night-light on in my room. I don't want any unexpected visitors. When Trinity's mother finds out what she's up to, she freaks.

"Trinity, you are a crazy girl! Don't you remember when my own Mamang, God rest her soul, died last year?"

Trinity says, "How could I forget?"

"Ah!" says Mrs. Turner. "It was dreadpul. I had to sleep in one room with all six of my sisters por protection. Our Mamang was not so nice, huh? We thought she was going to come back and haunt us, she was so miserable. Por a whole week, we did this. You leave the dead alone!"

"Mama," Trinity says, "Lola didn't come back to haunt anyone. Besides, I'm trying to send Safira's ghost on, not bring her back."

Mrs. Turner frowns. She calls Mr. Turner into the kitchen and tries to get him to convince Trinity. Instead, he laughs and puts his arm around Mrs. Turner. "You are so cute. Did I ever tell you how cute you are?" Then he gives her a great big kiss. Trin and I hustle out of there.

"They are so weird," Trinity mutters.

"Um," I say. "Not really."

"Oh, come on, Safira. Look at how *old* they are. Shouldn't they be over that stuff by now?"

She has a point.

As more days trickle past, an awful feeling rumbles in the pit of my stomach and I get the shivers more and more. I've never been the sickly sort, but I start to wonder if there's something seriously wrong with me. Maybe I have a rare form of cancer or some other awful disease? I finally tell Mom about it.

She sighs, pats my arm and says, "We're all feeling nervous, Safira. It's only two more days until the wedding." She looks at me and adds, "Just make sure you get lots of rest and exercise. And don't forget to eat right."

Talk about your standard Mom advice. But since I don't have any better ideas, I follow her advice and go for a run. When I get home, the only one in the house is Mya. As I walk past her room on the way to mine, I notice her door is open. Not normal. Even less normal is the silence. Mya always plays music when she's in her room. I pause at the open door and say, "Hey."

There's the distinct sound of a nose being blown, and a muffled, "What?"

I take a huge risk and step inside. "Are you okay, Mya?"

She's scrunched up on her bed with her back to the door. She says, "Does it look like I'm okay?"

I can't believe she actually said so many words to me. Carefully, I say, "No."

She doesn't answer.

"What's wrong?" I ask.

A huge shuddery sigh comes from the bed. "You wouldn't understand."

"I might," I say. "I could try."

She sits up and squints at me through red puffy eyes. "What the heck. It's this whole deal with Lino and Jill. I mean, I thought we'd worked it out, but Jill's still being strange. And she's been my best friend forever. Like you and Trinity, right?"

I nod.

"But she and Lino hate each other. And it's all so…I don't know. Impossible!"

"I've always liked Jill," I say. "She's nice."

Her dark eyes narrow. Her face pales and her nose turns pink and starts to quiver. Uh-oh. That's the red alert Mom face! The one a smart person avoids. Too late, I realize I should have said I also like Lino. The thing is, I'm too surprised to run. "Do I look like that when I'm mad too?" I ask.

"What?" Mya hisses.

"You look just like Mom right now," I tell her.

Whatever she was going to say is lost. Instead, she leaps from the bed and races to her mirror. "Omigod!" she wails. "I *do* look like her. My nose…!" She places a finger on her nose and squashes it flat, as if she's trying to squeeze out the pink. It doesn't work. When she removes the finger, her nose is pinker than ever.

"Jill always told me I was like her," she moans. "I thought she was just kidding."

"It's not as if you're exactly like Mom," I say. "I mean, there are plenty of ways you're different."

"Too right." she says. Then her expression gets thoughtful. "What do *you* think of Lino?"

Something must be seriously wrong with her. She's asking me this question, like what I say might actually matter? I feel a huge rush of gratitude that is swiftly washed away in a cold bath of confusion. Do I lie and say Lino's great? I want this sisterly moment to continue. I do. But I can't lie that big. I say, "I don't really know him."

Mya stares at me. She blinks. "Right. Thanks for nothing, Safira."

I blurt, "I mean, I wish I did. Because then I'm sure I'd like him."

She allows herself a small smile. "Oh, yeah, you'd like him. Cuz if you *did* know him, you'd see what a sweetie he is. He cares about me so much and he's always talking about how he's going to look after me."

Now I want to say she's old enough to look after herself, but I don't. I just nod.

Mya goes on. "See, if Jill got to know him better, I'm sure she'd like him too.

We just haven't hung out together often enough. Lino always wants me to himself."

"Oh," I say.

She gathers up a section of her hair and studies it. Mya has amazing hair: long, dark, all one even glossy length. Abruptly she says, "I'm going to call Jill right now. I want to get my hair cut for the wedding and I want it to be a surprise for Lino. Maybe Jill will come with me and then we can go for coffee. Like old times."

"Sounds good," I tell her.

And then she turns away, like I just ceased to exist again.

I say, "Catch you later," and slip out of her room. My own room feels safe and, at the same time, boring. I plop onto my bed, stretch out and stare at the ceiling. I should have lied. Then maybe Mya would still be talking to me. Maybe she'd even ask *me* to go with her for the haircut and coffee. I replay the whole scene and get snagged on one thing.

Mya *is* like Mom. She's even getting married at the same age. Not that Lino is anything like Dad. Mom and Dad were both only twenty when they got married; Lino is twenty-six. I picture his face, that chilling blankness he wore when Trinity asked him if he was for real. And I get that shiver again.

Is it true that Mya wants out of our family? Are we really so bad? I don't think so. Okay, Mom and Mya have always fought a lot; it's as if Mya has *always* been fighting to be apart. To be different. Only it seems like there are some things that just can't be wished away, or thought away or even fought away. They're just there, part of who you are. I mean, what do you do about a nose that turns pink when you're mad?

Nothing, I guess.

Obviously, there are some things we *can* change. Mya found plenty. When she graduated from high school, she had big plans to travel and go to university. She got a job and started saving up for a trip to Europe. And then she met Lino and all that changed. Not for the better, so far as I can tell. Does love screw you up like that?

I changed how I felt about swimming. I *did* love it. Dad says it was plain as day when he took me to a toddler class. There was no stopping me. Being in water was like being at home. I swam every chance I got, in pools, lakes, rivers, the ocean. The ocean was the best. It was amazing to be immersed in that huge body of water, to know that it went on, around the earth. It was crazy beautiful, a place of endless possibility.

But last year, it all got twisted. My swim coach pushed me to compete. And practice. And compete. The only place

I ever swam was in a pool, and the stop-watch was always ticking. Time became my enemy. At first, I usually won. But when it stopped being fun I started to lose, lose, lose. I hated it! It wasn't just the losing I hated. I could deal with that. It was more like I'd taken the best part of me and made it into a machine. Dad used to laugh so much when we were just goofing around in the water. The competition took his smiles away too. I wonder if he knows that.

Or was it Mya getting engaged to Lino that took Dad's smile away? I never thought of that before. Now that I know he isn't happy about that, I wonder. It all happened around the same time, didn't it?

I'm confusing myself. Maybe I should call Trinity. What was that smart remark she made about the ghost being like swimming? Something about having experiences I can't explain.

No, I can't explain it, but I do remember every detail. It was the final meet. I qualified since I'd done well early in the season. I told Dad and the coach that I didn't want to go, but they both just basically patted my head and said I'd be fine. I wasn't fine.

It happened during the backstroke race. I was doing okay, keeping up with the others, but on the final turn, when I went under, it felt like I'd never come up again. Through the water, I saw my dad waving me on. I glimpsed my coach yelling from the side. There was the stroke-and-turn judge above me, a watery pillar of detached opinion. And then *I* was detached, from myself. I wanted to take a breath. I wanted to go up, not on. I *needed* to break the surface but my push off the wall sent me deep.

I shouldn't have gone so deep. The world exploded into a thousand crazy colors. The colors swirled around me and wrapped around my legs, my chest and my head. As they closed in and squeezed, intense pain ripped through my brain. Then a cloud of black poured over the colors, the cold black of deep shade, and I was dead.

I wasn't dead. They said it was a panic attack, not too common, but not unheard of. It was nothing to worry about. These things happen.

I haven't been in the water since then. I know everyone thinks I'm scared, but that's not it. It's more like… what? Let's see. Maybe it's like having a dog die and then getting it stuffed and keeping it in the living room? I've heard of people being weird like that. They can't let go of the much-loved dead. If I kept trying to swim, it would be like holding on to something that's dead.

Chapter Ten

Trinity is on the phone. "Safira, you won't believe it! I think I've found our victim."

"Are you serious?" I ask.

"Yes! For real! Can you come over right now?"

I consider this. "You're not saying you've found, like, an actual body, are you?"

Trinity snorts. "No, goof. Well, maybe. But it's buried."

I feel the need for further clarity. "But we're not going to look at this, um, grave or anything, are we?" With Trinity, one needs to be careful.

"It's possible. Some day. Jeez, Safira, right now I just want to show you a newspaper article, okay?"

I sigh with relief. "Okay. I'll be over in a bit."

When I arrive at Trinity's, she's vibrating with excitement. She waves a piece of paper in my face and says, "Read this."

I take the paper, flop down in a chair and read a copy of an old newspaper article.

LOCAL WOMAN KILLED BY FALL FROM WINDOW

Miss Myra Norton, 20 years old, was instantly killed late last evening when she fell from a second-story window of her home. It is believed that she may have been attempting to exit through the bathroom window. Scuff marks on the washstand suggest that she used this as a stepping-off point. Dr. Kandt pronounced her dead at the scene.

—Times Colonist, August 20, 1940.

I look up at Trinity. "So? This doesn't mean anything."

She smiles. "Wanna bet? Check this out." And she sets another piece of paper in my lap.

QUESTIONS ARISE IN YOUNG WOMAN'S DEATH

Miss Sarah Norton, sister of the recently deceased, Myra Norton, was detained by police for questioning. A neighbor reported that she overheard the sisters shouting early on the evening of Myra Norton's death. She said the sisters were arguing over the affections of a young man. Police say this person has also been questioned. While it has not been confirmed, it is thought that Myra was attempting to sneak out of the family home for a clandestine meeting with the young man.

—Times Colonist, August 25, 1940.

Further down the page, there is a third blurb about Myra.

FUNERAL SERVICE HELD, QUESTIONS LINGER

Following a small funeral service, Miss Myra Norton was laid to rest today at Mountain View Cemetery. Earlier reports raised questions regarding the circumstances of her death. However, police say the case has now been closed. A neighbor reports that the family has plans to demolish the old family home. They have stated that the old house holds too many painful memories and they wish to build a modern, one-story house.

—Times Colonist, August 29, 1940.

I drop the paper. Trinity, who has been hovering over me, says, "So? What do you think?"

"Where did you find this?" I ask.

She shrugs. "It took a while, but I just kept searching the net until I found it. Then I printed it out. I think Myra is your ghost."

A prickle runs over my scalp. "It does fit, doesn't it?"

"Too right it fits. We've got sisters, death by falling—or being pushed!—off a washstand. I mean, the family probably sold it when the house was demolished, right? And Myra must have stayed with the washstand!"

"Wow. This is creepy. Now what?"

"Now, we need to use the Ouija to get in touch with her. We'll ask if her sister pushed her out the window. Because if that's what happened we'll have to get the policc to reopen the case."

I glance down at the date on the article. "Um, Trin? This happened a *long* time ago. Even if her sister did it, and even if she's still alive, she would be ancient by now."

"Yeah," Trinity says, "but if Myra needs justice to be at peace, what else can we do?"

"I don't know," I mutter. "Tell her Elvis is dead now too, and if she moves on she might get to meet him?"

"Safira! That's terrible." She pauses for half a second, and then adds, "It's also dumb. Elvis wasn't big until the nineteen-fifties, before Myra's time. Anyway, how can you joke about this?"

I sigh. "I'm not joking. Think about it. Don't you think she's a few bubbles short of a bath? Would *you* hang out in a washstand for almost seventy years?"

Trinity shrugs. "I doubt it. But possibly she injured her head in the fall and she isn't thinking clearly. Or—she was robbed of her one true love and never got to experience the life she was meant to have. That would really mess up her karma. How can we judge? Oh! I almost forgot! There's a picture of her too, on the net. I couldn't get it to print properly, so you need to check it out on the screen."

I follow her to the computer and wait, with a feeling of dread, while she brings up the picture. But the second I see it…

"That's not her. That is *so* not her."

"What?" Trinity screeches. "Are you sure? It must be her. It's too perfect."

"Sorry," I say. "This is not the same girl. Not a chance. The hair, the chin, the nose—nothing like my ghost."

Trinity gives me a sour look. "You don't have to look so happy about it."

I'm not happy. I'm just super-relieved.

Chapter Eleven

I'm wakened by a sharp clatter. And just like that time in the cabin, I'm not just sort of awake—I'm *wide* awake. I grab my sheets, draw them up to my chin and then slowly sit up. Carefully, I examine every inch of my room. The night-light provides enough glow for me to see into each corner. I find nothing unusual. I strain to hear, but there's only silence. I take a deep breath in and let it out slowly. Whew. Probably just a racoon knocking over a garbage can. I lie back.

And then I hear a low moan. Every molecule in my body turns to ice with this certain knowledge: *She's here, in my house*! The moan came from the washroom next to my bedroom. Of course she's in the washroom. Where else would she be? I clutch at my sheets and stare at the door. She could decide to come in here, couldn't she? I switch my stare to the wall. She could come right through the wall, couldn't she? Oh, God. Why me? I hear Trinity's voice in my head saying, "You have to help her, Safira."

I ignore Trinity's voice. I can't do this. Not only that, I can't tell Trinity the ghost came back. She'll never forgive me for being a wimp. I'll have to carry this secret with me to my grave. Argh!

What a thought. I don't want to think about my grave.

I realize I've been holding my breath, and take in a little gulp of air. What was that? Another sound from the bathroom! I hold my breath again. Oh God, oh God, oh God! Do I believe in God? Yes, I do. I mean, if there's a ghost in the bathroom, God must exist too, right? What would God do? I have no idea what God would do.

Another sound! A sob. That was a sob; I know a sob when I hear one. Oh, I am such a coward. That poor girl. Enough already. All I have to do is tell her she made a wrong turn somewhere. Happens all the time. People don't get good directions, and bam, they're lost. I can tell her that. I'll tell her to look for the light. That's it. Dead people are supposed to follow the light.

I place one foot on the floor. I place the other foot. I stand. Step. Step.

I'm doing it. I'm at my door, I'm opening it. I'm in the hall. There's the bathroom door. There it is. It's half closed. I reach for the knob. Pull back. Reach for the knob. Pull back. Listen. Anything?

Nothing.

I'm probably too late. I dawdled, and now she's drifted out into the street. She's going back to her dingy washstand because I took too long. I failed her.

I reach for the knob and this time, I take hold of it. I push the door open. The faint light coming from the window is all there is. I take a deep breath. Shall I switch on the light? No. That would scare her away for sure. I inch forward and poke my head around the door frame.

And there she is! The stripes. The dark jagged hair across her forehead. I feel my mouth open wide, feel a scream gathering, and it takes every ounce of willpower I possess to swallow it back down. I don't quite stifle the scream. A gurgle comes out of my throat. She's standing on the toilet, gazing out the window, and when I gurgle, she turns. The hair shadows her eyes. There's that unbearable sadness. It's her all right. It's…

It's…

"Mya?"

"Leave me alone!"

I sag against the door frame. I feel woozy, like maybe I'm going to faint. I stare at my sister and gasp, "Are you dead?"

"Are you nuts?" Mya asks.

"But…," I stammer. "You…She had…Your hair!"

"I got it cut, remember?" she says. And then a giant tear, glistening like a bead of silver, slides down her cheek.

"And you got a new striped top?" I ask.

"Omigod," she moans. She turns back to the window. Her voice crumbles around a sob as she adds, "Please, Safira. Just leave me alone."

In that moment, when she turns her profile to me again, I see something else. "What happened to you? To your face?"

"Nothing! Crap! Would you just go?"

I go. I climb back into my bed and I lie awake for a long time. I think about a lot of things. I think about calling Trinity, but it's the middle of the night. I'm not even sure I'd know what to say. Mostly I think that tomorrow is the day my sister gets married. At some point, I drift into a half sleep and wake from it, startled. I dreamt that I was trying to dive, but my feet were stuck to the ground.

Chapter Twelve

I wake up early. I peek into Mya's room and once I'm certain that she's really just sleeping, I run to Trinity's house.

Mrs. Turner answers my knock. "Sapira! You are here bright and early. Trinity is still sleeping."

"Do you mind if I go wake her?" I ask.

She grins. "Go ahead. I don't mind one bit. She's the one who may mind, so be carepul."

"I will," I say. But I'm not careful. I jump on Trinity's bed and start shaking her. "Trin! Wake up! Hurry!"

"Wha…? Oh. Go away." She flaps an arm at me and her eyes remain shut.

"I know who she is, Trin. The ghost. Or whatever. I know."

That gets her attention. Both eyes pop open. "What? You do? How? She came back?"

"She was always there," I say.

Trinity rubs her eyes and sits up. "Huh?"

There's no way to explain it, so I just tell her, "It was Mya."

Trinity collapses back onto her pillow. "You're not making any sense."

"I know. But I'm telling you, I saw Mya in the dark last night. She got her hair cut and she was wearing this striped shirt, and it was exactly her."

"And she looked sad?" Trinity asks.

I nod. "Oh, yeah. Really sad."

Trinity is frowning now. "Have you seen Mya yet today?"

"Yup," she said. "I checked on her. She is in bed sleeping."

"Sleeping?" Trinity squints at me. "Ah. Um. I don't know how to put this, exactly. Safira, are you *sure* Mya wasn't dead?"

"I'm sure."

"And," Trinity says carefully, "did this person speak to you?"

"The person this morning or the person last night?" I ask.

She blinks. "Both, I guess."

"The person last night, Mya, yes. She told me to go away. The person this morning, Mya, no. She snored."

"Whew," Trinity sighs. "That's good. At least for the moment."

"Why is it good?" I ask. I have my own reasons for thinking that, but I want to hear Trinity's too.

"Okay, here's the thing. If the person who visited you at camp was Mya, and if you're sure she didn't actually go there in the flesh to play a trick on you…"

"She didn't have that haircut then," I say.

"Right. And your sister isn't exactly the practical joker type, either, is she? Plus you definitely said the camp visitor was not of this world." Trinity pauses. "I'm afraid that only leaves us with one explanation. The Mya at camp was her shade."

"Her what?"

"It had to be her shade. A shade is something like a ghost, only it's really more like a fetch. Like a shadow of the living person." Trinity takes my hand. "The thing is…a shade sometimes appears to a loved one to say goodbye…just before they're about to die."

"Mya's not going to die," I say.

Trinity looks down. "No," she says softly, "you're probably right."

"She's not!" I say. "I'm not going to let her."

"I believe you," Trinity says.

I can see that she doesn't believe me. She looks sadder than Mya. "Listen, Trin. I did a lot of thinking last night. I didn't know that the thing I saw was called a shade. But I know that if it was my sister, she was asking for help. See, there was another thing too. It looked like Mya had a bruise on her face last night."

"So you think the shade was a warning for the bruise?" Trinity gazes at me with pity.

"No. I think that jerk of a boyfriend, Lino, hit her. I think he didn't like her surprise haircut or her going out with her friend, Jill. I think Mya *will* die if she marries him. I'm not going to let that happen."

Trinity stares at me. "You're serious, aren't you? And you know, I think you could be right. Why couldn't a shade appear to ask for help? That makes sense."

"Too right it makes sense. I think it goes even further than that. I think that when Mya appeared at camp, part of her was dying then. Her spirit. You know how horrible she's been with the wedding—a total Bridezilla? And even though she's always argued with Mom, this past while it's been way worse. And she was upset about losing Jill. And she's lost all her dreams. It's all been killing her!"

"Why didn't she just call it off and break up with Lino, then?" Trinity asks.

"Probably because she couldn't do it on her own. Either she was scared or because her spirit was dying, she was weak."

Trinity shakes her head. "Wow. That's amazing. You're amazing."

"I'm amazing?" I ask.

"Yes. You go deep, Safira. That's what I love about you." Then her eyes widen and she screeches, "The wedding is today!"

"I know," I tell her. "So you're coming with me. I've got it all figured out. When they come to that part in the ceremony—the one when they ask if anyone knows a reason why the couple shouldn't get married…"

Trinity jumps in. "You're going to tell them?"

"Yup. That's exactly what I'm going to do. In front of everyone. So that slimeball Lino can't stop me."

"All right, girlfriend." Trinity says. She gets to her feet and stands tall, all five feet two inches of her. "I'll be there to watch your back."

Chapter Thirteen

I look closely at Mya before we leave for the church. There might be a faint mark on her cheek, but it's mostly hidden under a smooth layer of makeup. She looks gorgeous in the elegant gown. I find it interesting that she hasn't chosen the lace and pink ribbon dress. I give her a chance to speak for herself and say, "So, I guess you're not feeling romantic today, Mya?"

She looks at me with dazed eyes and says, "I feel fine, thanks."

I want to answer, "Hello? Anybody home?" but before I can, Mom frowns and tells me to get into my aunt's car. "We'll see you at the church, all right?"

When we get to the church I'm ordered to sit in the family row. Luckily, Trinity is able to slip into the row right behind me. Then we sit there, waiting, for what feels like hours. I start to have doubts. I was so certain that I had it all figured out last night. I was still certain when I explained it to Trinity. But sitting here in the church, with a hundred people all decked out in fancy clothes, I'm not so sure. What if I'm wrong?

I'm wrong. Trinity and all her wacky ideas have made me crazy. Do I really intend to stop a wedding that cost my parents a fortune? Do I really have the courage to stand up in front of all these people and tell them my sister sent her shade so I could save her? They'll probably send an ambulance to save me.

And then Lino slides in. He and his groomsmen emerge from a side door at the front like snakes slithering out from under a rock. Yuck. He's wearing black and his sneer. His sunglasses dangle from his jacket pocket. He takes up his position and stands there like he owns the place. I catch him glancing sideways at one of his pals and rolling his eyes. Oh, yeah, I'm taking that puppy down. I'm right.

The music starts. The minister takes his place. And here come the brides-maids, wafting up the center aisle like flowers on a breeze. They are so pretty. Okay, Jill doesn't look her best; she's not even smiling. And finally, there's Mya, eyes glazed, smile frozen. Dad walks beside her, holding her arm. There's this strange moment when it looks like he's pulling her along. Like she's a little girl who doesn't want to go. I'm right.

The ceremony starts. I glance back at Trinity, and her eyes are enormous. She looks poised for flight as she gives me a fluttery thumbs-up. Right. I can do this. I listen carefully. There are prayers. The minister speaks about love and the meaning of marriage. I wait. Any minute now, he's going to ask that question. My body feels like a thread pulled tight, to the breaking point.

But wait a minute. He's starting the vows. He's got Mya and Lino facing each other. He's saying, "Repeat after me. Do you, Lino…"

"Wait!" I scream. "Stop! You didn't ask if anyone knows a reason why they shouldn't get married. I know a reason."

I don't know how I got here, but I'm standing in front of the minister, right beside my sister. She's staring at me, her face pale with shock—so pale under that makeup that I can see the bruise clearly.

"Look!" I point at her cheek. "He hit her."

"Good heavens...," the minister sputters.

All around me, I hear the rise of voices, the gasps and murmurs, and my mother saying, "Safira! What...?"

I'm aware of Trinity at my side, her hand clasping my arm. There's a blur of black, Lino reaching out, and I shout, "If she marries him, he's going to kill her!"

The black blur connects with my shoulder. I'm shoved hard, sent staggering backward. "You little snot!" Lino roars.

I don't fall. Trinity holds me up. And then my sister's bouquet, her beautiful bouquet of roses is squashed into Lino's chest. Mya holds it there like a shield and screams, "Don't you dare touch my sister!"

She glares at him, face pale, nose pink and quivering. "You! Look at you. What was I thinking?"

"Babe," he says. But it isn't said sweetly. It sounds like a warning.

Mya snorts. "I'm not your babe. You pushed my little *sister*? That's sick."

He raises his hand again, but it goes nowhere. My dad is there, one of the groomsmen too, and Jill pulls Mya out of range. To Lino, Dad says, very softly, "You better go now." For half a second, Lino looks like he's going to argue. But the groomsman tugs on his arm, and Lino leaves. Every eye in the church follows him out the door.

Mom is with us now too, clasping my hand, clasping Mya's. Her voice trembles as she asks, "Did he really hit you?"

In a clear voice she says, "No." She touches the bruise on her cheek. "This is just a giant zit I tried to get rid of and it sort of..." She stops, glances at the watching crowd and gives an embarrassed little shrug. Then she looks at me. "But Safira was right. If I'd married him, I would have died."

Chapter Fourteen

Trinity and I are in my room, replaying every detail of the events at the church. Trinity tells me my nose was bright pink. I'm trying to decide if this makes me happy or not, when Mya and Jill walk in. Wow. They've never visited my room before.

Mya says, "So, Sis. I need to know. How did *you* know?"

"It's like this," I say. I start at the beginning, telling them about Mya's appearance at camp. They're completely stunned, hanging on my every word. It's great.

Trinity jumps in. "Can I tell the next part? Please?"

I nod and Trinity picks up the story. That girl is destined for a career on the stage or maybe in politics. Her performance is incredible. She makes me proud. Mya and Jill are amazed at the amount of research Trinity did. They're speechless over the message of the Ouija. They puzzle over Myra Norton.

"Her name was *Myra*?" Mya asks. "That's freaky."

"Yeah," Jill agrees. "Just take one letter out of the name and you've got Mya. Makes you wonder."

"True," Trinity says, "but it's also a heads up for me. In the realm of the paranormal, coincidence can lead us astray."

I grin at her. "Like auras in pictures? You're saying we can read too much into some things?"

She giggles, then grows serious again. "So maybe there wasn't an aura around the washstand. But there *was* a real mystery. And someone did need your help, right? The main thing is, you figured it out, Safira."

She's right. But at the moment, there's something else I need to figure out. "Mya? What happened to you? With Lino, I mean."

She gazes out the window and shakes her head. "I don't know. I think it's going to take a while to understand. It hurts."

I press on. "Did you love him?"

She nods. "I think I did. But then... it wasn't *right*. At first, he seemed so mysterious. He was such a cool guy, and I was so flattered that he was interested in me. He seemed more exciting than anything I had going on, ever. And then he started to take over, you know? He thought university was a waste of time. He thought Europe was just a bunch of boring old buildings. He wanted me with him, every minute."

She pauses and shakes her head again. "He even had me convinced that my family and friends were a bunch of control freaks. I think that was the weirdest part about it. Every time I told him about something that didn't fit in with the Lino way, he mocked it. He twisted things. I'd feel like what he was saying was wrong, yet I couldn't find the flaw. Like when I got my haircut. He was furious that I hadn't asked him. He said he loved my hair just the way it was and how could I go behind his back like that? Didn't I care how he felt?"

"It's *your* hair," I say.

"I know. He was even angrier that I'd gone with Jill. He said she's the sneaky one. She must have talked me into it because she wants to be in charge of me."

"What?" Jill screeches. "*He* was the control freak."

"Yeah," Mya says softly. "He was. And somewhere along the way, I lost myself. I guess that sounds stupid, but it's as if I was living in his shadow. I didn't know who I was anymore."

"Except Bridezilla?" Trinity asks.

Mya bursts out laughing. "That bad, eh?"

There are nods all around.

"But I still don't get it," I say. "You always seemed strong, Mya. Confident. How could this happen to you?"

She shrugs. "Like I said, I still don't know. It wasn't sudden—it was gradual. And obviously I wasn't as strong as I pretended to be. Mom was right. I wasn't ready. She and Dad tried to talk me out of getting married. Did you know that? But I threw it in their faces, how they'd gotten married young. And of course Lino made sure I saw them as controlling."

I get that shiver. "I hope that never happens to me," I mutter.

Mya looks at me. "Safira, if you're ever in trouble, promise me something."

"What?"

"Promise you'll send me your shade, okay? I'll be there in a heartbeat."

"You'll be scared," I tell her.

"Of you?" she scoffs. "I don't think so."

Chapter Fifteen

A week rolls by, enough time for me to start feeling restless again. It's not exactly boredom. I've been doing a lot of thinking when I'm not listening to Mom and Mya argue. That doesn't happen too often anymore, but they're at it again today.

Mom says, "We don't expect you to pay us back, Mya."

"But I have to," Mya says. "I know it means you'll have to put up with me living at home for a couple more years—"

"Put up with you?" Mom interrupts. "Mya, it's not like that. We just want you to get on with your life, follow those dreams you have."

"First, I need to pay you back," Mya says.

Mom sighs. "We'll work something out. I just hope you can be happy. Be all you can be."

Be happy. Be all you can be. Those words ring and echo and bug me, big time. I'm not really happy. I'm not really unhappy. I have no idea what I can be. I only know something I *can't* be. I do feel good about saving Mya from Lino, but it's not like that's going to happen again. At least, I hope not.

The problem is that I still don't understand some things. And no matter how hard I try to figure out how a shade is possible or how a panic attack can happen, I can't. I'd really like it if things went back to normal. Whatever that is.

I call Trinity and ask her, "What is normal?"

She says, "I'll be right over. We can decide when I get there."

I wait for her in the backyard. It's a warm day, the sun shining in a wide-open blue sky. I lie down on the grass and gaze upward, trying to decide if *I'm* normal. I'm thinking so hard that I don't notice Mya until she speaks.

"Must be a big question," she says.

"What?"

She laughs. "You look like you're trying to figure out quantum physics."

I frown at her. "Huh?"

"Never mind. You'll get to that later." She studies me for a minute. "For now, just enjoy being a kid, okay?"

"Um. Yeah." I return my gaze to the sky. "Now all I need to know is how to do that."

"You used to love swimming," she says.

"Right," I mutter. "I *used* to."

"So," she says, "maybe you just need to try something else."

"Like what?"

She shrugs. "That's for you to figure out. And you will. I need to do the same thing."

This surprises me. "You don't know what you want to do?"

"Nope." She sighs. "I'm not the same person I was. I guess that's life, eh? The only thing you can count on staying the same is that everything changes."

I wrinkle my nose. "That stinks."

"Not really." She smiles. "Look at how great it is that we can talk like this now."

I smile back. "Yeah. That is pretty great."

We sit in silence for a few minutes. Then I blurt, "I just didn't like competing. I still love the water." What is it with this stuff that comes out of nowhere?

She raises an eyebrow. "Yeah? So what are you going to do about it?"

"I don't know. I feel like I let Dad down."

"I know what that's like," she says. "But if you tell him the truth you might be surprised at how cool he can be."

Before I can answer, Trinity flies into the backyard. "Hey, Safira. Hey, Mya. So I figured it out."

Mya and I look at her. In unison, we ask, "What?"

Trinity grins. "There's no such thing as normal."

"Okay," Mya says. "I'll go along with that."

I groan. "No normal. Everything changes."

"For sure," Trinity says. "So, what do you want to do?"

I look at her. I look at Mya. I say, "Let's go for a walk. To the beach."

"All right!" Trinity leans down and grabs my hand. "On your feet, girl, before you change your mind."

I let her pull me up and turn to Mya. She shakes her head. "You two go ahead. I'll catch you later."

We set out walking, but after a few minutes, Trinity says, "Uh, Safira? Can you slow down just a bit?"

"What do you mean?" I ask.

She gives me an eye roll. "You're practically running. What's the rush?"

I glare at her. "I'm not running."

"If you say so," she says.

I mimic the movie version of running in slow motion. "Is this better?"

"Fine with me." She gives me a sideways look. "So. Things seem good with you and Mya."

"Yeah. It's nice." I return the sideways look. "And I figured out something about the shade."

"You did? What?"

"It's sort of hard to put into words," I say. "But I think people in the same family have a special connection. It's like we're tied to each other."

"For sure. My family is like that." Her brow wrinkles. "Do you think it's just being in the same gene pool that makes the connection?"

"No," I say slowly. "I think it's how much we care. I bet if you sent me a shade, I'd notice."

"That's good to know. Thanks!"

"Hey, anytime." I turn to look at her. "But there's something else I figured out. You know how I stopped believing in anything mystical? I thought it was kid stuff? Mya's shade didn't just save her—it saved that part of me too. I believe again. In possibility. And you helped me see that."

Trinity shrieks with delight, "That's awesome, Safira!"

I giggle. "Yeah. *Awe*-some!" With a jolt, I realize my feet have landed on sand. The beach. I look up and feast my eyes on the ocean. "And there's something else. Do you think we can send ourselves a shade?"

Trinity ponders. "Maybe. I mean, we can't really understand how shades work, anyway, can we?"

I keep my gaze fixed on the water. "No. We can't. But we don't need to understand *everything*, do we?"

"Nope," Trinity says. "That would be boring."

The water looks cool, blue. Inviting. There's the sun and sky, the whole world here above. And then there's that watery, shadowy place below: the mysterious world beneath the surface.

Softly, I say, "It really would be boring."

Trinity grins.

"So, why not let some things go?" I kick off my shoes and curl my toes into the soft sand. "And just go for some things?"

As I wade into the water and gather myself for a dive, I'm so happy I start laughing. That's not good because when I dive in, salt water goes up my nose and down my throat. I come up spluttering.

Right. I *do* know a few things about water: There might be undercurrents. Keep trusted companions nearby. Never take it for granted. Always allow for wonder.

I dive again.

Acknowledgments

My gratitude to the generous spirits of the Great Aunties, Diane and Shelley. Very special thanks to Kimm Tarampi for the Filipino flavors, and to Nicole Foulkes for sharing a certain anecdote. The fine work of Melanie Jeffs, Orca Editor, is deeply appreciated too.

Once, long ago, K.L. Denman saw a ghost that was very much like the apparition who appears in this story. Although K.L. never learned the identity of her visitor or the meaning of that strange incident, writing *The Shade* provided her with an enjoyable dip back into the inexplicable. While she hopes never to meet a ghost again, she's delighted that they and many other mysteries exist. She lives and writes in Powell River, British Columbia.

"**F**rank Corso is irresistible,
part Sam Spade, part
Hunter S. Thompson . . . You're in the
hands of a superior storyteller."
Martha C. Lawrence

"**P**lenty of page-turning thrills . . .
G.M. Ford has vaulted into the
forefront of [crime] writers."
<u>Seattle Post-Intelligencer</u>

"<u>**R**ed Tide</u> depicts bioterror attacks
on the Pacific Norhwest, and it does so
in troubling, believable detail . . .
Ford has clearly done his homework.
He pulls no punches . . . Readers
may never travel comfortably again
on any mass-transit system."
<u>San Francisco Chronicle</u>

"**F**ord's intelligently constructed
story . . . gathers momentum like
a runaway monorail car. You simply
can't get off until the ride is over."
<u>Booklist</u> (*Starred Review*)

"**G.M.** Ford is a writer of great
acuity and power . . . The real deal."
Jonathan Kellerman

"**[A]** steely-eyed and speedy series."
<u>Seattle Times</u>

"**F**ord hits the ground running with his
fourth solid Frank Corso novel . . .
Ford creates likable characters,
whom he has the nerve to subject to
the worst, no matter how attached the
reader has become to them . . . [He]
keeps the pace fast and the characters
in the foreground, making this an
entertaining read in a dependable series."
<u>Publishers Weekly</u>

"**C**orso is a terrific, unpredictable
character worth spending time with."
<u>Albany Times-Union</u>

"**S**eattle takes on more
interesting shades from Corso's
darker perspective."
<u>New York Times Book Review</u>

"**T**he action is well-paced . . .
Frank Corso [is] as hard-boiled as his name."
<u>St. Louis Post-Dispatch</u>

"**F**ord is making a deservedly
big splash in the genre's pond."
<u>Minneapolis Star Tribune</u>

BOOKS BY G. M. FORD

The Frank Corso Series
NO MAN'S LAND
RED TIDE
A BLIND EYE
BLACK RIVER
FURY

The Leo Waterman Series
THE DEADER THE BETTER
LAST DITCH
SLOW BURN
THE BUM'S RUSH
CAST IN STONE
WHO IN HELL IS WANDA FUCA?

RED TIDE

G.M. FORD

AVON BOOKS
An Imprint of HarperCollinsPublishers

AVON BOOKS
An Imprint of HarperCollins*Publishers*
10 East 53rd Street
New York, New York 10022-5299

Copyright © 2004 by G.M. Ford
Excerpt from *No Man's Land* copyright © 2005 by G.M. Ford
Author photograph by Skye Moody
ISBN: 0-06-055481-9
www.avonbooks.com

First Avon Books paperback printing: June 2005
First William Morrow hardcover printing: July 2004

Avon Trademark Reg. U.S. Pat. Off. and in Other Countries, Marca Registrada, Hecho en U.S.A.
HarperCollins ® is a trademark of HarperCollins Publishers Inc.

Printed in the U.S.A.

10 9 8 7 6 5 4 3 2 1

To Kathy Ann and those little white shoes.
Now and Forever.
—GMF

RED
TIDE

1

"*The native son is missing.*"

"*Missing how?*"

"*Packed his gear and drove off in the van.*"

For thirty seconds the only sound on the line was static.

"*He was always the weak link.*"

"*A weak link with a personal ax to grind.*"

"*They all have an ax to grind. That's why they were chosen.*"

"*We were hoping his local knowledge would be of use.*"

"*It was. The house is perfect.*"

"*He was always a loose cannon.*"

"*We knew that going in.*"

"*Yes, we did.*"

"*Should we abort?*"

He thought about it. "*No way he goes to the authorities.*"

"*The authorities are not what he has in mind.*"

Something in the tone served as an alert. "*Is there a problem?*"

"*He took the rest of the accelerated material.*"

A longer silence ensued.

"Could have been worse, I suppose."

"Yeah, he could have taken the other."

"And we'd be booking flights to the Falklands."

A dry cough scratched the silence.

"Can you find him?"

"I put a transponder under the front seat."

"A judicious move."

"I'm an untrusting man."

"Find him then . . . and see to it he's not going to be a problem."

"The others say he was getting crazy. Wanted to start things going right now. Didn't want to wait anymore."

"Find him before he does something stupid."

2

The last moments of Carson Moody's life were silent. Surely, other conversations must have swirled about him in those final minutes. It was, after all, rush hour and the bus was full, but, as he so often did in public, Carson Moody had tuned it all out. His full lips moved as he listened to his inner voice run down the dessert column of the Alexis Hotel's room service menu. He'd already settled on the Veal Picatta entree and was debating the wisdom of finishing with a nice crème brûlée when the gruff voice came rattling out of the overhead speaker. "Pioneer Square Station," the bus driver rasped.

Pulled from his gastronomic ruminations, Moody reached between his legs, slipped his fingers over the handle of his briefcase and lifted it into his lap. As the bus silently slid past the white tile walls, he turned his eyes toward the window. His distracted gaze ran over the string of bodies standing in knots along the bus tunnel's northbound concourse. He was still staring at this random assemblage of humanity when, as often happened in his pensive moments, he heard his mother's voice reciting one of the hundreds of homilies by which he primarily remembered her. "If you're going to Rome, you might as well see the Pope," he heard her say and smiled. It was settled then. Definitely the crème brûlée. He stifled an inner chuckle. Couldn't tell Wendy about it though. Oh, no. Since last May, when he'd been diagnosed with diabetes, she'd become the food police. Ever vigilant. No excuses. No . . . the crème brûlée was most certainly destined to remain his little secret.

Carson Moody got to his feet as the bus approached the center of the station. He used his free hand to smooth his overcoat. Satisfied with his appearance, he straightened his shoulders and turned his attention to the automatic doors directly across the aisle from his seat. Staring through the door's plastic ovals, his eyes were drawn to an elderly couple in bright black and yellow ski parkas. He watched as they hurried across the floor, toward the open mouth of the elevator. The old man raised a hand and mouthed a plea at the thirty-something guy standing inside.

Moody watched as the younger man reached out and pushed a button. Quite naturally, he assumed the young fellow was holding the doors open for the couple, a misconception which perhaps explained why he went slack-jawed when the sliding doors snapped shut and the green light began to rise.

As the bus slid along, Moody was forced to turn his head and watch the unfolding scene through the bus's dirty back window. Watch the old folks shuffle to a stop. Watch the woman bring her hands to her hips and say something to the man. And then watch the old guy shake his tousled head in disgusted disbelief.

He was still watching the pair when he caught sight of a puff of smoke. Not smoke exactly. Something thicker. More substantial. In the artificial light, it looked for a moment like his boyhood in Iowa, when the afternoon breeze rustled the late summer dandelions and filled the air with squadrons of tiny white parachutes.

Although Moody didn't personally hear a noise, it was plain to him that whatever had launched the smoke must have made a sound of some sort. Everyone on the platform stiffened for an instant and then turned toward the spiraling cloud of white. Hands rose to throats. People pointed. Forty yards down the platform, the old man seemed to wobble on his feet. "Some damn fool with a firecracker," Carson Moody thought to himself.

The bus hissed to a stop. Moody collected his thoughts, picked his way carefully down the trio of stairs and stepped out onto the platform. To his right, the crowd milled around, staring upward at the rapidly dissipating cloud. The elderly couple were screened from his view by an uneasy wall of humanity. Carson Moody surveyed the scene for a full minute before striding off in the opposite direction, toward the long escalator at the south end of the station and the mezzanine above.

He hadn't walked more than thirty feet before he suddenly felt a dry patch at the back of his throat. Almost as if someone had affixed a postage stamp to his tonsils. He hawked twice and tried to swallow. When his efforts failed . . . when, in fact, his entire throat suddenly felt constricted and inflamed, he began to conjure more dire possibilities. Wondering first if he weren't perhaps coming down with a cold, or worse yet . . . the flu . . . or . . . even . . . God forbid . . . he wondered if perhaps he hadn't contracted this most recent strain of flu, which, if the media were to be believed, presently ravaged the country.

He gathered himself and managed another half a dozen steps toward the escalator before stopping again. The roots of his teeth had begun to throb, as if they had suddenly become loose and were about to fall from his gums. He brought a hand to his lips. Or at least that was the plan. Instead of reaching its intended destination, his hand bounced off his forehead and then flopped back to his side, like a fish dying on a riverbank.

His muscles felt rubbery and barely under control. Certain that his distress must be obvious to his fellow travelers, he turned back toward the station, only to find that no one was looking his way. That, in fact, everyone in view seemed to be suffering something quite similar to his present malady. He blinked his eyes several times, and then shook his head, but the scene remained the same.

Several people had fallen down and now writhed about on the white marble floor, legs scissoring, arms flapping as muscle contractions propelled them in smooth stone circles. Closest to him, a Hispanic woman, her face fire engine red, had dropped to one knee as she tended to her spasming daughter. Half a football field away, the black and yellow ski parkas lay silent and still. Closer, the driver of his bus sat . . . head thrown back . . . mouth agape . . . staring at the ceiling of his bus. A river of blood poured from the man's mouth, down over his chin and onto his crisp blue shirt.

Carson Moody coughed heavily. He felt something thick and warm in his mouth . . . thought to reach for it and then changed his mind, instead turning and lurching toward the escalator, staggering toward the silver salvation and the light at the top of the stairs.

As he moved forward, he felt as if liquid were shifting in his innards, almost as if he had a bucket of water in his chest, slopping back and forth as he made his unsteady way, shuffling his feet in the last yards before grabbing the moving handrail, allowing the black plastic to jerk him forward onto the escalator, where he wobbled but kept his feet as the soundless machinery carried him upward, above the level of the platform, where his backward glance caught no movement at all, only stillness, dotted here and there with uneven patches of red. He turned away. Looked upward.

He was trying to feel the light on his face and wondering about the red patches when the shifting ocean in his chest dragged him to his knees. His trembling fingers lost their grip on the briefcase, which tumbled end-over-end down the moving stairs toward the mother and child, still and silent in the quavering red spotlight.

He forced his gaze upward again. Out over the expanse of the bus tunnel. Nothing moved but his eyes, which, for unknown reasons, proved incapable of coming to rest on any single scene, but instead rolled relentlessly from body to body, rolled along the walls and over the ceiling to the pair of buses standing idle on the tracks, rolling from one abhorrent picture to another as if, by constant movement, his brain could avoid processing the details of the carnage.

His arm gave way. He felt the ribbed metal of the stair against his cheek, felt the machinery in its guts as it carried him upward toward the bright light at the top of the stairs. He willed himself to reach out for the glow, but was unable to summon the strength. He felt a need to say something but his mouth was full of soup.

He lay with his body wedged across the electric treads at such an ungainly angle that the escalator was unable to push him off onto the floor when he reached the top. Instead, he found himself paralyzed, his unmoving form undulating above the steel steps as they sank in upon themselves and disappeared beneath his body, leaving only a series of bright clicks to drum his passing, as each succeeding stair clipped the underside of his jaw and clicked his teeth together . . . over and over . . . click after click after click . . . like the rhythmic rolling of bones. He closed his eyes, took a final shuddering breath and, with a sound not unlike a child's rattle, died there on the moving metal stairway.

3

When the hand grasped her elbow, she twitched at the touch, caught her breath and aimed an icy stare down at her arm. She'd seen him many times before but could never recall his name. Always at some artsy-fartsy social function or other. Invariably, he came over to chat, like they were long-lost friends or something. Worse yet, he not only recalled her name but also remembered whatever it was they'd talked about the last time, almost like the previous season's inanities were part of an ongoing dialogue to which they alone were privy. A wave of musky fragrance arrived a moment later, as if his cologne had followed him across the room like a stray cat. He gave her elbow a second little squeeze and treated her to a baby grand worth of teeth. "It's fabu, darling. Absolutely fabu." He slid the hand up to her shoulder and began to gently knead her flesh.

"I told you so," he said knowingly. "Remember . . . I told you so."

She didn't remember and had no idea what he was talking about.

He was late-forty-something and quite obviously

had spent more time primping for the evening's events than she had. Perfect gray suit and hair. Custom-made shirt. Cufflinks no less. Probably had his tootsies pedicured inside the tasseled Bally loafers. Very slick. Very money. Very annoying.

Meg Dougherty mustered a tight smile. "Thanks," she said. For the umpteenth time in the past hour, a sigh escaped from her chest. She caught herself. Made a rueful face. "I guess I'm a little nervous," she offered.

He reproached her with a scoff. "Don't be silly. You're the star, my dear." He wagged a reminding finger. "As I predicted," he intoned. Having made his point, he used the finger to point along the length of the nearest wall. "Look at all the red dots. Looks like the show's got measles or something." He flashed another toothy grimace and laughed at his own little joke.

He was referring to the little red stickers used by the Cecil Taylor Gallery to denote items which had been sold. Whatshisname was right. Fully two-thirds of her photographs were sporting little red dots in the lower right-hand corners. For some reason, the sight failed to cheer her.

She threw a glance over the man's shoulder. To the far side of the room where Corso stood alone . . . looking her way. He could sense her discomfort, and found it amusing . . . caught in the act, he swallowed a smile and looked down into his wineglass.

She heard her name being called. "Meg. Meg," the insistent voice repeated. She peered out over the sea of heads. There was no mistaking Cecil Taylor, resplendent in a gold brocade caftan, winding his way through the crowd with a flourish denied all but the most unrepentant drag queens. As he moved, his pear-shaped body seemed to take on a life of its own, rippling and rolling this way and that beneath the flowing folds of fabric, coming fully to rest a second or two after his feet slid to a stop at her side. He smelled of cognac and baby powder.

"I've got some patrons who are just dying to meet you," he announced.

Before she could respond, he took notice of the man with his hand on Dougherty's shoulder. "Ah . . . Michael. I'm so sorry to have to pull her away from you, but . . ."

Reluctantly, the hand left her shoulder. "No problem at all, Cecil," the guy said. "I understand. Business always comes first."

Cecil Taylor rearranged his agile features into an understanding face. "A regrettable factoid of the trade, I'm afraid."

Using her other arm for leverage, Taylor began to move Meg Dougherty toward the north side of the room, where the collection of art enthusiasts was a bit thinner and the roar of conversation a bit dimmer. They allowed the crowd to wash their footsteps and then stopped and watched the other man make his way to the wine bar by the window.

"You looked like you needed a rescue," Taylor said.

She nodded wearily. "Thanks."

"The least I could do," he said. "Michael can be quite a bore."

"I can *never* remember that man's name."

"Michael Marton."

"He a member of the Arts Commission or something? I see him at nearly every opening I go to."

"If you went to more events, you'd see him more often. Michael lets no opening go unattended." His lip began to curl. "Never buys a piece either." He waved a dismissive hand. "Just another little man with too much money and not enough to occupy his time." He anticipated her next question. "His grand-daddy made a bundle in sand and gravel down in Portland and, as far as I've heard, nobody in the family has done much of anything useful since the interest began to accrue." He looked across the room toward Corso. "Quite the opposite of your famous friend Mr. Corso there."

Dougherty glanced at Corso, who now stood with his back to the room, staring out through the drizzle onto First Avenue.

"Amazing how he commands a room by ignoring it," Cecil Taylor observed. The sound of his own words caused him to flinch slightly. He looked down at his sandals. When he looked up Dougherty was regarding him in amusement. He chuckled. "It's those big strong silent types. The ones with all that hurt locked up inside. Always bring out the bitch in me."

Dougherty heaved another sigh. "I shouldn't have badgered him into coming," she said. "He hates this kind of thing."

As if on cue, Corso turned back to face the room. His eyes found Dougherty's. She shivered as a finger of electricity coursed down her spine. From fifty feet away, she could feel the icy, silent space at the center of him and again wondered at his ability to be alone in a roomful of people. His need to stay disconnected from his fellow creatures in the very way they strove so insistently to be connected to one another. She turned her eyes away and then shivered again.

Cecil Taylor cleared his throat and changed the subject. "Well, my dear . . . it's official. You're a hit. By the time the papers make the streets in the morning you'll be the darling of the Northwest art scene once again."

She cast him a skeptical glance.

"Pleeeeease," he insisted. "Look around you. These people are in awe of you . . . of your talent. The show's going to be completely sold out by the end of the week." He patted her arm. "It doesn't get any better than this, my dear. I'd suggest you wallow in it while you have the chance." He gave her a wink. "As you, above all people, know so well . . . fame is fleeting."

Something back over her shoulder caught his eye. She turned that way. Cecil's partner Maury Caulkin waved a diffident hand. "Seems I'm needed," Cecil said with a smile. He excused himself and started for the back of the room. Glad-handing as he went along, he left no hand unshaken, no elbow unfondled, no smile unreturned.

Dougherty watched for a moment and then started across the room toward Corso. She watched as a woman in a red sweater said something to him. Saw Corso step aside, allowing her to retrieve a pair of coats from the antique rack behind the door. The man she was with hung his black raincoat from the crook of his arm and then helped her into her gray wool coat. "Great stuff," she heard the man say.

"Wonderful."

"She finds life in things . . . you know . . . you normally . . . wouldn't . . ."

She shrugged herself into her coat. "Some people just have the eye."

"I feel like I've seen her before somewhere." He waved his keys. "Maybe one of Todd's pool parties or something."

"In the papers, silly," his companion said.

The man suddenly noticed Dougherty's approach, closed his mouth and stood at attention. He cleared his throat once and then again . . . louder.

Busy with her purse and gloves, his companion failed to pick up on the distress signals. "Her boyfriend doped her up and tattooed her all over. Remember?"

The man didn't respond.

"Guy looked like Billy Idol," she went on.

"Uh-huh," he mumbled.

"They say she's got some really bizarre stuff tattooed on her. You know what I heard? I heard . . . she's got . . ."

Finally, she glanced up at his face and got the message. She looked around; the sight of Dougherty standing so close stopped the breath in her throat. "Oh," she began, "I didn't realize . . . I . . ." A pair of red spots appeared on her cheeks. "I mean . . ." she stammered. The air was suddenly thick.

The guy recovered first, gave a couple of uncomfortable nods, pulled open the door and ushered his stiff-legged companion outside. Meg watched as they hurried away, chattering between themselves and casting furtive glances over their shoulders as they hurried down the sidewalk. "Loose lips sink ships," Corso said.

Dougherty took the final three steps to his side, looped her arm through his and leaned her head on his shoulder.

"I probably should have tried to make them feel better," she said.

"Why would you want to do a thing like that?"

"Cause it's what people do when other people are embarrassed."

"Funny. I always figured they just gloated and thanked their lucky stars it wasn't them with the mouthful of foot."

"You always think the worst of people."

"And they never let me down."

She stepped back a pace and looked up into his cold blue eyes. "You can go," she said. "I know these things drive you crazy."

"And miss your moment of triumph? You gotta be crazy."

She made a rude noise with her lips.

His eyes got serious. "Don't be snatching defeat from the jaws of victory," he said. "You're knocking 'em dead here tonight. You've waited a long time for this. Worked real hard. Enjoy it while you can."

Another sigh escaped. "That's what Cecil said."

"Cecil was right."

She let go of his arm. Shrugged. "It just doesn't feel like I thought it would."

"Things never do."

Before Dougherty could respond, the tinkle of a bell drew Corso's attention toward the door. He put his hand around Dougherty's waist and pulled her aside as a pair of Seattle police officers pushed their way into the room. He sipped at his wine, watched one of the cops lean over and speak to a woman in a green sequined dress who stood just inside the door. She moved her wineglass to her left hand and waggled a long manicured finger out over the crowd, toward Cecil Taylor, now entertaining the multitudes along the back wall. The woman said something, but, by then, the cops had begun to elbow their way through the crowd, showing considerably less finesse than was usually exhibited at gallery openings, thus leaving a trail of wrinkled brows and jostled drinks as they forced their way toward the rear of the room.

Something in the way they moved stiffened Corso's spine.

Dougherty felt the sudden tension in his arm. "What?" she said.

He inclined his head toward the back of the room where the taller of the two officers leaned over and whispered something into Cecil Taylor's ear. The roiling din of conversation prevented them from hearing what was said, but whatever it was most certainly pissed Taylor off. His diffuse features gathered themselves in the center of his round face before the cop was through talking. His jaw was set like a bass. He snapped a response. Then another, before chopping the air with the edge of his hand in a gesture of finality. The cop held up a hand of his own . . . fingers spread, as if to indicate five of something.

An older woman in a shiny black dress swooshed up to Dougherty.

"This is wonderful work, my dear."

"Thank you so much," Dougherty said.

"You should be so proud of yourself. I've never seen—"

Ding. Ding. Ding. Cecil Taylor was tapping the rim of a glass with a spoon. The woman scowled and sought the source of the noise.

"People . . . people," Cecil Taylor shouted. *Ding. Ding. Ding.*

Slowly . . . in stages . . . the crowd noise began to diminish. *Ding. Ding. Ding.* "People. Please."

The room fell silent. "Apparently there's been some sort of . . ."—he looked over at the cop—"some sort of toxic spill or something in the neighborhood. It seems we're going to have to evacuate the building immediately." His tone suggested it was the most ridiculous thing he'd ever heard. "These gentlemen . . ."—he threw a glare at the pair of cops—"insist that we be out of here in the next five minutes." He set the glass and spoon down and raised his upturned palms to shoulder height. At that point the whispering cop took over.

"When you leave the building, please move south. Down toward the stadiums. The area between Cherry and King Streets has been cordoned off. Transportation is available at Safeco Field."

"My car—" someone in the crowd began. The cop waved him off. "If your car is parked between Cherry and King . . . from the waterfront to Fourth Avenue, you're going to have to find some other way home tonight."

A flurry of protests and questions filled the air. The cop shouted them down. "Move, people," he yelled. "Let's go. MOVE."

Slowly, one and two at a time, the crowd began to head for the door.

Cecil Taylor stood in the opening alternately offering agonized apologies and casting scowls at the cops, who continued shaking their heads at shouted questions and herding the disgruntled patrons like sheep.

As the final guest disappeared into the darkness, Taylor turned to the cops. "I know Chief Dobson personally," he was saying. "I'll be on the phone . . . first thing in the morning. This damn well better not be some goddamn training exercise . . . I'm telling you right now—"

The cop cut him off. "Let's go, sir," he insisted. "We'd appreciate it if you'd leave the lights on."

Before Taylor could muster a comeback, Maury Caulkin appeared carrying an armload of coats. He handed Corso two and kept a pair for himself. Cecil

Taylor shouldered his way into his long black cash-mere overcoat and then turned his attention to Dougherty. "I'm so sorry, my dear. I can only imagine how you must feel . . . on this of all nights . . . to have something like this—"

"Let's go, people," the short cop shouted. "Need you to move now."

4

"Give it a rest, huh?"

Corso stood in the street and watched a ragged pair of street people lurch around the corner and disappear. "What?" he said.

"You've braced every person we've run into. You're down to winos. Rate we're going neither of us will ever get home." She waved an arm. "Let's go."

"I'm just curious."

"Be curious while you're walking."

"I've got a feeling."

"You've always got a feeling."

The plan had been to walk down to the stadiums and grab a cab. Fifteen minutes . . . tops. That was an hour ago, before Corso began stopping everyone they encountered. Asking question after question. Picking everybody's brain. Getting absolutely nothing for his trouble, either. Nobody knew a thing.

The night air was heavy with mist. Fluid and gray, it dampened their cheeks as they walked. Behind them, a single strip of yellow police tape marked the southern edge of Occidental Park. Beyond the yellow plastic barrier, the park itself, normally awash in crack

dealers this time of night, was now completely deserted, its trimmed trees and tourist trap totem poles
swallowed whole by the liquid night. The sound of
hooves on stone heralded a pair of mounted cops.
Corso turned his head in time to watch the white-
helmeted officers bounce along the line of demarca-
tion at a brisk trot.

Dougherty kicked at a retreating pigeon and missed.
"I don't fucking believe it," she said. "This's gotta be a
joke."

Corso merely grunted. First Tuesday of the month—
Art Walk Night—and Occidental Square had taken on
the look of a science fiction movie. One of those end-
of-the-world disaster flicks where the city stands deserted after the Martians take over.

Inside the brightly lit galleries, bottles of wine and
trays of hors d'oeuvres waited like jilted lovers. In
front of the Parker-Holmes Gallery, a cigarette still
smoldered on the rough stones, sending its thin plume
of smoke up into the dark night sky.

"Don't worry about it," Corso offered.

"What do you mean don't worry about it? The most
important night of my life goes right down the toilet,
and you tell me not to worry about it?"

"It's out of our hands."

Her boot made another pass at the pigeon and, once
again, missed. "Easy for you to say. You're the big-
time famous author, not the town freak."

"Stop it."

She opened her mouth to speak, but Corso beat her
to it. "I can't imagine what somebody might have
spilled that would necessitate evacuating eight square
blocks of a major metropolitan area."

"That's what they always do. Evacuate the city."

"Only in the movies. Anybody in emergency response will tell you—"

"Whatever," she snapped. "All I know for sure is that my big show is going to sink beneath the waves without so much as a ripple. I'm gonna be back in obscurity so fast it'll—"

"Gotta be something super toxic."

"Four years of work, and there isn't gonna be one goddamn thing in tomorrow's paper but whatever disaster they've got going on back there." Before Corso could reply, she went on. "You know how they love a disaster. By now, they've worked up a fanfare and a logo." She lowered her voice. Waved an arm. "Spill Oh Three," she intoned. "They wait all year for something like this. A storm. A pileup . . . any damn thing they can beat to death for a week. It's like . . ."

She skidded to a halt, hands on hips. Corso had stopped and turned around. He looked up into the swirling fog and shook his head. "Where's all the sirens and lights?" he wanted to know. "This whole area ought to be lit up like a Christmas tree."

"Swear to God . . . I'm cursed."

"Stop it."

"It's true."

The sound of someone humming filled the spaces between their footsteps. What was the tune. "Time After Time," Corso thought. He stopped and watched as a middle-aged guy in a green canvas coat cut diagonally across Occidental Street and headed their way. "Looks like we're the last ones outta here," the guy said, looking around at the deserted streets.

"That's what I keep telling him," Dougherty said.

"Where were you?"

"Smith Tower," the guy said. "I'm the maintenance

supervisor. Had two guys call in sick, so I'm holding down the fort by myself . . . next thing I know the place is crawling with cops and firemen."

"They tell you what's going on?" Corso asked.

Guy shook his head. "Just told me I had to get out. Like right then. Said I had five minutes to beat it." He shook his craggy head. "Hell . . . I can't even get to my car."

"I hear every taxi and bus in town is down by the stadiums," Corso said.

"That's what the cop told me too."

Corso turned to Dougherty. Spread his hands. "What's all this tight-lipped shit about? A spill is a spill. You send in the haz-mat team; you clean it up. So what? B . . . F . . . D."

"It's on Yesler. That I know for sure," the guy volunteered.

"They told you that?"

"It's right behind the building. I was there when it first started."

"When was that?"

"Coupla hours ago. Buncha aid cars. Fire trucks. The whole nine yards."

"Where on Yesler?"

Corso heard Dougherty cough. Could sense the heat of her impatience.

"Down in the bus tunnel. They got the whole entrance sealed over with plastic. Everybody's wearing gas masks. Cops got their little robot thing out."

"You saw this?"

"Damn right." The guy shook his head again. "What a pain in the ass."

"Let's go," Dougherty said through bared teeth.

She turned and walked away, her black cape fanning out behind her like a pair of ebony wings. Corso and the other guy fell in beside her, striding out now, stretching their legs as they stepped out into King Street. To the east, a pair of SPD patrol cars blocked the street. Two more down at the waterfront.

"Lotsa overtime tonight," Corso said.

"You think maybe it's got something to do with that terrorism thing they're having up at the Weston?" the guy asked as they walked along.

Corso stopped in his tracks. Looked north. Up toward the center of the city, where the International Symposium on Chemical and Biological Weapons was presently being held at the Weston Hotel. Experts from fifty countries were jammed into the Weston's twin towers doing whatever it was they did when experts got together. Predictably, the confab had brought the loonies out of the woodwork. Every political, environmental and social action group that could drive, walk or hitchhike its way to Seattle was in the streets demonstrating for and against everything from capitalist incursions into third world nations to the pitiful plight of sea turtles, leading to a series of day-long demonstrations which had virtually closed the center of the city for the past two days.

"Jesus . . . I hope not," Corso said.

A shout echoed through the silent streets. The sound of scuffling feet filled their ears like static. The new Seahawks Stadium loomed ahead, its metal brows arching a question into the gauzy night air. They angled across King Street, turned left onto the disjointed arm of Occidental and suddenly they weren't alone. Two blocks ahead, a couple dozen other stragglers moved south toward the bright lights on Royal Brougham. Seemed like everyone had a cell phone glued to his ear.

Halfway down the block, Safeco Field came into view; the field lights had been turned on, casting an eerie halogen glow over the herds of buses and cabs that filled the streets. The wail of a train whistle seemed to come from everywhere at once. Once . . . twice and then, after an interval . . . a third time. Ahead in the distance, the giant spoked locomotive wheel that opened and closed the stadium's retractable roof seemed to take kindred comfort in the sound.

"What can you spill in a tunnel?" Corso groused. The long shadows of their fellow refugees swirled around their legs. "There's no trucks, no tankers, no railroad cars. Nothing in there but buses. How do you get a haz-mat spill from a bus? I don't get it."

Half a block to go. The refugees began to fan out. Corso could hear people wishing one another well as they wandered off in all directions at once.

The cops had been correct. A herd of Metro buses lined up two deep along the north facade of the stadium. Corso read the signs as they walked along: Montlake Terrace. Kent via Southcenter. Northgate. Bellevue. Most were about two-thirds full. The acrid smell of diesel fumes now mixed with the mist, leaving the skin feeling oily and unclean. Inside the buses, people seemed more animated than usual. Looked like everybody was talking at once, instead of hiding behind newspapers and Walkmen. "Amazing what it takes to bring people together," Corso thought as he hurried along.

"See you guys." The guy in the green jacket waved good-bye and made a beeline for the number thirty-eight bus and the University District.

Corso and Dougherty cut in front of the buses, crossed First Avenue and made their way toward the line of cabs along the curb. As they approached, here and there along the line, cabs peeled off like yellow leaves blown south by the wind, rolling away from the city, toward the next freeway entrance five blocks down the road.

The three nearest cabs all cut their wheels and started down the street before Corso and Dougherty got there. The fourth was empty. Corso put his hands on the side of the cab and leaned down. The window slid open a crack. Driver seemed to be holding his breath. "Need to go up on the hill and then down to Eastlake," Corso said.

The crack in the window disappeared. The locks popped. Corso pulled open the door and ushered Dougherty inside. He waited while she scooted over and then put one leg into the cab. That's when he heard the voice. From across the street. Right away, Corso knew who it was. He stifled a shudder and pulled himself upright.

The voice was tentative. "Mr. Corso?" it called again. Corso looked around.

"Close the door," the cabby said. Corso did so.

His eyes found the figure. Standing alone in front of the first pair of buses. Slobodan Nisovic. Black raincoat. Long red scarf, looked to be hand-knitted, wound around his throat. Corso started across the street.

In his mind's eye, he could see them both. Walter Lee Himes and Albert Defeo. Two of the most disgusting human beings Corso had ever met. First time Corso saw Walter Lee in person was the week before his scheduled execution for a series of rapes and murders known as "The Trashman Killings." Ten young women savaged and then left lifeless in trash containers all over the city. Walter Lee Himes had been convicted of the crimes and was sentenced to die by lethal injection, when Corso got wind of another murder, same MO . . . same demeaning ovine ear tag hanging from the victim's ear. Much to nearly everyone's chagrin, turned out Walter Lee wasn't guilty. At least not of the murders for which he had been convicted. Turned out a skinny little gun nut had been getting back at his dear departed mother by raping and killing young women like Petra Nisovic. Made him feel better, he said.

Slobodan Nisovic was thinner than Corso remembered.

"You look well," Nisovic said.

"You too," Corso lied.

"Anna . . ." he said, naming his wife, "would want me to give you her regards." He looked down at his shoes. "We owe you a debt we can never—"

Corso cut him off. "How's the boys?"

"Nicholas entered high school, this year. Serge . . ." he smiled a little. "Serge is at that awkward age."

A moment passed. "I guess you saw the news about Albert Defeo," Corso said.

Nisovic nodded. Shifted his weight from one foot to the other.

Little less than a year ago. McNeil Island Penitentiary. Another inmate had beaten Albert Defeo to death with a mop handle in a dispute over a deck of cards.

Didn't much matter to Slobodan Nisovic, though. Either way, his only daughter was dead, and, no matter what else happened, life was never going to hold the bright promise he had once imagined. A refugee Croatian dentist, whose foreign credentials would not allow him to practice his profession in the United States, he'd risen from sweeping the floors in Doc Maynard's bar to owning the place. He ran the Seattle Underground tours out of a box office in the bar. Half a million tourists a year paid Slobodan Nisovic six bucks a head to stumble through the maze of dank cellars running beneath Pioneer Square. That the business was a gold mine . . . that he'd risen from the outhouse to the penthouse . . . that he was the living embodiment of the American Dream . . . none of it mattered anymore. He'd have traded it all for an hour . . . hell, a minute . . . with his beautiful daughter Petra, whose raped and sodomized body Albert Defeo had left decorating the top of a flower-strewn Dumpster behind Freddy's Flowers on the Ave.

Like Corso, Slobodan Nisovic was famous in a way he'd rather forget. In front of his wife, his mother, the five hundred or so people who packed the hotel ballroom for the press conference and a national TV audience numbering in the millions, Nisovic had pumped four bullets into Walter Lee Himes, as Walter Lee was explaining that in his worldview "them bitches that Defeo fella had kilt" probably deserved to die anyway. Just for being bitches. If'n you knew what he meant.

Fortunately or unfortunately, depending upon one's outlook, Himes had not only survived his wounds but had eventually extracted a four-million-dollar wrongful prosecution judgment from King County, a princely sum with which he had returned to his ancestral home in Husk, North Carolina, from whence, in a recent interview, he claimed to be "livin' high on the log."

After some deliberation King County decided it couldn't have people taking the law into their own hands and commenced to prosecute Nisovic for attempted murder, aggravated assault and reckless endangerment. Problem was it proved impossible to find a jury of his peers who were similarly disposed. The first two trials ended in hung juries. Convinced that the emotional climate in Seattle had poisoned an otherwise open-and-shut case, the prosecution requested and was granted a change of venue.

The third trial was moved twenty miles north to Everett. A blue-collar jury of seven men and five women, after being admonished at length by the judge . . . told that another hung jury could well lead to charges of contempt of court being filed against each and every one of them . . . thus chastened, deliberated for a full nineteen minutes before unanimously finding Slobodan Nisovic not guilty of all charges.

"Hell of a mess," Corso said.

Nisovic nodded agreement. The wind swirled around them, lifting the tails of Nisovic's overcoat, prompting Corso to raise his collar.

Corso cleared his throat and said, "Well, hey . . . I gotta go . . . Dougherty's . . ." he inclined his head toward the line of cabs.

"Please give Ms. Dougherty my regards," Nisovic said. "And those of my family."

Corso assured him he would. Nisovic turned and started for the bus. Corso's brow furrowed as he stood on the sidewalk and watched Nisovic walk away.

"Mr. Nisovic," Corso shouted.

The little man had one foot on the bus. He stopped and then stepped out of the way so the Chinese woman behind him could board.

Corso hurried over. "You got the key with you?" he asked.

"The key?"

"To the Underground."

Slobodan Nisovic looked Corso over as if he were

breaking in a new set of eyes. "They say it's a very hazardous material," he said finally.

"I know."

"Is it so important to know?" he asked.

"It's my nature," Corso replied.

Nisovic thought for a long moment and then dropped into a squatting position. He set his briefcase in the street, popped the locks and pulled out a monstrous ring of keys. With great deliberation, he selected one and separated it from the others. He looked up at Corso. Offered the key. "Take the master key. I have another at home."

He began to close his briefcase. Stopped and again reached inside. He pulled out what looked like a brochure. "You want a map?" He got to his feet. "We give them to the tourists." He shrugged. "Mostly it's too dark to read."

"There's a Groucho Marx joke in there somewhere."

"Excuse?"

"Don't suppose you've got a flashlight," Corso said with a smirk.

"We keep it lit all the time," Nisovic said, with a touch of annoyance. "Insurance insists."

"Thanks," Corso said.

Nisovic bowed stiffly at the waist before crossing the sidewalk and mounting the bus. Corso watched as he found a seat up in front, against the far window, then strode back across the pavement to the taxi. He pulled open the door, leaned down and spoke to Dougherty. Her face told him she knew what was coming.

"I'm gonna run a little errand."

She rolled her eyes and grabbed the door handle.

Corso jerked his head back just in time to avoid losing his face to the slamming door. He walked up to the driver's window, peeled off a hundred-dollar bill and waved it at the driver. The window opened just far enough to accommodate the cash. Corso said, "Take her anywhere she wants to go."

5

"Her new boyfriend plays the saxophone in one of those Vegas shows," the cabdriver said. "I haven't seen my kids since July."

"Must be tough," was all Dougherty could think to say.

"Specially around the holidays," the guy said. "Talkin' to them on the phone was almost worse than not hearing from them at all." He took one hand off the wheel and waved it in the air. "They're telling me all the stuff they're getting for Christmas . . . like you know they're all excited and all . . . and I'm like . . ." He shook his head sadly. Checked the rearview mirror. "You got kids?" he asked.

She emitted a short, dry laugh. "Me? Kids? No . . . not me."

Her tone caught his attention. "Never too late," he said. "Nice-lookin' lady like you. I bet you got lotsa—" The look in her reflected eyes stopped the words in his throat and sent his attention scurrying back out over the hood.

She checked the side window. The mist had cleared. Traffic was beginning to thin as they inched steeply uphill on Cherry Street.

The cabdriver snapped the radio on. War doing "Lowrider."

"Where on the hill?" he asked above the rhythm.

"Thirteenth Avenue East and Republican."

"Nice neighborhood," he tried.

She flicked her eyes down at the laminated plastic ID card hanging from the back of the seat. His name was Steveland Gerkey. He'd grown his wiry black hair out since the picture was taken. "Steveland, huh?" she muttered.

"My mom named me after Stevie Wonder," the driver said. "She named all of us that way. I've got a brother Marvin and a sister Diana . . . named after Marvin Gaye and Diana Ross. Mom was real big into Motown."

Dougherty let herself sink into the seat. Only a couple of cars at a time were getting through the intersections. She sat in silence for five minutes as they inched forward, and then suddenly she leaned closer. Put her hands on the back of the seat.

"You happy with what you're doing, Steveland?" she asked.

His eyes fixed on the mirror again. Trying to tell if she was serious. "Stevie," he said. "Everybody calls me Stevie."

"You happy with what you're doing, Stevie?"

"You mean like driving a cab?"

"I mean like with your life."

He thought it over. "Depends on what you mean," he said after a minute. "You know . . . it's not like this was what I was planning when I was a little kid or anything."

"What'd you want to be when you were a little kid?" she asked.

"A cowboy," he said. "I really wanted to be a cowboy."

"What about later? After you grew up."

He twitched his shoulders but did not speak. His long-term aspirations were not a subject upon which he allowed himself to dwell. Not because they were in any way bad or bizarre, but because he had come to realize he didn't have any. Nothing specific anyway. He'd never pictured himself as anything in particular. Just a situation where he made enough money doing something ... anything ... enough to have whatever he wanted. A nice new Dodge pickup. A boat or maybe a little house someplace. The kind of things people wanted.

He looked in the mirror again. "What about you?"

"A ballerina."

"I was gonna go to community college. They got a real good culinary arts program at South Seattle," he volunteered. "But then ... you know ... I met Janie ... we ended up getting married." He seemed to shrink slightly in the seat. "Next thing you know we got two kids and there ain't no going back to school after that."

"How long you been driving a cab?"

"Last coupla years. Ever since they laid me off at Boeing."

"What'd you do at Boeing?"

"Worked the tool crib ... up in Everett. Janie's dad ... Harvey ... he got me on. Harvey's been with the Busy B thirty-two years. Knew the foreman."

He slid the car forward three car lengths. They were second in line to cross Broadway. "Got my pink slip in the first big wave of layoffs." He checked the mirror again to make sure she was listening. "That's when it all started to come apart for Janie and me. I look at it now . . . you know like in hindsight . . . it was mostly about money, but, you know . . . at the time . . . seemed like we couldn't agree on anything anymore." He caught himself rambling and changed the subject.

"Whata you do?" he asked.

"I'm a photographer."

"You mean like for one of the papers or something?"

"Freelance," she said. "I work for myself." She read the question in his eyes. "Sometimes I work for a famous writer. I take the pictures for his books."

"What's his name?"

"Frank Corso. He writes—"

"The crime books," he interrupted her. He smiled for the first time and flicked on the overhead light. Opened the glove compartment. Rummaged around inside. Came out with a battered paperback copy of *A Blind Eye,* which he held up like a trophy. "I read all of 'em," he proclaimed. "Soon as they come out in paper, I'm right there."

The light changed. He kept the cab about four inches from the blue Volvo in front as they crept through the intersection and began to roll downhill, along the north side of Seattle University. A blinking yellow light marked the walkway leading from the university's parking garage to the main campus. They stopped and waited as a solid line of chattering students crossed in front of the cab. While they waited, he thumbed his way into the center of the book, found the photos, turned the book sideways.

"Margaret Dougherty," he read.

"Meg."

That's when it hit him. He moved his eyes upward for a second and then buried them in the book. She'd seen the expression so many times before there was no mistaking the look. That combination of palpable pity and carnal curiosity her story seemed to inspire. Especially in guys. They always seemed torn between offering their condolences and begging for a peek.

"They ever catch the guy?" he asked. "You know, the one who . . ."

She had the answer ready. It was like a part in a long-running play. A part where she never forgot her lines. "He left the country. France they think."

He opened his mouth to speak, but, mercifully, changed his mind. The last student passed in front of the cab. He lifted his foot from the brake, allowing the cab to roll downhill, where they made the light and turned north on Twelfth Avenue. The meter read six dollars and ninety cents. An idea nearly brought a smile to her lips. She'd give Steveland Gerkey the rest of Corso's hundred bucks as a tip. Make his whole damn day. Because Corso was such a goddamn fool and because Steveland had a well-developed sense of when to shut up. The song changed to Norah Jones. "Don't know why I didn't call . . ." Dougherty sat back in the seat and closed her eyes. The singer's husky voice tickled her insides.

She kept her eyes closed, rolling around inside the music until she felt herself pressed back in the seat by the steep slope of East Republican Street.

"Left at the top of the hill," she said.

He eased the cab over to the curb and brought it to a halt. "Which building?" he wanted to know.

She scooted forward in the seat and pointed out over his shoulder. "The little house with the gate," she said.

He took his foot off the brake and the cab began to roll forward. "What gate?"

"Between the apartment buildings," she said, pointing again. "See the white sign above the gate?" He peered out through the semidarkness. GRAVEN IMAGES, the sign said. PHOTOGRAPHY BY M. DOUGHERTY. BY APPOINTMENT ONLY, and a phone number.

"Jeez," he said. "All the times I been down this street and I never noticed that little place way back in there."

"Most people don't," she said. "It's what I like about it."

"All the trees and bushes and stuff makes it real hard to see."

He lifted his foot from the brake again. As the car began to move forward, the gate bordering the street opened and a shadowy figure stepped out onto the sidewalk.

Without thinking, Dougherty put a hand on the driver's shoulder. He stopped again. The figure caught the flash of brake lights. His head swiveled. He stared intently at the cab, but did not move.

"You expecting company?" Stevie asked.

"No."

"You know him?" he asked, switching off the car's interior lights.

She started to say she didn't when the apparition took a step forward, profiling his features against the security lights of the apartment building next door.

Her breath came quicker now. She heard it, but couldn't control herself.

"Can't be."

"What can't be?"

She shook her head in disbelief, as if the sudden movement would improve her vision or, better yet, make the apparition disappear altogether. The figure stopped on the sidewalk, pulled a pack of cigarettes from the pocket of his jacket and lit one. Now she was sure. The old-fashioned Zippo lighter. The way he posed for a second before extinguishing the flame. Just in case he had an audience. It was him. No doubt about it.

"Holy shit," escaped her lips. "I don't believe it."

The visitor cast another long glance at the darkened cab and then started up the street. Walking north along Thirteenth Avenue. She waited a moment, then pulled the door handle and stepped out into the street, nudging the door closed with her hip.

"Something wrong?" the driver wanted to know.

She didn't answer. Just stood in the street watching intently as the dark figure walked away. "I don't believe it," she mumbled to herself.

"You okay?" the driver asked.

Before she could muster a reply, a movement in her peripheral vision snapped her head around. Someone was moving soundlessly along the sidewalk. Just as her eyes were beginning to focus, the apparition slid behind the massive oak tree and disappeared. She waited . . . squinting out into the gloom at the spot where he should emerge from behind the tree. Nothing. The silent stroller had stopped. Hiding? She looked at Stevie, who had gotten out of the car and now stood by her side; his attention was riveted on her.

"Listen, lady . . . ," he began, "I gotta get going here. I gotta . . ."

She tore her eyes from the sidewalk. Jabbed a finger in the direction of the retreating figure. "That's the guy," she hissed. "That's Brian." With her other hand she pulled down the front of her dress, revealing the cleft between her breasts, covered with tattoos. He squinted in the darkness until he could make out the images and the words that swirled around on her chest. His lips moved as he read the tattooed script until the language embarrassed him and he turned his face away.

"That's the guy did this to me. Brian Bohannon. That's him right there."

"You sure?"

"Like I could ever forget."

"I thought you said he moved to France."

"He did."

"Jesus." He hesitated and then pulled a cell phone from the dash. "Maybe we oughta call the cops."

She thought it over. Shook her head. Got back in the cab. "Every cop in town is downtown at the Weston or back there in the square. They're not coming up here for a five-year-old assault beef that they never took seriously anyway."

"Whata you mean they didn't take it seriously?"

She waved a hand in the darkness. "They always treated it like some kind of lover's quarrel. Like I was just another weirdo who got what was coming to her."

"You're kidding me."

"Said I had a marginal lifestyle."

"Whata you want to do?"

She thought for a long moment. "Let's follow him," she said finally. "See where he goes."

"What for?"

"I don't know," she snapped. "Let's just do it."

"Hey, lady . . . I'm just a cabdriver. I'm not good for any of that . . ."—he used his fingers to make quotation marks in the air—"follow that car' stuff. I'm just tryin' to make a living here."

Dougherty leaned forward. Put her face in his. "I'm freaked out here, Stevie. I don't know what to do." She made eye contact. "Please. Help me out."

A van's headlights came on. They sat in silence,

watching as the van pulled up to the intersection, turned right and disappeared down Mercer Street.

"Come on, Stevie," she pleaded. She pointed at the meter. It read nine dollars and seventy-six cents. "I've got ninety-three bucks to go."

"Okay, lady," he said finally. "If you put it that way." He put the cab into gear and roared down the street, headlights off, poking the hood out into Mercer Street just in time to watch the van's taillights turn left and disappear from view.

"But . . . you know . . . like no car chases or nothing like that."

"Just drive."

6

At first, he'd attributed the sound to echoes. Told himself the noise was nothing more than the ricochet sound of his own feet bouncing around and around the tunnel walls. Or maybe something mundane like the rush of traffic overhead. Or something organic and benign like the settling of the earth. He'd successfully held that thought until the first time he'd had occasion to come to a full stop. At that point . . . despite his fervent wish that it not be so, he'd been forced to acknowledge that what he'd been hearing was the skitter of claws along the stone floor.

He winced, took a deep breath and reached above his head, grabbing the metal cage surrounding one of the thousands of lightbulbs festooning the ceiling of the tunnels. He tilted the light in the direction of the noise. The sight of a trio of harbor rats, their narrow eyes gleaming red in the beam, sent a steel shiver rolling down his spine. "Shoo," he rasped. And then again . . . louder. Nothing. Not only didn't they scurry off, but the largest of the three stood on his hind legs, bared his long yellow teeth and grunted out what Corso felt certain was a challenge.

He left the overhead light swinging to and fro as he hurried down the tunnel. Moving north toward Yesler Street, he focused on the corridor ahead and whistled out of tune as he walked along, filling his mind with thoughts of how nearly every city denotes the place where the community was first settled. About how they always seemed to give it a quaint-sounding name. Old Town, the Gaslight District, the French Quarter, the Mission District, or, in Seattle's case, Pioneer Square. Soon as they got it properly named, seemed like they immediately turned it over to the tourist trade, before moving on to newer and greener pastures.

Corso was still pondering this historical anomaly when he came to a three-way junction in the tunnel. On his left lay the tattered remains of a turn-of-the-century dry goods store. The broken sign read: *Jensen's Pr—*. . . its counter was empty and expectant, its shelves toppled down, rolling a collection of cans and bottles haphazardly out onto the floor. That the cobwebs were plastic and the cans crude reproductions mattered not a whit to the foreign throngs who flowed through these dank tunnels six days a week, year-round, hearing the story of how, after the city burned down in 1898, they'd rebuilt Pioneer Square from the second floor up, thus providing some measure of relief from the omnipresent dampness and ensuring that their newfangled flush toilets would operate as designed, a fateful decision which had simultaneously improved sanitation and interned a ghost city beneath eight square blocks of south Seattle.

Ahead a steep set of stone stairs led up to the street. On the left, beyond Jensen's, a thick steel door held a bright orange NO ADMITTANCE notice. To the right, a narrow tunnel led slightly uphill. He nodded contentedly to himself, tilted the map in his hand, found where he was and then rotated it in his hand so that Jensen's Provisioners was on his left. If the map were to be believed, and if he hadn't seriously fucked up, those ought to be the stairs at the base of Yesler Street. He looked to the right again. Seventy yards that way ought to be the Underground entrance directly across the street from the bus tunnel. He'd thought it over and decided that one was too risky. Better to have a look from down here first, he'd decided, and then play it by ear from there.

As he rechecked his bearings, something in the darkness squealed. Corso frowned, jammed the map into his pocket and began climbing the stairs. Once at the top, he twisted the brass handle on the lock and eased the door open. Slowly. A quarter inch at a time, until finally there was room to poke his head through the opening.

Second Avenue was awash in metallic blue police cars. He listened for a moment. Heard nothing and then wondered why. No wailing sirens. No static crackle of radio transmissions. The only sound splitting the night was the *whop whop* of rotor blades. He poked his head out a little more and looked up. A pair of police helicopters circled lazily in the night sky. He craned his neck in a circle and wondered where the news choppers were. Why they weren't up there giving their "eye in the sky" perspective. "High above downtown Seattle" and all that crap.

A pair of Seattle's finest stood whispering, no more than thirty feet away, their attention riveted half a block uphill on Yesler, between Second and Third, where what little he could see of the bus tunnel appeared to be covered in plastic. Whatever was going on in the street outside the tunnel entrance was blocked from view by a pair of fire trucks parked nose to nose across Yesler Street. Another pair blocked the street farther up the hill, making sure nobody came blundering down from the freeway.

And then he heard the voices. Raised voices coming from his left. He pushed his head farther out the door. A KING-TV remote truck sat angled into the police barricade two blocks up Second Avenue, its yellow lights blazing. The guy with the red hair. What was his name? The one who was always broadcasting from the summit at Snoqualmie. The snow conditions guy. In his mind's eye, Corso could see the red ski jacket . . . the collar flapping in the stiff breeze. Parka Boy Something they called him. He was standing out in front of the truck, trying to talk his way past the cops. The cops looked like they were hoping he'd step around the barricade so's they could kick his ass.

Corso pulled his head back inside and snapped the lock. Took a deep breath. No doubt about it. If he was going to get a look at what was going on, he was going to have to walk up and poke his nose out smack in the middle of it.

He looked down the passage. Overhead lights threw oblong pools of yellow light along the floor of the tunnel. At the far end, he could just make out the landing and the half a dozen stairs rising to the street. Something disturbed one of the tin cans in Jensen's long-ago store, bouncing a metallic *ping* around the walls and sending Corso on his way.

He walked quickly up the corridor, moving from light to darkness and back again a dozen times as he covered the seventy or so yards up to the next Underground entrance.

End of the line. It was either walk up the stairs and open the door or retrace his steps back to the foot of Yesler Street. He climbed the stairs. Put his ear to the door and listened. Nothing. Not surprising. The doors were steel and solid. Kept the winos from turning the place into the Homeless Hilton. He grabbed the knob on the brass lock and twisted. The door stuck in its warped wooden casing. He pulled harder. And then harder still, until finally the upper corner came loose and the door popped open with a rattle.

He held his breath, used his other hand to quiet the door. A cool breeze fanned his face through the crack. The sounds of angry voices filled his ears. Cops using that command voice they practice. "Down," one of them was yelling. "Get down right now."

A yelp of pain. The scratch of boots on concrete. And then . . . other voices. Cautionary . . . outraged. The sound of running now, followed by the unmistakable sounds of a struggle. He eased the door inward and stuck his head out.

The street was lit up like a ball game at night. He was staring at the red and white side of an SFD aid car, parked along the curb. A huge van was parked in the middle of the street, its nose pointing down the hill, its sliding doors thrown open, revealing a rack of orange jumpsuits quivering slightly in the breeze. The lettering on the side read: CRITICAL INCIDENT MOBILE SQUAD ROOM.

To his right, an unruly crowd of about fifty citizens was being held behind a double line of police barriers. At the moment, they were clustered at the upper end of the enclosure, where one of their number was being subdued by a trio of burly SWAT storm troopers. One knelt on the back of the man's neck while the other two jerked his hands behind his back and clicked on a pair of cuffs.

"You got no damn right," somebody shouted.

"Leave him alone," a woman's voice pleaded.

A foot came swinging out from the crowd, catching one of the kneeling cops in the side of the helmet with a crack. He turned his visored gaze toward the cluster of people and growled. The seething mob surged forward to meet the challenge, bringing another half dozen officers sprinting across the street. The mingle of voices grew more strident now, the sounds of struggle more violent.

With all eyes trained on the scuffle, Corso took a chance. He stepped out into the street and closed the door behind himself. Up at the scuffle, the newly arrived squad of cops held their batons before them in both hands as they forced the mob away from the struggle on the sidewalk. The crowd resisted. Cursing, shouting, lashing out here and there as the phalanx of officers moved them inexorably across the sidewalk until the rearmost members of the pack had their backs pressed to the buildings on the south side of Yesler Street.

Corso looked around. He was just outside the enclosure. To the left, a pair of firemen knelt in the street behind the aid car. They were fiddling with a wheeled metal cart, upon which a nineteen-inch TV monitor flickered. A braid of cables as thick as a man's arm led from the cart, across Yesler Street, over the sidewalk, right up to the mouth of the bus tunnel, where what had to be a robot of some sort sat unmoving on the concrete, its rubber-tracked feet still, its articulated metal arms held forward as if in supplication. Only the blinking green light on top of the contraption suggested the possibility of movement.

The decorative blue arches of the tunnel entrance had been completely enshrouded in thick plastic film, creating the illusion of a giant opaque cocoon. Half a block uphill, Government Park was deserted; its worn grass, usually a haven for the homeless, lay limp and empty, littered here and there by backpacks, sleeping bags and scattered piles of debris.

He looked upward. Only the pale blue light at the top of the building announced the Smith Tower's stab into the night sky. A shouted threat pulled his attention down to earth. Down the hill to that pair of cops who'd been whispering at the base of the street. They'd noticed his sudden appearance and were now running up the hill, pointing his way, coming as fast as their baggy motorcycle pants and high black boots would allow.

Corso moved quickly uphill toward the enclosure. He stepped in front of the aid car, raised the strand of yellow plastic police tape above his head and then bent over, as if to duck under the collection of tape and barriers that formed the downhill edge of the enclosure. As if to step inside and lose himself in the crowd.

Another shout split the air. The sound of boots was nearly upon him when, instead of ducking under the barriers, he lay down in the gutter and forced himself backward on his belly, sliding between the front tires of the ambulance, inching toward the rear of the vehicle, his head half an inch beneath the oil pan by the time the boots arrived. Four of them. He lay still, his breathing short and silent.

"You see him?" he heard somebody shout.

Another pair of boots, shinier than the others, arrived at the front of the aid car. "See who?" a voice demanded. "Somebody get out?"

"Looked to me more like he got in," a third voice offered.

"Guy was just standin' there on the sidewalk."

"We looked up and there he was."

"Tryin' to get inside?"

"He lifted the tape. I saw him." The other cop agreed.

"Sure it was a *him?*"

"Too tall for a woman."

Corso rested his chin on the street and watched as the new pair of boots turned uphill toward the crowd. In the momentary silence, he could hear a jumble of voices raised in protest and the rustle of bodies in motion. "Musta been trying to get out when you guys spotted him. Musta changed his mind and got back where he belonged."

"You'd think they'd understand," a voice complained, "it's for their own damn good. You'd think—"

"We need more containment."

Corso heard a sigh. "I already made three requests. Brass don't want to hear about it. They're sayin' they want to send the robot inside before they decide what to do next. All I'm getting is a bunch of crap about minimum personnel exposure."

The feet turned to the left. One toe tapped the pavement.

"Exposure to what?" The voice was now half an octave higher.

The toe stopped tapping. "Nobody's saying," came the answer. "Just that we got a couple of missing buses and some dead citizens down inside the station."

The boots began to shuffle. Corso could sense their mutual uneasiness.

"You two better get back to your posts."

They didn't have to be asked twice. From the corner of his eye, Corso watched the pair start down the hill toward the foot of Yesler Street. The third cop hesitated for a moment, then shouted something Corso couldn't make out before moving uphill at a lope.

Corso used the heels of his hands to move himself backward. Out from under the engine, to a place in the middle of the undercarriage where he had room to lever himself up onto his side. The pitch of the hill gave him an unobstructed view of the firemen as they fiddled with the robot's control panel.

He watched as the men spoke to one another and as the taller of the two then began to walk his way. As the feet approached, Corso shrank deeper into the darkness beneath the ambulance, lying still until the feet disappeared.

Corso waited a moment and then crawled over to the edge of the chassis and looked up. The guy had stepped up into the haz-mat van. He had his back to the street as he pushed a leg into one of the orange bio-hazard suits. And then the other. Then up over the shoulders with a wiggle. And the zipper and the Velcro. Until finally he pulled the orange hood over his head just before disappearing inside the truck.

When the fireman stepped back into the street his entire face was covered with a black rubber mask. Corso watched as the guy adjusted the straps, satisfied himself that the filter was working and headed back toward his buddy.

He rolled over and watched between the rear wheels as the pair exchanged a much practiced collection of nods and hand gestures. Watched as the orange apparition started across the street toward the robot and the mouth of the bus tunnel. Watched as his partner picked up what looked like one of those virtual reality helmets and fitted it over his close-cropped head.

Corso was cursing the fact that the huge blue van blocked his view when he heard the sound of engines starting and then the slap of soles on concrete. He cringed as two pairs of black shoes skidded to a stop on either side of the ambulance. He heard the doors open and felt the aid car rock on its springs as its occupants levered themselves inside.

The engine started with a roar. Corso heard the click of the transmission being dropped into gear. His throat tightened. If they backed up, he'd surely be dragged to his death beneath the vehicle. Without thinking, he rolled left. Toward the haz-mat van and the safety of the open sky. Kept rolling as he covered the five feet of bare pavement separating the vehicles. Rolling until he was completely beneath the Critical Incident van.

He scooted back between the giant rear tires and waited. Despite the temperature, beads of sweat rolled down his face. He mopped his brow with his sleeve as the ambulance began to move uphill toward the freeway.

Across the street, the fireman in the biohazard suit had pulled back enough of the plastic to allow the robot to roll inside. He looked over at his buddy in the street and gave a two-fingered salute.

The guy in the helmet adjusted the wire-thin microphone so that it hung just under his lower lip, grabbed the joystick in both hands and spoke.

"We're ready, sir," he said.

7

Assistant Fire Chief Ben Gardener sat down in front of the quavering TV monitor, laced his fingers together and cracked his knuckles. At fifty-eight, he was still ramrod straight and in possession of a full head of wiry salt-and-pepper hair. Less than a year and a half from retirement, he and his wife Cyndi planned to spend their golden years in Port St. Lucie, Florida, where their divorced daughter Tracy and their three grandsons had finally taken root. He unbuttoned his suit jacket, started to remove the coat and then thought better of it. Even with the chief on vacation, it probably wasn't a good idea. Recent SFD policy had mandated that he give up wearing his uniform and instead report for duty in a business suit. More professional, the chief said. More twenty-first century. Gardener hated the idea. Said it made him feel like an insurance salesman. In a subtle act of defiance, he'd purchased three suits . . . all the same color . . . all the same deep blue hue of his beloved uniform. He bent low over the desk and pushed the green button on the telephone. A hiss of static filled the tiny speaker.

"What's your status, Hamilton?"

"We're ready, sir," came the electronic reply.

Gardener swiveled in the chair and looked around the room. That's when it hit him. There was nobody there. Not downstairs in the lobby and not up here in the Special Operations Room either. No press. No publicity seekers. No nothing. He shook his head in wonder. What could well be the defining moment in the city's history and only six people were going to be present to bear witness. Seven if he counted himself.

Somebody was pulling serious strings to keep this one under their collective hats. Probably the mayor. Lord knew nobody liked to jerk the reins of power more than Gary Dean, and nobody was better at controlling the spin than Dean's press liaison Harlan Sykes. This had all the earmarks of what Sykes liked to refer to as "optimum information control."

Dean and Sykes were huddled together in the far corner, their body language making it abundantly clear they weren't looking to chitchat. Over by the door, Police Chief Harry Dobson of the SPD was waving a blunt finger as he made a point to a tall guy in a blue blazer. Dobson was built like a fire hydrant and wore so many departmental commendations on his uniform he looked like an admiral. Good man though. A stand-up guy and a very capable administrator who had a knack for ending up with what Gardener always figured was just a little bit more than the SPD's share of the public pie.

Out in the middle of the room Mike Morningway from Emergency Management shared a whispered conversation with a moderately attractive blonde woman in a pale green lab coat. Harborview Medical Center was stitched on the coat in red. Gardener had seen her before someplace, but couldn't remember where or when. He thought she might have been a speaker at one of the many conferences he'd attended in the past few months, nearly all of which had been aimed at preparing for a moment just such as this, but which, at this point, all ran together in Gardener's head as little more than an endless series of presentations, punctuated here and there by bleak rubber chicken lunches.

Gardener watched Morningway think it over before responding to whatever the woman was saying. He wondered how Morningway felt about administering a program everybody hoped never to need. Wondered how one kept his troops battle ready when all they were ever called upon to do was clean up moderately toxic spills from the highways and help with household recycling.

The mayor looked Gardener's way and cocked an eyebrow in an exaggerated manner which made it plain he'd spent hours practicing the move in the mirror.

"I believe we're good to go," Gardener said.

Just as he uttered the phrase, at the moment when people began to cross the room, the TV picture started to roll. Gardener kept his face intact as his innards collapsed like a dying star. This was the first time the SFD had patched directly into the robot for a remote video feed. The department had put a lot of money into the technology, money most of city government would have preferred to spend elsewhere. Any kind of failure here would surely not bode well for next year's appropriations. He crossed his fingers and smiled.

When the screen went blank, Gardener pretended not to notice, busying himself, instead, in the top drawer of the desk. Before anyone could speak, however, the screen reappeared, rolled once and then again, before suddenly coming to rest. Mercifully, the picture was considerably better than Gardener could have hoped. Far from the grainy images of the past, the picture on the screen was crisp and clear. The sound was so good they could hear the crinkle of the plastic when the gloved hand pulled the film aside to allow the robot to enter. Gardener adjusted his expression to suggest he'd known all along the system was going to function properly and refocused on the screen.

They were now looking at the world through the robot's eyes. The Pioneer Square Station lay deserted. Everything seemed huge and ominous from the robot's three-foot-high point of view. The safety railings looked like a forest of blue metal trees receding to the horizon, the stone floors like a wide, polished runway, leading off in all directions.

"Give us a little background, will you, Ben?" It was Harlan Sykes, doing what he got paid to do . . . making people feel informed whether it was true or not.

Gardener stifled a sigh and began to speak. "First call came into the downtown station at three thirty-six P.M. Said we had a dead guy on the escalator in the bus tunnel. We dispatched an aid car to the scene."

"Only one?" the mayor interrupted.

Gardener kept his voice neutral. His dislike of the mayor was well known within governmental circles. The way he saw it, Dean was a habitual self-promoter, a sycophant, whose only real interest in public service was in his own reelection. Worse yet, he was a man who always seemed more interested in fixing the blame than fixing the problem. This close to making his thirty, however, Gardener could see no sense in baiting the bear, so he kept his face clear and his voice flat.

"At that point, the call was nothing more than a standard request for assistance," he said.

A low-frequency electrical hum announced that the robot was moving. All eyes fell on the screen. Gardener spoke as he watched. "The aid car arrived six minutes later. By that time a pair of SPD officers were on the scene. They confirmed the guy on the stairs."

"Who called Emergency Services?" Sykes wanted to know.

"The SPD officers," Gardener said. "While they were satisfying themselves the guy on the stairs was beyond help, they observed a pair of victims at the bottom of the escalator. Apparently there was some visible discharge, so they went downstairs for a look." He hesitated, looking around the room. "According to the officers . . ." he started again, "both the northbound and southbound concourses are full of bodies."

"How many . . ." the mayor began.

"Too many for conventional violence. That's when they realized they were dealing with something . . . something unusual."

"Jesus," somebody in the back whispered.

"They backed off, immediately called Emergency Services and sealed off the tunnel as best they could from that end," Gardener finished.

"Good move," the mayor commented.

"Good training," Chief Dobson quickly corrected. "Both men had been through Emergency Incidents Training within the past ninety days."

Dobson enjoyed his self-congratulatory moment as they watched the robot round the corner and head toward the escalator at the far end of the frame.

"Where are they now?" Sykes wanted to know.

"Up at Harborview," answered Dobson. "The

medics are keeping both the cops and the EMTs in complete isolation until we know what we're dealing with here."

"Far as we know, those four are the only people who've actually been *inside* the station since the incident," Sykes said.

Dobson spread his hands as he spoke. "We're detaining about fifty civilians who were in the area at the time." He looked over at the mayor. "Fifty very unhappy civilians, I'm given to understand," he said.

The guy in the blue blazer spoke up. "Your people did a heck of a job, Chief." Dobson nodded his appreciation of the compliment . . . at which point Mike Morningway from Emergency Management piped in. "We immediately called Metro and closed down the tunnel. Got a crew started in sealing off the entrance."

Gardener took over again. "We've got the tunnel sealed off. Metro reversed the ventilation output from both the University Street Station and the International Street Station, which should keep whatever we've got down there pretty much confined to the—"

"Pretty much?" the mayor interrupted.

Gardener's voice tightened. "It's not a closed system, Mayor. It's a tunnel. It connects one thing to another. It was never designed to be completely isolated."

The robot approached the top of the escalator from an oblique angle. The top of a man's head was visible . . . resting on the upper landing. The remainder of the body was hidden behind the silver side of the escalator. The robot stopped.

"Hutchinson." Gardener spoke into the phone again.

"Hamilton," the voice corrected.

"Take us around the far side," Gardener said.

The robot began to move again. Skirting around the

top of the corpse until it was looking at the body from
the opposite side. The victim lay splayed across the
metal stairs. The powerful mechanism had wedged the
body between the rails at an inhuman angle, contorting
the spine and preventing the stairway from dumping
the lifeless form onto the upper landing. The right side
of the man's face was visible. The sight of his silhouette against the ribbed metal background of the tread
stopped their collective breaths.

His face was beet red and contorted into a grimace
which left little doubt as to the painful manner of his
passing.

"What the hell is with his face?" Harlan Sykes muttered, brushing shoulders with the mayor as he leaned
closer to the screen.

The woman from Harborview slid her pastel smock
past both the mayor and Sykes and peered down into
the screen. She cupped her chin in her hand and narrowed her eyes as she gazed at the image before her.
Half a minute passed before she took a step backward
and looked over at Gardener.

"Can you get us a close-up?" she asked.

Gardener spoke into the telephone. A moment later
the camera began to move, jumping one electronic
magnification step at a time . . . closer and closer . . .
As the successive images appeared, a buzz of whispered anxiety filled the air.

At the point when the victim's head filled the entire
screen, his malady seemed little more than a general ir-
ritation of the skin, which, as the camera moved closer,
appeared puckered and shiny in places like a burn. Two
jumps later, however, everyone in the room stiffened,
as it became evident that the redness was, in fact,
caused by thousands of puss-filled lesions, many of

which had burst, leaving a waxy red film coating the surrounding tissue. Another magnification . . . and then another until the stubble on the victim's chin looked like shrubbery and they could make out that the blemishes were shaped like bones . . . thin at the center, widening out into knobby ends. The woman's involuntary groan brought silence to the room. "Stop," she said.

"Dr. Stafford . . ." Sykes began.

She held up a hand and leaned closer to the screen. "Can't be," she muttered.

When she looked back over her shoulder, her face was the color of oatmeal and her lower lip was beginning to tremble. "You said the officers saw other victims at the bottom of this escalator?"

"According to the report," Dobson said carefully.

"Can you get me a look?" she asked.

Gardener relayed the request. After a ten-second interval, the robot began to move, wheeling around to the top of the escalator and moving forward until the victim's head must have been directly between the machine's rubber treads.

The view down the frozen metal stairway revealed little more than a single dark smudge on the floor at the base of the stairs.

The robot's operator anticipated her next request. A bright halogen light suddenly snapped on; the camera zoomed, and the smudges on the floor became a woman and a little girl. Matching blue jackets and matching red faces. Only this time their heads were surrounded by a wide halo of coagulated blood, spread out black and sticky-looking in the harsh artificial light. The doctor turned her gaze back toward the room.

"Call Atlanta," she said. "Get the Centers for Disease Control."

The mayor opened his mouth in protest. She cut him off.

"Hurry," she said. "Get them here now."

8

Meg Dougherty spoke directly into the driver's ear. "Don't lose him," she whispered.

"Traffic like this . . ." Stevie said, "there ain't much I can do."

As he spoke, the gray van suddenly turned downhill and disappeared from view. Stevie gave it a little gas, pushing the cab up Broadway toward the brightly lit drugstore on the corner.

"Come on," Dougherty chanted.

They'd spent the past forty minutes winding around the top of Capitol Hill in an endless series of loops and whorls seemingly headed nowhere. He'd stopped four times. Twice in the street, where he just sat in the van and looked around. Once at the Summit Tavern, where he'd gone inside and had a couple of beers, and finally up on Twelfth and Pine, where he'd spent a full five minutes parked in front of the first apartment they'd rented together. For the first time in nearly six years, she'd wondered what he was thinking.

Stevie swung the cab out into the turn lane, floored it past an ancient Chinese man driving at the speed of lava, and then again to pass an empty police car, light

bar ablaze, parked in the middle of the street. They
were roaring toward the intersection when suddenly
the light cycled to red. Instantly the street was filled
with pedestrians. Stevie jerked the cab to a halt, the
front bumper halfway across the crosswalk. He banged
the heel of his hand on the steering wheel in disgust,
caught her eyes in the mirror and shrugged a silent
apology.

"Shit," Dougherty hissed. She threw herself backward in the seat, bouncing off the cushions. "He's
gone," she said. "Goddamn it."

A cycle dyke slammed her hand on the hood of the
cab as she crossed the street, her narrow eyes etching
displeasure at the cab's intrusion into the crosswalk.

"Fuck you," Stevie muttered, racing the engine.

She stopped, making like she was going to come
back and kick his ass; Stevie was reaching for the lock
button when she smirked, shot him the finger and
strode away.

A pair of red dots appeared on Stevie's cheeks. A moment later, a slight break in the stream of humanity
proved to be all the encouragement he needed. He nosed
the cab the rest of the way through the crowded intersection, waited another moment for side street pedestrians to pass and then squealed around the corner.

The rear of a tandem Metro bus loomed like a mechanical mountain. "Wash Me" had been fingered into
the thick dirt on the back window. Stevie screeched to
a halt, throwing Dougherty forward in the seat, bouncing his chest off the steering wheel.

The cab's interior was hot with their frustrated
breathing as slowly . . . incrementally . . . the knot of
traffic began to unwind and the bus began to nose into
the curb, the front coach sliding along the bus stop,

leaving the rear hanging out into traffic, until suddenly the air was filled with the sound of squeaking brakes and the hissing of hydraulic doors. "Goddamn it," Dougherty said again, slapping the seat.

Stevie hit the gas, throwing the cab toward a narrow opening between the bus's big ass and the steady stream of oncoming traffic. The breath caught in Dougherty's throat. It seemed certain they were going to have a head-on with a red Dodge pickup. The truck's driver jerked the wheel to the right, narrowly avoiding a line of parked cars as the truck fishtailed in the street. Stevie kept the cab so close to the bus Dougherty could see the screws that held the advertising signs. Then *bang!* And the tinkling sound of broken glass. Stevie looked around, as confused as she was. Couple of blocks later she saw him wince.

"We hit mirrors," Stevie said disgustedly.

Dougherty slid across the seat and peered along the side of the cab. Where the side view mirror had once been was now nothing more than a jagged pair of torn-out screw holes in the yellow sheet metal. She turned in the seat, looking for the truck, but the bus completely blocked her view.

"Oh . . . man . . . I'm gonna be in deep shit over the mirror," Stevie said as he wheeled wildly down the street. "Gonna get my ass fired for sure."

"The damage is on me," Dougherty breathed. "You just catch him."

He snuck a peek over his shoulder, making sure she was serious, and then floored it.

The street ahead was temporarily clear. "Come on . . . come on," she whispered as they raced down Denny Way, her hopes fading with every passing block.

Halfway down the hill, a yellow Penske truck was trying to turn left onto Summit Avenue, holding a dozen vehicles hostage as a steady stream of uphill traffic prevented the maneuver. Brian Bohannon and the gray van were third in line behind the truck.

"There's our boy," Stevie said.

Dougherty dove forward, once again hanging over the driver's seat and peering intently out through the windshield. "Sure is," she said. She clapped him on the shoulder.

The van was ten cars in front of them. They sat and waited. Another dozen vehicles crawled uphill before the truck was able to make the turn onto Summit.

Stevie glanced over at the torn metal where the side view mirror used to be and then turned to meet her gaze. "You sure you don't wanna just call the cops on this guy?" he wanted to know. "This is getting hairy."

"No," was all she said.

He lifted his hands from the wheel in an unspoken question. She answered.

"I don't know, man," she said. She stared straight ahead as the traffic began to move. "I used to dream about what I'd do to him . . . all the ways I'd make him pay for turning me into a freak . . ." Stevie began to object, but she kept on. "How I'd sit in court and watch him get sent off to prison. Or even better how I'd take care of him myself. How I'd . . ." She stopped . . . shook her head once and clamped her mouth shut.

Stevie fed the cab some gas. Several cars turned off, disappearing this way and that, reducing the number of vehicles between the cab and the van to five. Stevie closed the gap.

"What were you gonna do to him?" he asked.

She shook her head again. Made a wry face. "It all seems so silly now," she said.

"And you ain't no freak," Stevie said with a mock frown. "That's no way to be talkin' about yourself." He waved a hand and put on a boyish smile. "You keep that kinda talk up and I'm gonna have to ask you to vacate the cab."

Before she could reply, the van made a sharp left. The cab hustled up the street and followed suit. By the time they rounded the corner, the van was making another turn, right, downhill again, toward Olive Way. "He used to live on this block," Dougherty said. "Back when we first met." Stevie snapped off the headlights.

A series of images flashed across her mind's eye. Of parties that ran long into the night, parties where nobody ever had to be anywhere in the morning, where the politics involved ridding the world of corporations, and their long-range plans never ventured further than the following week. She could see him there with his Billy Idol hair and that smug smirk on his lips, as if to say he had no doubt about anything, when if you knew him at all, you could see right away it was just for show, and under all the bullshit was a scared little boy who knew he was never going to live up to his rich parents' expectations and so had decided not to try, had decided to go the other way so that nobody, not even his worst tormentors, could say he'd failed . . . only that he'd chosen a different path.

Stevie pulled to a stop. A block down, the van was backing into a parking space. They sat in the darkness, watching Bohannon take three tries to work the van to the curb.

"Shitty driver," Stevie commented as they watched the lights go out and Brian Bohannon's shadowed form appear on the sidewalk, hands thrust deep in his jacket pockets as he headed down the hill at a loose-jointed shamble.

Dougherty popped the door handle and stepped out. A car rounded the corner at the head of the street, its ultrabright halogen lights sending Dougherty's shadow halfway down the block. She shaded her eyes and waited for the car to pass, but apparently the driver was otherwise occupied. The car didn't move. Just sat there, lights ablaze, throwing a painful purple glare over the entire block.

Dougherty leaned down and looked into the cab. In the bright artificial light, Stevie looked like he had only half a face. "I'm gonna . . ." she began.

He nodded. "I'll meet you at the Starbucks on Olive," he whispered.

And then, without warning, the lights went out and the street faded to black. She jerked her eyes in that direction. Blinked a couple of times. The car was gone. No headlights. No taillights. No nothing.

She had only a split second to wonder. Brian Bohannon had nearly a full block lead on her. Another short stretch of sidewalk and he'd be down on East Olive, where the lights grew brighter while her chances of going unnoticed grew dimmer.

She reached down, pulled off her shoes and began to jog down the street with the black pumps bouncing in her hand like a scuffed bouquet.

The sidewalk was uneven, cracked by time, heaved by tree roots, the concrete slabs tilted this way and that like some funhouse promenade. She kept her eyes on the uneven ground as gravity pulled her into a full run that stretched her long legs until her hip joints began to loosen and she settled into her stride.

Her bouncing eyes watched him turn right, up the little sliver of street that fronted the Hillcrest Market. She was thirty yards away and closing quickly when he turned along the front of the market and disappeared from her view.

She short-legged it to a stop. She could feel the rough sidewalk through the freshly worn holes in the bottoms of her stockings. Her mouth hung open, but she was breathing easily as she peeked around the corner. No Brian.

Another step forward and she could see into the store. He was at the counter, buying cigarettes. Waving his hands around, making small talk with the four hundred pounder on the other side of the counter.

Dougherty crossed the side street, angling over to a small traffic island and a pair of battered utility poles. She settled into the semidarkness just in time to watch Brian emerge from the market. Through the space between the poles, she watched as he opened the cigarettes, shook one out into his hand and then lit it with his silver Zippo lighter and a practiced flip of the wrist. He liked to think he smoked like James Dean. All cool and casual like. His hair was dark now and combed forward in a series of waves. Working the butt, he watched the passing parade until he spotted a break in the oncoming traffic and then stepped off the curb, all squinty-eyed, cigarette dangling from the corner of his mouth.

He got three steps into the street when she heard the roar of an engine rise above the hiss of traffic. Brian must have heard it at just about the same time because he snapped his head around toward the dark blue Mercedes sedan screaming up the hill, full-tilt boogie, lights out, coming right at him like a high-end German missile. He started back for the sidewalk, but slipped and went to one knee in the street, before scrambling to his feet and limping back the way he'd come.

The driver must have been drunk. As he rocketed closer and closer, he began to veer toward the right almost as if he was intentionally trying to catch Brian before he made it to the curb. Nearly on him now, the driver snapped on the headlights as if to fix his quarry in the beam at the moment of collision.

Involuntarily, Dougherty turned to face the terror. She pressed her back into the rough surface of the poles. The car, lights ablaze, engine screaming, was now coming right at her. She opened her mouth to scream, but all that came out was a hoarse croak, the sound of which was swallowed whole by the scream of the approaching Mercedes.

The right front tire bounced over the curb six feet away from her. She closed her eyes and waited for the impact . . . and then . . . a violent *whoosh* of air stirred her clothes and the heat of an engine rose to her cheeks as the driver veered back into the street, missing Dougherty and the telephone poles by no more than a couple of feet.

Breath raced like a hurricane in her chest. Her knees shook so badly that, had it not been for the utility poles, she would have dropped to the ground. And then she remembered Brian. And the evils she'd mentally visited upon him over the years. The horrific pictures she'd savored. Pictures of his bent and broken body as it paid in blood for what he'd done to her in ink. And . . . she began to cry.

She turned slowly and flattened her chest against the poles. The smell of creosote filled her nostrils as she drew in a long breath and held it. And then she heard his labored breathing and the small keening sound that was coming from his chest. He sat on the pavement, gathering himself. She watched as he struggled to his feet and then staggered out of view. Dougherty pressed her cheek against the rough wood and listened to his heels clicking on the pavement. After a moment she peeked around the utility poles and watched Bohannon limp back up the side street toward the van. His gait was unsteady and his line crooked as he moved from shadow to streetlight and back until finally, about halfway back to the van, he stepped into a thick blotch of shadow and . . . then . . . somehow . . . never stepped out. She waited, staring intently into the darkness. Her eyes thought they detected a sudden rush of movement in the darkness, almost as if he was dancing, and then, above the rumble of traffic, perhaps the sound of a strangled cry. And then nothing. Nothing at all.

She hurried up the street, taking advantage of a break in the traffic, loping diagonally through the intersection, all the way to the far curb and then up the opposite side of the street, staying in the deep shadows as she moved abreast of the spot where she'd lost sight of him. A narrow alley running between apartment buildings. At the far end of the passage, a glint of light on metal caught her attention and she thought she could make out a car, its headlights dark, as it bounced backward across the sidewalk and disappeared from view.

9

Corso rested his cheek on one of the rear tires and watched as the robot rolled back out onto the sidewalk. The fireman in the orange haz-mat suit and breathing apparatus waved his arms, signaling the operator to stop while he untangled the plastic from the rear of the device. Then waved again when the robot was free.

The operator spoke into his microphone. His partner in the suit nodded that he'd heard and reached for the back of the robot, where he pulled open a panel and reached inside. Corso didn't get a chance to see what the guy was removing. Up the street, where the cops had all the people collected, all hell suddenly broke loose.

A woman screamed, not in agony, not in pain, but with a guttural bellow of outrage and hate. Corso rolled over twice and peered uphill between the front wheels. A riot had broken out. Hoarse shouts filled the night air. He inched forward for a better view. A deep voice was screaming the same thing over and over, something about fascist Nazi bastards.

The crowd had pushed over the sawhorses and

spilled out of the enclosure, battling the cops hand to hand in the street. At the front of the impromptu skirmish line, a middle-aged man wore a strip of yellow police tape across his chest like a beauty queen while swinging wildly with a briefcase, lashing back and forth, then finally coming straight down as if he were chopping wood, until the case shattered on the nearest cop's plastic helmet, driving the cop to his knees with the force of the blow, breaking open the case, spewing the contents into the street, where the swirling breeze separated sheet from sheet until the spilled paperwork roiled around their ankles like an angry flock of pigeons.

The cop was halfway back to his feet when an angular African-American woman threw herself onto his back, driving him down again, forcing him to duck and cover himself from the hail of fists and knees and elbows which she directed his way. She was screaming at the top of her lungs. Something about her children, Corso thought. Totally out of control, tight black skirt forced up over her ample hips, her pantyhose torn to pieces by the violence, she windmilled her fists and knees into the downed cop with a strength generally only seen in moments when maddened mothers summon sufficient adrenaline to lift automobiles from their stricken children.

Corso pulled his eyes upward. The scene he'd been watching was being repeated all over the street as enraged citizens fought the police in a frenzy. He watched as another line of helmeted cops waded into the fray, holding their batons in front of them like steel offerings, only to be driven back by the frenzy of the mob.

The nearest of the reinforcements spotted the

downed cop and moved directly to the rescue. He threw his baton around the kneeling woman's throat and lifted her completely off the ground. Her eyes bulged in her head as she clawed desperately at the steel shank crushing her throat. Her long legs flailed in the air as she fought for breath.

Corso watched her eyes roll back in her head, and still the cop applied more pressure. He wanted to shout but stopped himself. He could see the moist pink interior of her mouth when, without willing it so, he found himself moving. Scuttling forward on his belly until he was out from under the front of the van and then on his feet. Took him three long strides to get to the barrier and another second to duck beneath. She hung limp now, only her twitching fingers in motion. That's when things got dicey up on the hill, pulling the cop's head around, loosening his choke hold until the woman dropped on the pavement in a heap and he hurried toward the riot. Corso slid to a stop.

He felt the blood heat in his face. His breath was shallow and his hands were knotted so tightly his fingers ached. The woman had rolled to her knees and was puking in the street. In between heaves, she looked around uncomprehendingly and gasped for air. Corso pulled his eyes from her and looked up the hill toward the flailing mass of bodies filling Yesler Street.

The crowd had taken the street. Outnumbered and outgunned, they were nonetheless pushing the line of cops backward. Batons swung wildly in the night. Screams and curses assaulted the ears. The crowd had taken on the look of a single beast, a throbbing collection of arms and legs moving to and fro and nowhere at all as the give and take surged from curb to curb and back again.

An SFD SUV bounced over the curb, rocked to a halt on the sidewalk, wedged between the mammoth cop van and the boarded-up windows of a defunct bodega. The doors burst open and four firemen clomped up the hill to reinforce the cops. The sight of their brethren in motion sent the robot's operator and his orange-clad partner hurrying up the street to join the fray. Corso watched as the arrival of the reinforcements stopped the retreat and, by sheer weight of numbers, began to force the crowd backward.

At the crucial moment in the conflict, when things could have gone either way, something flickered in his peripheral vision. He swung a glance over in the direction of the robot . . . and there she was. Like she'd been beamed down from space. Stepping out of the mouth of an alley on the north side of Yesler Street. Maybe five-eight in her low heels. Striking features, blonde hair cut short, wearing a black raincoat that stopped just above her shapely ankles. Her eyes met his, sending a chill down his spine. Even at a distance, something cold and disinterested rolled from her gaze. A gaze that made it clear . . . if it was mercy you were looking for, you'd better look someplace else because around here that shit was in short supply. She looked him over like a lunch menu. As her eyes crawled over him, he thought he saw a slight flicker, as if in recognition, before she began to move, covering the ten yards to the mouth of the bus tunnel, where she pushed the plastic back, threw Corso one last look and stepped inside. Corso watched dumbfounded as the apparition slid across the concourse, hesitated for a moment at the top of the stairs and then disappeared from view.

He never got a chance to decide what came next.

"You," the rough voice boomed. "Over against the wall. Now! Move it."

Another half dozen officers had abandoned their motorcycles and squad cars to help with the battle in the street. A burly motorcycle cop pointed a black glove at Corso. "Get up there with the others," he screamed.

Corso gestured toward the puking woman, whose lower lip was now joined to the pavement by a silver filament of spit. "She's hurt," he said.

He fixed Corso with an angry stare. The cop was torn. Part of him wanted to vent his rage . . . right there . . . right then. Another part wanted to throw his anger into the surging crowd. A sudden series of shouts and curses and a final surge from the crowd helped him make up his mind.

"You stay right here," he yelled, shaking a fist at Corso. "You hear me?"

He was already running uphill by the time Corso assured him he wasn't going anywhere. Corso stepped over and went to one knee at the woman's side. Uphill . . . away from the path of the thick stream of vomit.

She twisted her neck far enough to look into his eyes. Beneath the dark roast brown, her complexion had taken on a burgundy tinge, as if the skin were merely floating on an ocean of blood. Her eyes had leaked water down her cheeks, and she'd lost one of her gold hoop earrings.

"You gonna be okay?" Corso asked.

She gave a small nod and then reached out and grabbed his sleeve. "My . . ." she croaked. Swallowed twice and tried again. "My children . . ."

Corso put his hand on her shoulder. She was trembling like an idling engine.

"I gotta go," he said. "Everything's gonna be all right."

She reached for him again, as he got to his feet. He took a step back and looked around. The crowd had turned its collective shoulder and was grudgingly giving ground. An umbrella lashed out from the crowd, its wicked point deflected by a black visor. Out in the middle of the melee somebody bull-rushed the officers and was quickly thrown back.

Corso groped in his pocket and found Slobodan Nisovic's key. Satisfied, he ducked under the barrier and veered left, heading for the door to the Underground.

The second he stepped out from behind the SUV, a shout stopped him in his tracks.

"You there," the voice boomed.

He didn't stick around to check out the source. Instead, he turned on his heel and retreated down the narrow alley between the vehicles. When he looked uphill again, the woman had risen to one knee and was looking directly at him as he lifted his foot and stepped up into the huge van.

Bigger than the biggest motor home, the Critical Incident Mobile Squad Room was a cornucopia of cop equipment. On the left, a compact communications center ran a third of the way along the wall. Lots of colored lights. Every kind of radio and telephone known to man. Across the aisle, half a dozen orange haz-mat suits hung on a steel bar, black breathing devices on a narrow shelf above. On the left, a series of shelves and bins bursting with god knows what. On the right, four closets about the size of airplane bathrooms. The rear of the coach consisted of four individual holding cells, each with its own little seat allowing the occupant to rest in relative comfort.

The sound of scuffing feet sent Corso across the aisle to the closet doors. He went down the line, trying the doors. Locked. Locked. "Shit." Here they come. Locked. "Fuck." The fourth door wasn't quite latched. It swung open at a touch. The walls were covered with tools. Picks, shovels, axes . . . a winch hung from the back panel. In the center of the floor sat a wicked-looking device Corso thought he recognized as the Jaws of Life. He fit his legs around the mechanical pincers, wiggled his shoulders inside and closed the door.

Five seconds and the van rocked hard. Heavy breathing. Corso listened as an arm rifled through the orange coveralls, sending the suits swinging and squeaking on their metal hangers. Then the rattle of the first closet door and then the next and the next and then, finally, the one he was in. The door had locked itself. Corso held his breath.

The van rocked again. "What the hell are you doing in here?" came a voice.

Corso heard somebody swallow hard. "Thought I saw one of them duck in here, Captain. I was . . ."

"Everything locked?" the captain asked.

"Yessir."

A short silence ensued. "They need you up the street," was all he said, but the sense of disapproval was palpable.

"Yessir."

Footsteps and the clank of boots on the metal stairs. The squeak of a chair and the flat click of a button. "Patch me through to the chief," the captain said.

Didn't take but half a minute. "Harry . . . it's George. Yeah . . . but listen . . . we're stretched way too thin. I need another . . ." Corso could hear the scratch of conversation coming through the line, but could not make out the words. "I'm not kidding, Harry . . . I've got a serious problem down here. I don't get some help . . ." The scratching interrupted him again. This time for good. "Yes. Yes sir. Yes I do."

Ten seconds passed. Long enough to be sure the circuit was broken.

"Goddammit," the captain bellowed.

10

It was with great trepidation that SPD Chief Harry Dobson put down the telephone receiver and crossed the room to the mayor's side. Gary Dean wasn't the kind of man who took bad news well. It was almost as if he was unable to attack a problem until he had first expended his anger and frustration on some underling and thus, in his own mind at least, deflected a major portion of the attendant guilt.

"We've got serious crowd control problems in the square," he whispered.

The mayor folded his arms across his chest, pursed his lips and blew out a long breath. He kept his lips puckered as he looked around the room.

Dobson went on. "What with maintaining control at the Weston and this new incident downtown, we're stretched too thin."

"So . . . you're saying what?" Harlan Sykes asked.

"I'm saying we need to examine our priorities."

The mayor began shaking his head before the words were out of Dobson's mouth. "You need more people down there, pull them off the Weston and send them downtown until we get things back under control."

"I've got no personnel to spare. We're completely maxed out."

Sykes opened his mouth to speak, but Dobson cut him off. "Besides which"—he waved a hand—"I'm not putting any more of my people at that kind of risk until I know exactly what's going on down there."

"You heard what the doctor said," the mayor said.

"I heard," he scoffed. "She was every bit as confused as we were."

"How goddamn hard can it be to get fifty civilians packed up to Harborview for observation?" Harlan Sykes whispered accusingly.

Dobson met his gaze. "Pretty damn hard," he said. "You don't think so . . . maybe we ought to get you a helmet, and a baton and send you . . ."

The mayor waved him off. "What's the holdup?" he demanded.

"Harborview isn't quite ready for them yet. They're clearing two whole floors, so they can keep them in strict barrier isolation. They're saying it's going to be another hour . . . at least."

The mayor shot a glance at his watch. "It's been over two hours since this thing started." He looked around the room and lowered his voice. "I thought we were prepared for this type of situation. I thought—"

Dobson cut him off. "This is the big time, your honor." His face had taken on that ashen hue his subordinates often saw in times of crisis. "We've got something here that kills people in their tracks, then bleeds them out on the way down. Our local epidemiologist thinks it's a hemorrhagic fever. Some relative of Ebola . . ." He waited a second for the word to sink in. "Just about the deadliest disease ever discovered on the planet."

"She wasn't sure," the mayor said. "She said—"

"She said she wanted some backup on this thing." He looked from Dean to Sykes and back. "And, unless I'm mistaken, the good Dr. Stafford looked pretty much scared shitless when she wheeled out of here."

Dean and Sykes were momentarily taken aback. Neither could remember Harry Dobson ever having used profanity before, just as neither had ever heard the undercurrent of bitterness which had worked its way into his tone. Now Dobson lowered his voice. "Harborview's doing the right thing," he said. "This stuff is worse than the plague. It's killed health care workers all over the world. They're breaking out the space suits, which is just exactly what I'd be doing if I was in their place."

Sykes was shaking his head. "What a mess."

"Which rhymes with press," Dobson snapped. "I've got seventy press queries sitting in my mailbox. I'm getting heat from the nationals. CNN's starting to nose around. Our detainees are using cell phones. We're getting flooded by calls from families." He rolled his eyes. "Some of whom are also calling the press. I think it's time we threw everybody a bone."

Again, the mayor disagreed. "We're keeping a lid on this thing," he insisted.

"It's bad policy," Dobson said.

"We're not keeping a damn thing from them," Sykes threw in.

"With all due respect—"

"We don't know squat," the mayor hissed. "Anything we released at this point would be pure speculation."

Dobson shrugged. "You know how they are."

The mayor waved an impatient hand. "There's nothing we can do about that. If the press wants to fabricate facts, that's their business. What we need to be absolutely certain about is that we don't appear to have been even remotely guilty of misinformation."

Sykes did what he did best. He agreed wholeheartedly. "We need better medical data. Until then . . ." He began to ramble on about the need for accurate information.

Harry felt his pager buzzing on his hip. He pulled it from his belt and brought it close enough to read the number without his glasses. Eastern Washington area code. His wife Kathleen. With all that had been going on, he'd forgotten to call her this morning. Ever since she'd left for Pullman, ten days ago, they'd spoken on the phone every day. Gave her an outlet for the frustrations of nursing her ninety-six-year-old father through the final stages of Alzheimer's. Gave Harry a connection to the day-to-day universe that cops often lost somewhere in the shuffle of the job.

Harry sidled over toward the corner of the room, where he pulled out his cell phone and dialed. She answered on the third ring. "Is everything okay?" she wanted to know.

"Real busy," he answered. "How's by you?"

"Same here."

"How's Tom?"

She sighed. Same old. Some days he's clear as a bell. Some days he has no idea who I am. Thinks I'm some state worker going to take him to a nursing home."

"What about Nancy?" he asked, bringing up the sore subject of Kathleen's older sister, who while living in nearby Coeur d'Alene, Idaho, had thus far provided little or no support for their dying father, insisting instead that he'd be better off in a nursing home, a notion which Kathleen vehemently opposed.

He heard his wife heave another sigh. "Nancy's out for Nancy," his wife said. She caught the bitterness in her own voice. "Sometimes I think that maybe she's right. Maybe . . ." Her voice trailed off.

Harry knew better than to get involved in the family tug of war. Wasn't his business anyway. Wasn't like he and Tom Green were close or anything. Truth was they'd pretty much detested one another for the past thirty years or so. Harry clamped his jaw closed and looked around the room.

As if on cue, the conference room door opened and Dr. Helen Stafford pushed her way back into the room.

"I've got a situation here," Harry said. "I've gotta go."

He could sense her anxiety. "Maybe you ought to . . ." he began.

"I'm gonna stick it out," she said.

"Gotta go," he said again.

"Bye," she said and broke the connection.

Harry turned his attention back to the room just in time to check out the dozen or so people who trailed Stafford into the room. The body language said the three guys in front were the heavies. One was an elderly gentleman in gray slacks and a black cashmere blazer. He'd reached that stage in life where he was no longer required to keep his long white hair properly combed, and his leonine mane was beginning to take on the disheveled look of Albert Einstein during his later years at Princeton.

The second man wore a black yarmulke and a full set of side whiskers. He had that vaguely unkempt look of lifetime academics, as if the niceties of careful grooming were, to some extent at least, either beneath his dignity or so far down his list of priorities he never quite got that far.

The third guy was just the opposite. An army officer. A bird colonel. Hat tucked under his arm, chin tucked to his chest, he entered the room with an erectness of bearing and a seriousness of purpose that seemed to bring the very air to attention.

Without so much as a word, the trio made a beeline for Ben Gardener and the TV monitor. As the entourage spread out along the back wall, Harry Dobson checked them out. Six men and a woman. Harry made the two on the near end to be low-key security types. There seemed to be a general understanding that they would occupy the positions closest to the luminaries. They showed a lot of teeth, but their quick little eyes rolled relentlessly over the room like searchlights.

The rest of the men were surely functionaries. Secretaries, drivers. People accustomed to standing around waiting.

From where he stood, Harry's view of the woman was obstructed by the tallest of the toadies. Short blonde hair and a good-looking pair of legs were as far as he'd gotten when Dr. Stafford appeared at his shoulder.

"I take it we're about to get a second opinion," Dobson whispered.

"And a third and a fourth," she said.

"Who we got here?"

"The old guy with the hair's Dr. Hans Belder, president and founder of the Nehring Works, a German firm specializing in vaccines for exotic viral infections. Probably knows more about viral infection than anybody else on the planet. He's delivering the keynote speech at the convention."

"The rabbi?"

"Isaac Klugeman," she said. "He's the Israeli version of Belder."

"What about GI Joe?"

She sighed. "Colonel David Hines, used to be assistant director of"—Stafford spelled it out—"U-S-A-M-R-I-I-D . . . U.S. Army Medical Research Institute of Infectious Diseases, in Fort Detrick, Maryland."

"Used to be?"

She turned her back on the others and lowered her voice. "Got to be such a pain in the butt, the army removed him from his post."

"Pain in the butt how?"

"Strident," she said. "All gloom and doom. We're all gonna die." She shot Harry a quick look. "You know the type."

"So how come he's here?"

"He invited himself along."

"No . . . I mean how come he's still a part of the scene if he's been removed from his position."

"He's on the UN inspection team. The people who travel around the world making sure nobody is playing with biological matches." She rolled her eyes and then put her lips close to Harry's ear. "I hear the army would love to get rid of him but he's got a friend somewhere inside the Joint Chiefs who won't let it happen. I was told he's under direct orders not to speak with the press."

From the corner of his eye Harry caught sight of Ben Gardener, who, not coincidentally, was also looking his way. He read the glance and had to turn away so Ben wouldn't see the smile. Gardener had watched Harry getting into it with the mayor and his monkey and desperately wanted to know what was going on. Except, these days Ben Gardener was a careful man . . . the kind who wanted to play it safe . . . to keep out of it . . . to let Dobson handle the dirty work.

"Could you run the tape for us?" Dr. Klugeman

asked. When Ben Gardener moved to comply, the crowd along the wall shuffled forward for a look. A single image shuddered on the screen for a moment and then they were inside the bus tunnel again, rolling toward the victim on the escalator, looking at the world from an eerie close-to-the-ground vantage that warped things out of perspective. And then they moved around to the far side of the cadaver, and three quick zooms into the side of the victim's face, where the magnification made the stubble of his beard appear the size of wires. Where the redness of the face could now be seen as an interconnected series of bone-shaped blotches rather than as a uniform field of color, and the yellow discharge which had leaked from many of the lesions suddenly became visible.

Belder shot his colleagues a glance. "Hemorrhagic fever to be sure," he whispered. Looking now from one to the other as if inviting argument. "Can there be any doubt?" he asked. If there was, nobody said it out loud.

"Doesn't look like this one bled out," Colonel Hines said pointing at the screen.

"The escalator was moving when the officers found him," said Dobson.

"Ah," Belder said, nodding.

Colonel Hines stood stiff-legged and ashen-faced. "You've called Atlanta?" Discretion phrased it as a question. Fear made it sound like an order.

"They're on the way," Stafford assured him. She checked her watch. "They should be here in a little over four hours." She anticipated Belder's next question. "Level Four containment lab and all," she said.

Again Belder nodded his shaggy head. He tapped the screen with a well-manicured fingernail and, as if scripted, the picture moved to the bodies at the bottom of the stairs. Hans Belder put his nose nearly on the screen. He blinked several times as the camera zoomed in closer and closer.

"We have a police officer's report that says the tunnel's full of bodies," Stafford narrated. "Perhaps as many as a hundred."

Belder furrowed his brow. "I don't understand," he said, pulling his face back and looking around the room. "Were all of these people traveling together?"

"No," Dr. Stafford said. "Not as far as we know."

The old man made a dismissive noise with his lips. "Not possible," he said.

"That time of the afternoon, most of them are going to be commuters trying to get back home after a long day," Dobson said. "They're almost certainly strangers to each other. Maybe a few of them . . ." he began and then waved the notion off.

The old man shook his head. "You don't understand," he said throwing a hand at the screen. "Hemorrhagic fever does not work this way. In order for this many people to have contracted hemorrhagic fever at the same time, they must either have contracted it from the same source . . ."—he tapped the screen with the backs of his fingers—"most certainly somewhere in Central Africa . . . or they must have spent sufficient time in one another's company to have infected one another." He blew out a thick breath. "And even that doesn't begin to explain the complete lack of variance in incubation period and the absolute mortality rate."

The mayor lost patience. "I don't understand," he sputtered. "What is it . . . how do we . . ."

"Hemorrhagic fever doesn't sneak up on a person," the colonel offered with a scowl. "It comes on with a very definite and very unpleasant set of symptoms."

"In seven to twenty-two days," Belder threw in.

Hines went on. "You come down with a terrible headache. Your eyes feel like they're going to burst from your head. You get a fever. You begin to bleed from the nose and mouth. You become delusional." He moved his shoulders slightly. "Not the sort of symptoms one can ignore, or put off treating," he said finally.

Klugeman straightened up and looked around. "Hemorrhagic fever liquefies the body. Your capillaries and mucous membranes dissolve. The chest cavity fills with blood. And then your intestines." He paused for effect. "Then you either bleed out through your nose and mouth or through your anus." He pointed at the screen. At the halo of blood fanning out from the women's heads. "In all probability . . . that single pool of blood contains sufficient virus to kill off most of the world's population."

"Ninety percent," the colonel said. "Ebola Zaire killed ninety percent of its untreated victims."

Mike Morningway from Emergency Management cleared his throat. "So what you're saying is that if we've got a hundred dead people down in the tunnel, the chances are . . . we've got another ten infected people who walked out alive and are strolling around the streets somewhere."

"Chances are," Hines said.

A low-key buzz filled the room.

"Except!" Belder said it in a loud voice, bringing the room to silence. "Except that none of this makes any sense," he went on. "Hemorrhagic fever does not kill people in their tracks. It is passed only through the bodily fluids of an infected person. It does not fly through the air like a pox virus." He looked up at Chief

Dobson. "And even if it did . . . there's the matter of your officers," Belder said.

"They're under strict quarantine."

"But showing no ill effects?"

"Not yet."

"So why aren't they dead too?" Hines wanted to know.

Belder pondered the question for a moment and then stepped back from the screen. "You're going to need to send a team in there. The CDC is going to require blood . . ."—he began counting on the fingers of his right hand—"tissue and skin samples. Also we'll need to use wipe kits on the walls and any other flat surfaces."

"I've got a team that can do that," Dobson said.

Ben Gardener found himself rising from the chair. From the corner of his eye he watched Mike Morningway raise a finger as if to volunteer the services of his organization. Gardener's mouth began to move before his brain was fully in gear. "I've got people specially trained for this sort of thing," he said.

Dobson stiffened. Hesitated for a moment. "We've already got personnel at risk here, Ben . . . probably best if we—"

Gardener interrupted. "All the more reason you ought to let us handle it. Your guys have already—"

Morningway cleared his considerable throat.

"Put something joint together," Harlan Sykes snapped.

"What do we do about the possible carriers we may have walking around? People who were in the tunnel at the time and walked out just before people started dropping in their tracks," Mike Morningway asked.

"We pray," the colonel said.

11

Dougherty chewed at her lower lip as she trudged up Olive Street with her shoes still dangling from her hand. The jetsam of the city wore gritty on the soles of her feet as she moved along. Her torn stockings circled her ankles like kittens. As she came abreast of Starbucks, she caught sight of Stevie's taxi backed into the shrubbery at the top of the parking lot. He was standing on the pavement smoking a cigarette, watching the smoke rise up into what had turned out to be a clear night sky.

At the sight of her, he dropped the cigarette to the pavement and pulverized the butt beneath the sole of his boot. "So?"

She shook her head. "I lost him," she said.

"Where?"

She threw a thumb back over her shoulder. "Right back there in the street. It was like . . . one second he was there and the next second he was gone." She snapped her fingers. "Just like that."

He looked her up and down. "You don't look so good."

"Some drunken lunatic nearly ran us over," she said and then fed him the story in fifty words or less.

"For real?"

She held her thumb and forefinger an inch apart. "Missed me by this much."

Stevie sympathized, but she seemed not to hear. "I been watching for the van," he said after a moment of silence.

"The van's still there. It's *him* I lost." She looked downhill again.

"You said he used to live in the neighborhood. Maybe he went in someplace . . . you know like to see somebody he knew or something."

"Maybe," she said, without meaning it.

"Whata you wanna do?"

She shrugged. "I don't know."

"We could maybe keep an eye on the van for a while. See if he don't come back here pretty soon."

She looked at the jagged holes where the mirror used to rest and shook her head sadly. "How you gonna get the cab fixed?" she asked.

He looked down at the holes and winced. "The Somalis," he said. "They've got a shop up on Twelfth East. Open twenty-four/seven. Coupla hundred bucks and an hour . . . they'll have it back in shape." He patted the bright yellow fender. "They got a lot of this color already mixed," he said with a grin.

She looked up into the night sky. Saw a line of stars. Orion's belt, she thought. Low on the horizon, a thick train of clouds chugged north, toward Canada and the Arctic beyond. In her mind's eye she saw herself standing alone on the tundra, her cape fluttering around her as she watched the world through a shimmering curtain of blowing snow and ice, isolated from all sensation except the breathy wail of the wind. The shuffle of Stevie's feet pulled her out of her reverie.

She looked around the parking lot as if seeing the scene for the first time.

"Let's get your cab put back together," she said. She grabbed the door handle and pulled it open. Threw her shoes onto the far side of the backseat. "I don't know what the hell I was doing anyway," she said, as much to herself as to Stevie. "What I expected to accomplish by following him around."

She looked over at Stevie, as if he might have the answer. "Sometimes . . ." he said.

The word hung in the air like cannon smoke. "Yeah," she said. "Sometimes."

Whatever came next was lost in the squeal of tires and the roar of the engine. A red Dodge pickup truck came careening into the parking lot, banked hard to the right on its springs, its bright headlights blinding them both as it rocked to a halt in front of the cab. Wasn't until the guy was out of the truck and she noticed the shattered side view mirror hanging down from the door that Dougherty snapped to what was going on. By that time, Stevie was already backpedaling.

The guy was short, fat and redder than his truck. His shaven head gleamed purple in the unnatural overhead light. He had the remains of the cab's mirror in his hand. He brandished it at Stevie. Waved it in his face. "You gonna try to tell me you didn't notice we had a little accident," he shouted. "You stupid son of a bitch."

Stevie showed him a palm, calling for restraint.

Without warning, the guy hauled off and threw the mirror at Stevie's head. Hard as he could. Trying to flatten Stevie's skull with a five-pound hunk of twisted metal. But Stevie was quick as a mongoose, pulling his head aside, allowing the missile to whiz harmlessly past his face and smash against the cab. "Hey now . . . hey now," Stevie began to chant. "No need to get . . ."

At that point, the guy rushed him. Head down, arms flailing, he smashed into Stevie, throwing him backward over the hood, pummeling him alternately in the head and ribs as he kept him bent back over the car. As the guy gathered himself for another volley of punches, Stevie rolled left, sliding across the expanse of yellow sheet metal and off the front of the cab. He had balled his hands into fists and was dancing like a boxer.

"Come on, man . . . come on," he was saying. "You want a piece of me? I'll kick your ass, old man . . ."

Half a dozen pedestrians had interrupted their evening strolls and were watching the proceedings with mild interest. Pickup man took a deep breath, lowered his head again and charged. At least he started to. Halfway to Stevie he came to a stiff-legged stop. Almost like a mime confronting an imaginary wall. His eyes lost their furious focus and for a moment he appeared to be listening to distant voices. He clapped a thick hairy hand to his chest and then looked down at the appendage as if it belonged to someone else. He dropped to his knees. A groan escaped from somewhere deep in his innards.

His face was purple now. He coughed once and then spewed a thin line of phlegm onto his shirtfront. He was breathing in hiccups. He brought his other hand to his chest, fell over sideways and closed his eyes.

Stevie was at his side before Dougherty could collect her wits. "Guy's havin' a heart attack," he hollered. "Somebody call nine-one-one." Stevie had a bruise along his jawline and was developing a serious knot over his right eyebrow. He cleared the guy's mouth with his finger and then bent low over the man's chest, listening for a heartbeat.

"He's alive," Stevie reported.

On the sidewalk in front of the coffee shop, half a dozen people were calling for an aid car. The guy was on his back now, mouth hanging open, breathing like a locomotive. Stevie rolled up his jacket and put it under the guy's head. Off in the distance, a siren began to wail, and then a moment later another plaintive voice joined the chorus. Stevie looked over at Dougherty. "Jesus, lady," he said. "You gotta find yourself a new cabdriver."

12

A bead of sweat slipped out of Corso's hairline, slalomed down his forehead, rolled along the side of his nose and finally paused on his upper lip, where he corralled it with the tip of his tongue. Despite the cool of the evening and the louvers in front of his face, the closet had become quite humid and close. Wouldn't have been so bad if he'd been able to mop his brow once in a while. Unfortunately, the storage area was too narrow for that. The confined space would not allow him to raise his hands above his waist, which explained why, after ten minutes of silence in the van, he was so pleased to be stepping out into the aisle and why he was so disappointed when he heard new voices coming his way.

"Hey Bobby," the first voice said.

Corso took in a lungful of cool air and then stepped back into the closet and locked the door. "What we got?" a second voice wanted to know.

The van rocked on its springs as first one and then a second person stepped inside.

"What we got is a Level Four, Bobby. Biohazard of some sort. Full suits and full decom afterward."

"No shit."

"I'm thinking maybe we got victims down in the tunnel."

"They said that?"

"They didn't say shit, but I could tell. Just the way the captain sounded."

"Where's Boomer and Chico?"

"They're not coming along. We're working with a couple of firemen and a guy from Emergency Services."

"What the hell is that about?"

"You tell me."

"Weird."

"No shit. The whole thing's weird. All they'd tell me was who was going down and that we'd be briefed on the scene."

"Be a lot better working with our own people," Bobby said. "What's the point of all the training . . . if . . . we gotta . . ."

Corso heard the closet door swing open and then the rattle of hangers as the orange biohazard suits were pulled out. "Politics," the first guy said disgustedly. "Gotta be some kind of stupid-ass politics."

Corso pushed his head into the far corner of the closet and peeked through the door's narrow louvers. Bobby and the other guy were in their mid-thirties. Hair helmets and thick necks. He watched as they spread the elastic and pulled the suits on over their boots. In unison, they got to their feet and shrugged their shoulders into the shiny coveralls, before zipping up and pressing the Velcro covers in place. Before continuing, they took a moment to check one another out. Making sure they were properly sealed in the suits. Corso watched as they ran through their safety checklist.

"Fucking firemen better get here," Bobby said, pulling on a pair of black neoprene gloves. "Lest we have to handle this one on our own."

The van rocked. "Fucking firemen are here," a deep voice said. Somebody let loose a laugh. "I'm fucking fireman Bill Ensley. This miserable specimen is fucking fireman Tim Shultz."

Through the narrow slit, Corso watched a handshake get passed around.

"No offense intended," Bobby assured them.

"No problem," Shultz said.

"You know what we got here?" the first fireman asked.

Cop number one shared what he knew, which wasn't much.

"So where's the guy from EMS?" Shultz wanted to know.

"No idea," somebody said.

"We know who it is?"

"Nope."

"Hope to God they're not sending us a virgin."

"What else they got?" cop number one said as he pulled the orange hood over his head, leaving only an oval of exposed skin in the center of his face. Across the aisle, Bobby followed suit. Both cops stepped out of view for a moment. When they returned, each man was holding a black rubber breathing device in his hands.

"We'll gear up and meet you in the street," Ensley said.

"What about the EMS virgin?" Bobby wanted to know.

Ensley showed his palms to the ceiling. "He's here when we're ready . . . he comes along . . . if he's not . . ." He made a *c'est la vie* face and stepped out into the street.

A minute later, Bobby and his partner stepped out, leaving the van silent. Corso slid a hand across his torso and pushed the button on his watch. The dial lit up: it was ten twenty-seven. Give them six or seven minutes, he figured. Give them a chance to check their gear, get their orders and head inside. At that point everybody's attention ought to be focused on what the team was doing. Be a good time to make a quick break across the sidewalk to the door to the Underground. He could feel the sweat forming on his forehead. He took a deep breath and waited.

Four minutes in, he heard voices again and silently cursed. "Hey . . ." someone was calling. He squinted out through the louver just in time to see a blond guy in his late twenties step up into the van. He was so pale the freckles on his cheeks looked red as rouge.

"Hey . . ." someone outside called again. "You hear me?"

A tall man stopped in the doorway and turned toward the voice. A Seattle cop stepped into view. "This is an off-limits area," he said. "I don't know how the hell you got in here, but . . ."

The stranger sat down on the metal bench, fished a laminated ID card from his pocket and waved it at the cop. "I'm Colin Taylor from Emergency Services," he wheezed. "I'm supposed to meet some guys here and . . ." He looked fearfully over his shoulder. "I'm supposed to help out down in the station."

The cop leaned in far enough to scrutinize the plastic ID card. "You better hurry up. They're just about ready to rumble," he said. "I'll go tell 'em you're here."

Taylor got to his feet and pulled an orange outfit

from the closet. He plopped down heavily onto the bench, worked one foot into the suit and then suddenly stopped. He massaged his temples, leaned his head back against the wall and closed his eyes. His mouth hung open. His breathing was quick and shallow. He cradled his stomach with both hands as if he had an old-fashioned bellyache.

He was still in that position when the cop returned. "You okay?" the officer wanted to know. Although Corso didn't hear a response, Taylor must have indicated he was fine. "You sure?" the cop pushed. "You don't look so good to me."

"No . . . no. I'm good to go." His voice was flat and without conviction.

The cop wasn't buying it. Something about Taylor had the cop's radar buzzing. He looked downhill, dug his front teeth into his lower lip and whistled. He windmilled an arm a couple of times. "Come on up here," the gesture said. "Fast."

Half a minute later, a pair of blue-jacketed EMTs joined the officer in the doorway. "Have a look at this guy, will ya?" the cop said. "I don't like his color."

Taylor sat up. Tried to wave the medics off, but by that time they were kneeling on either side of him, checking his pulse and shining a penlight into his eyes. "I'm telling you I'm okay," he protested. "I'm just a little nervous is all." He looked from one guy to the other with a plea for understanding in his eyes. "I've never really . . . you know something like this . . ."

"You've got a heart rate of one eighty-five," one of the EMTs said.

"No way we can send you out with a rate like that," the other one said.

Seemed like a little confirmation was all his partner needed. He reached down and pulled the bottom of the haz-mat suit off of Taylor's shoe. "They're going to have enough to do down there without having to worry about you," he said.

He looked back over his shoulder at the cop. "Tell 'em he's not gonna make it today," he said. When the cop strode off, the EMT turned his attention back to Taylor. "Let's get you more comfortable," he said. "See if we can't get that heart rate down."

Taylor started to protest, but the more he talked, the more the sense of relief in his voice became palpable. They took hold of his elbows and raised him to his feet. His knees shook slightly as he stood in the center of the floor. Taylor pulled a cell phone from the pocket of his parachute pants. "I've got to call . . ." he began.

The nearest EMT slipped the phone from his fingers and dropped it back into his pocket. "We're gonna walk you down to the aid car," he said. "You can call whoever you need to call from there."

"There's no need . . ." Taylor protested. "Just a little air is all . . ."

Corso felt the van rock a couple of times as they took him out the door, then listened as Taylor's protests became fainter and farther away until, at last, it was silent inside, and he popped the lock and stuck his head out of the closet.

Empty. He stepped out of the closet and hurried over to the door. Ten yards downhill, Taylor's legs had turned to foam rubber. If the same cop hadn't showed up and lent a hand, Taylor might have fallen on his face. As it was, it took all three of them to keep him upright and moving forward. "Tough day for virgins," Corso whispered to himself.

Half a block up, the battle was over. The citizens had been herded back against the boarded-up bodega where they milled sullenly. Other than an infrequently shouted curse, they seemed to have vented their wrath and had now lapsed into some sort of postriotal repose.

At the top of Yesler Street, the fire engines had been pulled back far enough to allow a convoy of aid cars to pass between their front bumpers. Corso counted eight ambulances with others still cresting the top of the hill, before he turned and looked the other way, where Taylor was still being assisted down the street and the reinforcements had returned to their guard posts.

Corso stepped outside and quickly covered the narrow space between the van and the fire department SUV, still sitting with its doors flung open, half on, half off the sidewalk. He started to step around the front, heading for the door to the Underground, when he jerked himself to a stop and quickly squatted.

A motorcycle cop sat leaning back against the door, while an EMT tended to a nasty gash above his right eye. Corso held his breath. The pain had squeezed the cop's eyes shut. The medic was facing away from him, daubing away intently. Moving silently, Corso duckwalked back the way he'd come. Back to the van, where he peeked around the front to find that same police captain who'd been begging for help, now talking with Bobby and Ensley and the other haz-mat boys. For the first time, it crossed his mind that he had nowhere to go. That maybe the jig was up.

Corso was lamenting his paucity of options when a flash of orange in his peripheral vision brought his attention back to the floor of the van where Taylor's haz-mat suit lay in a crumpled heap. He ran his eyes up to the shelf above the closet. The black rubber breathing apparatus stared at him with oblong plastic eyes.

A smile spread slowly across Corso's thin lips.

13

Dr. Hans Belder buried his nose in the TV monitor again. At his request, Ben Gardener had rewound the tape to the first victim's cheek. Highest level of magnification. Belder used his fingernail to trace the outline of the lesion . . . first one and then another and another, as if by repetition alone he could convince himself that what he was seeing was real. He sat back in the chair and surveyed the room.

"I'm sure . . ." he began. "I'm sure you all remember the simulation your government ran with the pox virus."

He looked up at Colonel Hines, who anticipated the question. "Operation Dark Winter," Hines said. "Back in two thousand and one."

"Some sort of doomsday game," the mayor said.

"Doomsday indeed," Belder said, taking in the room with a bemused smirk on his face. "Game? I'm not so sure." He cast another glance at the colonel. "I seem to recall that your organization took part in the project, Colonel."

Hines nodded gravely. "Yes . . . we did."

"Perhaps it would be instructive for these ladies and

gentlemen if you would help them recall the results of this . . ."—he searched for a word—"of this game, as you people like to call it."

Hines took a deep breath and then began to speak. "The idea was to simulate a terrorist attack using smallpox spores as the agent. The exercise was conducted by the CDC, the CSIS, the MIPT, the Johns Hopkins Center for Civilian Biodefense Studies . . ." He noticed he was losing his audience and waved an impatient hand. "The best people we had at the time."

"Still the best you have," Belder added.

"Anyway . . ." Hines continued, "as I recall . . . the scenario went like this. They picked three cities. I think they were Atlanta, Philadelphia and Oklahoma City." His eyes made a quick sweep of the room. "This takes place in the weeks immediately preceding Christmas, so everybody's out and about. Anyway . . . they picked three shopping malls in the holiday season. Had three teams of terrorists posing as maintenance men go into the malls and spray smallpox onto the potted plants."

"You must understand . . ." Belder interrupted, "technically speaking, smallpox no longer exists on the planet. It has been eradicated in its natural state. The only known sources for the virus are the CDC in Atlanta and the Vector laboratory outside Novosibirsk, in Russia."

"So what we did . . ." the colonel said, "was to program everything we knew about smallpox, everything we were prepared to bring to bear on an epidemic . . ."—he used his fingers to count—"our vaccine supplies, our health care system, our emergency response agencies—all of it was programmed into a supercomputer, which was then asked to give us the most likely scenario of what would happen under those circumstances."

"The results were . . ." Again Belder searched for a word.

"Ignored," Hines said quickly. "The results were ignored."

Belder nodded. "For the most part . . . yes."

Hines reddened slightly. "All they did was to start vaccinating health care workers." He cut the air with the side of his hand. "Which lasted until one of their unions decided they didn't like the risk and then they stopped that too." He looked over at Belder. "God forbid we inconvenience anyone . . . embarrass anyone . . ." He shook his head in disgust. Closed his mouth hard.

"Tell them the results," Belder prompted.

"It went something like this," Hines said. "Two days into the game, the CDC had one confirmed case of smallpox in Oklahoma City and suspected about twenty more. Eight hours later, they'd confirmed the twenty cases and had fourteen more under the microscope. Similar results started coming in from Atlanta and Philadelphia."

Across the room, the phone buzzed. Gardener walked over, picked it up and began to whisper into the receiver.

Hines kept talking. "By the time a week had gone by, tens of thousands were showing symptoms. Hospital emergency rooms were overwhelmed by the volume."

Belder held up a finger. "Interestingly enough, in the early stages of an epidemic such as this, it does not much matter whether the symptoms are real or imagined. Both strain the system in precisely the same manner."

"Ten days in, we've got two thousand cases in fifteen states with more showing up in Canada, Mexico and Britain. Two weeks in, it's sixteen thousand cases in half the states in the country. A thousand people have died and we're completely out of vaccine. The health care system is a shambles. Violence is rampant in the streets."

He paused, as if inviting someone to contradict. "By February one . . . the computer estimates we've got three million cases of smallpox. A million Americans are dead and there's no end in sight."

"And this . . ." Belder said, "is with a disease for which there is a vaccine. An easily produced vaccine at that. Something where we can put a ring around outbreaks. Something where some of the population at least is immune." He reached over and tapped the TV screen with his fingers. "This," he said, tapping the screen harder now, "this has no cure. No treatment whatsoever. You cannot vaccinate against this. The virus keeps spreading until it runs out of hosts." He folded his arms. "Game over."

Gardener hung up the phone. He looked out over the room and caught Mike Morningway's eye. "Mike," he said, "it seems your man has turned up indisposed." He worked to keep his voice neutral. "We're sending in a four-man team."

Morningway waved a confirming finger but was unable to hide the disappointment in his eyes. This was the kind of failure the budget committee didn't forget. His expression said that some serious fence-mending was going to be required. As a preliminary step, he quickly changed the subject. "About the press . . ." he began, "my office is being flooded with—"

"We're not telling the press a thing until we have

something accurate to tell them," the mayor insisted. "It's bad enough they'll make up news. I'll be damned if we're going to assist them in the process."

The proclamation fanned a crackle of conversation within the room. Sykes whispered frantically into the mayor's ear as pronouncements of disagreement came from several quarters at once. As he so often did when faced with opposition, Gary Dean began to waffle, nodding almost imperceptibly at whatever pearls of wisdom Sykes was pouring into his ear and holding up a hand in the "yeah yeah . . . give me a minute" position.

That's when the colonel broke in. "He's right," Hines announced. "This has to be strictly 'need to know.' " The undertone of disagreement disappeared. The room was suddenly silent. "Keep it vague. Terrorist act in the bus tunnel. Unspecified number of victims. Ongoing investigation."

14

Fingers pulled the strings around Corso's face tight, leaving only a small oval with Corso's features bunched in the center of the opening.

"They told us you weren't gonna make it."

"Just a misunderstanding," Corso assured him.

The cop's orange haz-mat suit was now topped off by a red plastic miner's hat with a tiny TV camera mounted above the light. While his hands were busy checking Corso's protective suit, his eyes moved over Corso's face like searchlights.

"You got any experience at this sort of thing?"

"Coupla chemical spills," Corso said.

The policeman nodded knowingly. "Well then . . . you just stay close and do as you're told and everything will be all right." He took the breathing apparatus from Corso's hand and went over it carefully before handing it back. "We're going down on opposite sides of the station," he said. "These suits have built-in radios, but we don't run on the same frequency as the SFD, so you're coming down onto the south concourse with us. That way you can hear what's going on, and we can keep track of you. Okay?"

Corso said it was. "You don't rip the suit and you don't take off the mask for any reason." He waited for Corso to agree before going on. "We're gonna have you do the wall wipes. We're gonna want four from each end of the station." He drew in the air with his finger. "There's a central hall that bisects the station. It's where the elevators are located." He pointed at his imaginary drawing. "We're coming in here . . . down at the south end of the station. One set of stairs, two escalators to and from the mezzanine."

"I know what it looks like inside," Corso said.

The cop's expression said he was surprised. "So . . . you divide the space between the central corridor and the end walls into fours. Get a sample from each area. Put it in a tube and seal it. Write on the label where it came from. South concourse. East wall. Sample number one, number two . . ." He rolled his wrist to indicate "and so forth." "The samples closest to the elevators will both be number four."

"Got it," Corso assured him.

"Write it all out. Don't make up a secret code for yourself. Write it so some guy in the lab will know exactly where it came from without you having to translate."

Corso assured him he would and then followed him across the street to the mouth of the tunnel, where the rest of the team were making their final preparations.

They'd pulled everybody back. The street was nearly empty. The last three aid cars were rolling over the top of the hill, shuttling the civilians up to Harborview. Whatever was down in the tunnel had everybody spooked. He looked up. The moon had ducked under the clouds and now rode low in the sky like a tarnished nickel.

"He ready?" the cop called Bobby asked.

"Ready as he's gonna be," was the answer.

Corso watched as, one by one, they adjusted their breathing devices. He followed suit, pulling the straps until they felt tight on his face and then using his hands to wiggle the apparatus into place. Bobby came by for a final check, flipped a switch on the side of Corso's mask.

"You hear me?" came crackling from a tiny speaker somewhere near Corso's right ear. Corso nodded. Bobby pointed to a small black button beneath his filter canister. "You wanna talk . . . push this."

Corso pushed the button. "Okay."

Bobby nodded and handed Corso a clear plastic box, divided into a dozen small round compartments, one of which held a felt-tipped pen, the rest of which contained folded squares of gauze. "You make the wipe and then put your samples in here," crackled in Corso's ear. Bobby brandished a gloved finger. "Remember . . . good labels."

Corso pushed the button. "Got it."

"Let's roll."

The other cop pulled the plastic back and, one by one, everyone stepped inside. Without further conversation, the firemen headed directly over to the nearest victim, whose body lay half on, half off the escalator. Corso followed Bobby and his partner around the mezzanine, toward the wide set of stone stairs on the far side of the station. By the time they reached the top of the stairs, Ensley had rolled the victim over onto his back and was using swabs to take samples from the guy's blood-encrusted mouth and nose, while the other fireman took wipe samples from the walls.

They went down the stairs in single file, with Corso

bringing up the rear. Halfway down, the first bodies came into view; collapsed and colorful, they were strewn about the floor like carelessly discarded toys.

The team stopped for a moment and stood three abreast on the central landing, taking in the carnage that appeared before them. "Jesus," somebody whispered.

Another dozen stairs and they could begin to see the bus . . . and the driver, rigid in the seat, his head thrown back, mouth, filled with dark blood, shouting its silent outrage at the ceiling. As one, they turned their faces away and kept moving down until they could see the entire length of the station. Again, they stopped.

Fifty or sixty on this side alone, Corso figured. Something inside of him would not permit him to count, as if to reduce the situation to mere numbers would somehow constitute an act of desecration. Bobby stepped up into the bus and pulled out his test kit. The other cop walked to the nearest body and knelt by its side.

"Let's get this done and get the hell out of here," Bobby's voice said.

Corso began to pick his way among the corpses. Careful to keep his feet away from the thick pools of blood surrounding each and every body, pools which in places had run together, connecting these people more intimately in death than they would have allowed in life. Here, with the promise of the escalator so near, the concourse was full. Bodies collapsed upon bodies. He shuffled sideways, stepping over limbs and torsos, skirting the smears of black fluid where desperate people had tried to crawl forward through their own effluent, leaving wavy salutations of finger-painted horror on the smooth stone floor.

As he cleared the back of the bus, Corso could make

out the northbound concourse for the first time. He winced. Just as bad over there . . . maybe worse. The firemen came into view on the stairway landing. Corso ran his eyes the length of the floor. Over there, across the silent bus lanes, the victims were bunched up at the north end, as if they'd had an extra half a minute of terror and had made a collective run for the escalator.

He turned away and concentrated on the job at hand, eyeballing the long white tile wall. Using the artwork as a guide, he figured he was about a quarter of the way to the central exit sign when, moving with great deliberation, he stopped and took his first sample . . . wiping . . . folding . . . block-printing the label. One south. Southbound.

The air inside the suit was hot and dank; he moved along, treating the dead bodies like downed power lines as he sampled his way up to the elevators, wiping and sealing and printing his way along, accompanied only by the sound of his own measured breathing.

He managed to block it out. Keeping a loud, ongoing dialogue running in his head at all times. Doing everything by the numbers until he reached the elevators. Four South. Southbound. And the old folks in their bold black and yellow ski parkas, so bright and gay you wanted to tell them the game was over . . . that they could get up now and have a laugh with the rest of us . . . and . . . right there . . . her little hand reaching out . . . just a fingertip away from the old man's hand . . . a little Japanese girl in a red plaid skirt and a blue sweater . . . "Hello Kitty" proclaimed the front of her sweater.

Corso knelt by her side. Took him two tries to grasp the hem of her skirt with his gloved fingers and pull it down over her legs. He was about to rise when a gray stain on the floor caught his eye. Just outside the elevator door, a sunburst of gunpowder adorned the stone. Bits of brown paper bag had been blown about and here and there on the floor small pieces of glass glinted green and purple in the overhead lights.

Moving more carefully now, avoiding the shards of glass, Corso retraced his steps until he could see Bobby and his partner taking samples from a woman who'd fallen dead near the edge of the platform. Corso pushed the button on the front of his mask.

"Hey," he said.

Both of them looked his way.

"Whatever it was killed these folks was set off right here," Corso said.

"You sure?" Bobby's partner wanted to know.

"Yeah."

He touched his chest and the red light on his TV camera came on as he walked slowly in Corso's direction, swinging his head from side to side for the benefit of the video recorder. Corso pointed to the gray stain. Then at the bits of paper and finally at the small shards of glass. "Something like a glass vial . . . inside a paper bag . . . set it off with something like a cherry bomb," he said.

The cop agreed. "I'll get us a wipe on the explosion point and see if I can't come up with some of the paper and glass. You finish your wipes on the tunnel."

Corso did as he was told. Moving toward the north end of the tunnel where the bodies were fewer and farther between, he had, for the first time, a chance to wonder what he was going to do when they got topside again and discovered he wasn't Colin Taylor from Emergency Management Services.

He worked quickly as a sense of urgency began to

fill his veins. Four, three, two, one South and he was at the far end, staring into the gaping gullet of the deserted tunnel. He pushed the final piece of gauze into place, snapped the lid closed and turned back. That's when he saw her again.

Two floors up on the mezzanine. No mask. No hazmat suit. Just standing there taking it all in. Same "all there and in charge" look she had when she'd come out of the alley and disappeared into the tunnel. The look of a woman who knew something they didn't. She sensed his eyes and stepped back out of view.

Corso reached for the talk button. Stopped himself. He stepped out onto the platform and looked up. She was gone. He could feel it.

"Let's go," crackled in his ear. He nodded and started back toward the cops, who, by this time, were halfway to the far end of the station.

Corso stopped at the elevator, watching Bobby and his partner pick their way through a thicket of corpses. He pushed the up button. Waited. Bobby turned his way.

"Come on, man. Let's go!"

The elevator car arrived. The door slid open. Corso pulled the wipe kit from his pocket and held it up in front of his masked face, before ceremoniously bending over and setting it on the floor. The elevator door started to close. Corso used his arm as a lever to hold it open. Bobby and his partner were loping his way. "Hey . . . hey . . . what the hell are you doing?" He stepped into the car, pushed the up button with one hand and pulled his mask off with the other, just as the door slid shut.

15

Stevie had the radio on. KING 980. Action News. *"Jim Sexton reporting from downtown Seattle, where police have cordoned off a sixteen-square-block area of Pioneer Square."* His voice was strident and high-pitched. *"From where I stand on the corner of First Avenue and James Street, it appears that whatever has caused these extraordinary measures is a little farther downtown than I am being permitted to go,"* he intoned. *"I find it rather ironic that ten blocks north of here, Seattle police have prevented demonstrators from closing down the city streets surrounding the International Symposium on Chemical and Biological Weapons, while here in Pioneer Square they themselves have cordoned off the entire southern portion of the—"* Shouting could be heard in the background. Then his news voice again. *"I'm standing outside the barrier, officer. Look . . . I'm standing right here. I realize that. Yes. But . . . but . . . the people have a right to know. Well . . . could you just tell me . . ."* Sexton was saying. *"We have a right to report the news. We have a right to provide our viewers . . ."*

The sight of Dougherty coming out of the QFC supermarket with her hands full of twenty-dollar bills pulled Stevie's attention from the radio, which he'd been using to divert his attention from the dull ache in his head and the swollen purple lump which had formerly been his right eye.

She gave him a handful of money, which he stuffed into the pocket of his jeans without counting. "Comes to more than that, send me a bill . . . you know where I live."

She said the words with a bitterness that set Stevie's teeth on edge. "Wasn't *that* bad," he said with a shrug. "You know . . ."

She looked at him in amazement. Her mouth hung open. And then she started to laugh. One shake of the shoulders at first. Then another. Then three and so on until she was out of control, holding her face in her hands, shaking with laughter. "Not so bad," she brayed out between spasms. "You ought to see yourself," she said, wiping her eyes. "You look like you've been in one of those tough man contests. Your cab looks like it's been in the demolition derby." Another fit of laughter overtook her. "Not so bad . . ." she sputtered. "The whole city's in shambles. My life's a wreck. We just had a guy drop dead on us. We spent the past hour lying to the cops so we wouldn't end up in jail . . ."

"Aw come on now . . . they weren't gonna—"

"Trust me, Stevie . . . we were this close . . ." She held her fingers about a quarter inch apart. "I've had some experience being thrown in the can and believe me when I tell you, man, we were damn near there." She took a moment to compose herself, slipped the strap of her purse over her shoulder and wiped her eyes again. "I'll walk home from here," she said.

Stevie looked offended. Like this wasn't the way the

movie was supposed to end. "It's a hell of a long way back to your place," he said. "You sure you don't wanna . . ."

She waved him off. "God knows I could use the air," she said. "Maybe it'll clear my head."

"You sure?" he asked. "City's full of crazies tonight."

"City's always full of crazies."

Stevie shrugged in resignation. "Well then . . . I guess I'll . . ."

"Get the cab fixed," Dougherty said. She pointed a long manicured finger his way. "You probably ought to have somebody look at that eye too."

Stevie lied, said he would and then pulled open the cab door. "See ya," he said before ducking inside. "You be careful now."

Dougherty stood on the sidewalk and watched the cab's taillights dissolve into the tide of traffic. She sighed and then walked half a block up Broadway before realizing she wasn't wearing shoes. She opened her mouth to call out, but he was too far away now.

"Perfect," was all she could think to say.

"Jimbo," said the voice in his ear. Jim Sexton finished stowing the microphone before he answered. "Right here, Robert."

Not Bob or Rob but Robert Tilden. Only Robert. Anything else got you corrected, be it publicly or privately. Assistant News Director Robert Tilden. That's how the yutz answered the phone, for pity's sake. "Not much there," his voice said. "I need a little substance . . . something everybody else hasn't already got on the air. I need you to tap one of those sources of yours."

"It's a complete stonewall, Robert. Nothing going out. Nothing going in. Terrorist activity. Dead bodies in the bus tunnel. That's it. They're not giving us anything to work with."

"Seven's reporting a possible nerve gas scenario."

"They've got somebody inside?"

"Not that I know of."

"Then they're talking through their ass."

"Got to watch the potty mouth, Jim. Next thing you know you'll be doing it on the air."

He really, really wanted to explain to Robert how quaint phrases like "potty mouth" only have meaning when bandied among those under the age of seven, but decided against it. Instead, he stifled a sigh and said, "What have you got in mind, Robert?"

"News, Jimbo. Hard news."

He put his hand over the mouthpiece. Didn't want Robert to hear him gnashing his teeth. "Anything else we need tonight?" he inquired.

"I'm gonna send Sammy and a crew down."

Sammy Anacosta was the new kid on the block. The new Hispanic face at the station. The kid's ambition was so transparent, Jim could practically feel the hot breath on his neck. "Wish him luck," Jim said. "I'm going home."

"Yeah, Jimbo. You do that," and the connection was broken.

Jim Sexton sat back in the seat and stared at the headliner. What galled him most was that he'd done it by the book. Taken it one step at a time. Paid his dues. Spent five years in Pullman . . . earning that journalism degree at Wazoo . . . working two jobs in his spare time. Making it through Beth's first pregnancy, and then losing the baby. Another year as an intern at the station. And then, just like it was supposed to happen. They gave him a job. Reporting!

Okay . . . so maybe it was mostly the dog show stuff, the wind-whipped seventy-mile-an-hour gale remotes from the coast, flying high above the four-alarm warehouse fire in the International District, shouting into the mic with the clopping of the rotors punctuating his voice-over like hoofbeats. Back then it didn't matter. He was on the air. All that remained was to work hard and allow his innate talents to come to the fore. Way he figured it, attrition would take care of the rest.

Turned out he figured it wrong. About the time he began getting a little local notoriety, the girls started coming. Melissa in ninety-one. Two years later it was Kimberly and then little Meghan in ninety-six. After that . . . well . . . after that things were never the same. Whatever notions they might have had about moving on . . . about following his career path around the country as he moved up the affiliate ladder . . . well that was pretty much out of the question. Beth was already as far from her family in the Tri-Cities as she planned on being. Career took a backseat to family. Jim took a backseat period.

Thirteen years of pounding the pavement and nothing had changed. Yeah, the local market had lost Aaron Brown to the lure of New York, but nobody else in the entire Seattle media market had budged an inch. The same primped personages appeared on the screen . . . pronouncing and pontificating on the news every night. The same set of second bananas waited in the wings, doing the weekends and holidays . . . waiting . . . waiting for their hour to come round at last. But no. The time never came.

He heard the tag. Heard it all the time. Jim "Parka

Boy" Sexton. He'd become a local joke. Easing into middle age covering windstorms, slowdowns at the airport and icy streets. Mired in a midrange malaise. Nowhere to go but out the door the minute they could get anybody cheaper or younger . . . or both. And then what?

Pete Carrol, his cameraman, pulled open the back doors of the remote van, slid the camera and other gear up onto the deck and closed the doors again.

He slipped into the driver's seat and reached for the key. "We done for the night?" he asked, his eyes almost pleading. Probably had a date.

"Yeah," Jim said. "We're done. Let's go home."

16

"You see? Right here." Colonel Hines pointed at the close-up on the TV monitor. "The gray patches in the dried blood. That's the intestinal wall."

"The tissue can't support the volume of blood pouring in," Dr. Stafford said. "It simply collapses and the victim bleeds out through the anus."

"Hey." The electronic voice brought everyone up short. They watched intently as the helmet-mounted camera lifted its eye from the pool of blood on the floor and focused on the tall orange-clad apparition twenty yards away at the center of the station.

"Whatever it was killed these folks was set off right here." He pointed to an area directly in front of the elevator doors.

The knot of people huddled in front of the TV monitor tightened slightly as the camera approached the center of the station.

"Something like a glass vial . . . inside a paper bag . . . set it off with something like a cherry bomb," the voice said.

The camera bobbed up and down as the cop agreed. *"I'll get us a wipe on the explosion point and see if I can't come up with some of the paper and glass. You finish your wipes on the tunnel."*

After that, things got quiet again, as each man went about his tasks in silence, moving among the dead as if the bloodied corpses were no more significant than newly fallen leaves.

Harry Dobson looked back over his shoulder at Mike Morningway, who stood transfixed, chewing on a cuticle with his eyes glued to the screen. Been a while since he'd seen anyone look as relieved as Morningway when the word had come that his man Taylor had staged a recovery and was going along with the team after all. That he was performing well was the icing on the cake. "Your man Taylor's showing a lot of chops," Dobson said. "He's cool under pressure."

Morningway acknowledged the prop without taking his eyes from the screen. The phone rang, scaring the hell out of everybody. Ben Gardener picked it up. Slowly, his forehead began to furrow. Everyone in the room picked up on it. Beneath the dark brows, Gardener's bright blue eyes darted about. From Dobson, to Morningway, to the mayor and finally to the floor in front of his feet. "Just a minute," he said, looking out over the crowd. "It's for you, Mike," he said, proffering the phone.

"Me?"

Gardener reached over Dr. Belder's head and handed Morningway the receiver. He watched as Morningway opened his mouth to speak and then changed his mind as the voice began to rattle in his ear.

"Where is he now?" he said finally. "You're sure?"

He listened for a minute and then seemed to lose patience with the conversation. "I'll send his supervisor up. Okay. Yeah. Gotta go. Yeah. Gotta go."

Gardener reached out for the receiver, but Mike Morningway seemed to be lost somewhere inside himself. "Mike," Gardener prodded.

Morningway looked at him uncomprehendingly, then noticed the phone dangling from his fingers and handed it back. "Sorry," he said.

On the screen, the helmet camera was headed back for the escalator. The image bounced up and down as the cop worked his way over and around the maze of bodies.

The camera panned a one-eighty, coming to rest on the third man down by the elevator. *"Let's go,"* the cop said.

"Him," Mike Morningway sputtered. "That's not him."

While the words made no sense, something in Morningway's tone pulled everyone's eyes from the video monitor.

"Who's not who?" Harlan Sykes asked.

"Come on, man. Let's go," the cop on the screen said.

"That's not Colin Taylor," he said pointing at the screen. "Taylor's in a room up at Harborview sick as a dog."

A moment of stunned silence ensued before the mayor asked the obvious question, "Then who in hell is that?"

Morningway didn't answer. On the screen, the cops were running for the elevator. The third man had stepped inside the car. Just as the door began to close, the guy turned his face to the side and pulled off his breathing device. The room held its collective breath. Then the door slid closed and he was gone.

Harry Dobson was the first to recover his wits.

"So . . . what we've got here is a terrorist act for sure," he said. Nobody disagreed. He slid the papers back into his pocket.

"I better call the State Department," he said. "They're gonna want to hear about this."

17

Corso wadded the haz-mat suit into a ball and jammed it into the elevator door. Upon encountering the obstruction, the door emitted a chime, bounced back a few inches and tried again to close. Rebuffed for a second time, the mechanism stopped the door in the middle of the car where it seemed to pout as it pondered its next move.

By that time, Corso was gone, hugging the wall as he crossed to the northbound side. Keeping himself out of view from below, he made his way across the station. Moving quickly toward the sole break in the ocean of white tile surrounding him on three sides . . . to a solitary door adorning the north wall. A big solid brass door. A door so solid it didn't require any kind of written admonition. A door hanging half open.

He poked his head into the darkness and held his breath. He heard the slap of footsteps from somewhere within, before a fan clicked on and blew the sound to dust. He stepped all the way inside and pulled the door closed. Evenly spaced safety lights showed the way along the metal catwalk. Corso grabbed both handrails and hurried along.

The area was designed for the Metro engineers to be able to service the tunnel's ventilation system. Huge metal ducts ran this way and that. Everything tagged and marked and labeled. Twelve forty-six east. The catwalk turned hard right and then suddenly ended at a white metal ladder leading down to a lower level. From somewhere deep in the bowels of the machinery he heard distant footsteps again.

He swung out onto the ladder and began to descend. Moving quickly, using his long legs, he took two rungs at a time, until he reached the bottom, where he found himself in a dimly lit concrete corridor leading off in both directions. He listened. Felt a breeze on the left side of his face and so hurried in that direction. A sign on the wall proclaimed this to be a hard hat area. Eighty yards away, at the far end of the corridor, a dim patch of light suddenly appeared. And then the woman's soft silhouette filled the opening. She looked back over her shoulder at Corso and said something in a low voice. Something derisive in a language he didn't recognize. Then the light disappeared and she was gone. He began to run. At that moment, all the lights went out.

Corso came to a stop. He spread his hands for balance and waited for his eyes to adjust to the total darkness. When his pupils failed to gain a purchase on the inky blackness, he put his right shoulder against the wall and began to walk quickly along. Took him a full minute to negotiate the distance. By that time, his eyes had begun to come around and he was able to make out the black metal security door at the far end. And the red light switch on the wall.

He pulled the door open and stepped out into a much larger tunnel. The woman was nowhere in sight. He looked to his right and realized he was inside the bus tunnel, somewhere under Third Avenue. The sign on the wall announced Pioneer Square Station as the next stop. He began to run the other way. North toward University.

Maybe two hundred yards and he was starting to wheeze when he saw the sign, EMERGENCY EVACUATION EXIT. A series of metal rungs had been set directly into the concrete, forming a rudimentary ladder to the sidewalk above. In the second before he began to climb, he thought he might have heard laughter but couldn't, for the life of him, imagine what was funny.

Jim Sexton fumbled in his pocket for the key, then found it and tried to put it in the lock upside down. He cursed under his breath, reversed the damn thing and let himself in the door. The forced-air warmth of the room hit him in the face like a scratchy blanket. He had to square his shoulders and wade into the room like it was filled with Jell-O.

Beth stirred slightly in the armchair as he pulled the door closed and shrugged himself out of his jacket. It was nine-fifteen on a school night. The girls were off to bed. At least nominally. This time of night Melissa and Kimberly would be burning up the cellular airways chatting up their girlfriends regarding their boyfriends. Beth and the little one were asleep.

He hung his coat in the hall closet and then turned back to the room. The novel in Beth's lap had slipped over to one side and nearly closed itself. She'd ordered pizza for herself and the kids. He could smell it.

Motherhood had fulfilled Beth. Whatever dreams or aspirations she may have once harbored—he remembered vague talk of a career in fashion design . . . or was it office management . . . it seemed so long ago—anyway . . . the roles of wife and mother had provided Beth with sufficient cachet to allow her to get out of bed every morning and look at herself in the mirror with a certain degree of satisfaction. Different strokes for different folks, he reckoned in his finer moments. In his more pensive moments, he tried to recall exactly when he'd signed off on the oft-told tale of the rigors of wifedom and motherhood. The terrifying tale of tater tots and trauma that a full-time wife and mother was forced to endure day after day, year after year, while the wine of her youth spilled down the drain of life . . . drop by drop by drop. Wasn't like he could have disagreed anyway. Stepped up and said, "You know, honey, all in all I think you've got it pretty damn easy." No way that was going to float. No sir. "The trials and tribulations of the housewife" was one of those places in life where it was just plain easier to go along with the program.

A squeaky floorboard chirped under his feet as he crossed the living room and made his way to the kitchen. He could hear the girls chattering on the phones as he poured himself a glass of milk. He considered and then rejected the idea of poking his head in to say goodnight. In his mind's eye he could see the anguished looks they threw at the door these days, aghast that their privacy had been compromised by anything so trivial as a heartfelt greeting. Pleeeeeeease.

Jim turned out the kitchen light on his way to bed.

18

A hundred feet up, the maze of skeletal oak branches churned in the wind like ghostly dancers. Now and again their undulations were accompanied by a mournful creak from somewhere deep in the trunk, where its centuries-old essence stood rooted in a narrow strip of grass that separated the sidewalk from the street.

The clouds had blown north, leaving a desultory moon to compete for the sky. A fierce rush of wind stirred the highest branches, sending tiny bits of tree debris ticking and pinging down onto the cars parked below. Then, just as quickly, the wind stilled, leaving her alone on the street, listening to nothing more than the soft pad of her feet on the sidewalk as she moved along.

Meg Dougherty pulled open her front gate, stepped inside and then used the all-too-familiar loop of wire to hold it closed. As she had done every day for the past several weeks, she reminded herself to buy a new latch and then inwardly smiled as she remembered how long she'd been reminding herself. She was working on exactly whom she was going to rope into helping her put it on when the welcome sight of her own front door separated her from the thought, leaving her with nothing more than a sense of relief and an intense desire to crawl into bed and pull the covers over her head. She heaved a sigh of relief and let herself into the small foyer separating the house from the street.

She stopped in the foyer, sat down on the little antique bench and brushed off the soles of her bare feet. Then she stood and hiked her dress up over her hips, peeled the shredded pantyhose down and threw them onto the floor in a heap. She went inside, dropped her purse on the coffee table and was headed for the stairs when she noticed the strip of light coming from beneath the kitchen door. She shook her head disgustedly and chided herself again for being such a space case. She straight-armed the swinging kitchen door, sending it inward, bouncing it gently off the wall and then back onto her shoulder as she reached into the kitchen and flipped off the forgotten light.

She turned away and took two steps toward the stairs, when the taste in her mouth told her she wanted a drink before going to bed. Something cold and wet. She crossed the darkened kitchen, trying to recall what she had in the fridge. Last week's orange juice or maybe some more recent iced tea. She couldn't remember.

As she reached for the handle, her right foot slipped on the floor. She steadied herself, lifted her foot slightly and realized she was standing in a pool of something . . . something cold and sticky that clung to the bottoms of her feet like syrup. She stood on one foot and opened the refrigerator, sending a weak shaft of light cascading across the checkerboard floor, illuminating the room just enough to make out the dark oblong pool spread out across the floor . . . not coming from the refrigerator as she had feared. Her eyes followed the pool . . . coming from over by the back door. Over by the . . . was it . . . was that . . . that *thing* laughing?

Her legs turned to jelly. A hoarse cry escaped her throat. She tried to run from the room, only to slip and fall heavily on her side, rolling now in the sticky pool of liquid as she struggled to regain her feet. A high keening sound escaped from her chest as she crabbed across the linoleum on her hands and knees. "Oh God. Oh God," she chanted as she burst from the room and staggered back out the front door, out onto the walk, back through the gate into the street, where she turned toward the house, her face a mask of terror, her hands balled into fists, ready to fight for her life.

Nothing moved. Only the sound of the wind in the trees and her own lungs gasping the night air. She stood for a long moment. Waiting. For what she didn't know. Until she recovered some part of her senses and began to pat herself down, looking for her cell phone and then realizing it was in her purse. On the coffee table. In the house. She shuddered.

She looked around; the street was empty and, after another moment, when nothing moved and no sound reached her ears, she began to wonder about herself. Had she made it up? At the end of a long and difficult day, had she taken some odd configuration of light and shadow and mentally turned it into something hideous . . . some bloodless husk staring, mouth agape, at her kitchen ceiling?

Tears filled her eyes. She began to snuffle as she considered the possibility that her senses might have betrayed her. That she was sufficiently overwrought to have freaked herself out over nothing more than . . . nothing more than . . . what?

She approached the house again. Mounted the single stair and went directly to her purse where she grabbed the cell phone and quickly flipped it on. She started to dial . . . got as far as nine-one . . . and stopped. What if she was wrong? What if she called the cops and it turned out to be nothing more than her imagination?

Slowly, she walked to the kitchen door, pushed it open far enough to admit her arm and snapped on the overhead light. She pulled her arm back and stood and watched as the door wiggled to a stop, then took a deep breath and pushed it open again.

Her eyes were first drawn to the light switch and the smear of red she'd left on the wall. Then to the floor in front of the refrigerator where a pool of thick, nearly black liquid lay painted in places where she'd fallen in it. And finally her eyes moved to the far side of the room, to the kneeling figure.

She didn't recognize him at first. Couldn't pull her eyes from the wet collection of severed cords and tubes and muscle tissue that she'd mistaken for his gaping mouth. Wasn't until she came to grips with the fact that his nearly decapitated head, held in place by a single strand of tissue, was resting upside down on his back that her eyes traced the profile and her brain was able to process the data. Brian Bohannon.

19

"It's inert," the man said.

His name was Preston Novac, and, although his deep tan and rugged good looks spoke of a vigorous outdoor life, truth was he spent nearly all of his time in laboratories squinting into microscopes. The good looks were the product of three generations of Ivy League genes. The tan was accomplished during lunch hours, under the same lights they employed to grow viruses. Preston Novak was chief epidemiologist for the Centers for Disease Control in Atlanta, Georgia. His area of expertise was what they called "special pathogens." New germs. Invented germs.

"How can that be?" Hans Belder wanted to know. "It has been . . . not even twenty-four hours since . . ."

"Its timing sequence has been altered," Preston Novac said. His words hung in the air.

"Systemically?"

"On the protein level."

"How can that be?"

"Somebody with a great deal of expertise went to a great deal of trouble."

Novac reached into his pants pocket and came out

with half a dozen photographs, which he dropped onto the table in front of the TV monitor. The prospect of something new to look at roused the room. They'd been up most of the night. Run the tape from the tunnel at least a dozen times. Only Belder and Harlan Sykes had availed themselves of the couches in the room next door and taken naps. With the exception of Mike Morningway, who was up at Harborview looking after the real Colin Taylor, everybody else was still up, wrinkled and baggy-eyed, living on Starbucks and waiting for the CDC to pronounce judgment on whether life, as they knew it, had come to an end.

Belder used his spatulate thumbs to separate the photos. Everyone in the room shuffled forward for a look. Taken through a microscope, the photos showed what appeared to be a haphazard collection of threads; many were separate and distinct, others interwoven with one another . . . nearly all were curved at the extremities like a shepherd's crook.

"Magnified seventeen thousand times," Novac said. "There's no question about it. It's either Ebola Zaire or Ebola Reston." He made a face. "In the best of times, it's hard to tell them apart. With all the genetic manipulation we've got going on here, we'll probably never know for sure."

Belder pointed at a spiny-looking aberration in the top picture. "And this?"

"An airborne pollen spore of some sort. Something in the immediate vicinity of ragweed, we think." Novac used a finger to point. "Looks as if someone used the spore as both a host and a delivery system. Something to keep the virus alive but dormant. They freeze-dried the spore so it would be even lighter and more aerodynamic and then piggybacked the virus onto the spore so that the virus could be assimilated through the nose and lungs."

"So that something like hemorrhagic fever would no longer require direct human fluid contact in order to be spread," the mayor threw in.

"Exactly," Novac said. "Once the virus discovers lungs, you can get it out of the air. All it would take is someone to cough or sneeze in your face."

Belder shook his shaggy head. "Which . . . for all intents and purposes, is the equivalent of being able to contract AIDS over the telephone."

The analogy brought the buzz of conversation to a sudden halt.

"You realize what you're implying here," Colonel Hines said.

"Of course," Novac said. "This wasn't accomplished in anybody's garage. There aren't more than a dozen scientists in the world who could pull off something like this." He made a backhand gesture at the photographs. "This wasn't guesswork. These people had the genome for this virus." He looked around the room. "This isn't the work of some backwater terrorist. This is the work of nations."

"But why?" Belder asked incredulously. "Why would anyone go to such expense to create a virus whose effects last only a matter of moments. If one were trying to create a weapon . . . something that could be used . . ."

"I think what you see here is an experiment gone wrong," Novac interrupted. He looked around the room. "And quite possibly the first piece of clinical evidence that the Walsdorf Conjecture may actually be true."

Helen Stafford read the dazed facial expressions and

jumped in. "The Walsdorf Conjecture is an idea that's been bouncing around the genetic engineering community for the past ten years or so," she said. When no one else picked up the thread, she went on. "One of the difficulties in altering genes has always been that one invariably produces a series of effects in addition to the effects one is seeking."

"It suggests that genes are linked laterally in addition to sequentially," Hines said. "That there's an underlying connection we don't yet understand."

Belder got to his feet. "Johan Walsdorf suggested that certain aspects of a gene are tied together at the protein level and that to alter any one of these aspects is to unwittingly alter all other similar aspects."

"For instance," Novac said, "if one were to alter the genes of a tomato plant . . . trying to . . . say . . . increase the plant's tolerance to cold . . ."

"Which has already been done," Stafford said.

Novac nodded his agreement and said, "What they found was that when they altered the lower end of the plant's temperature sensitivity they also unwittingly altered the upper end of the scale. That to make the plant more resistant to cold was to make it less resistant to heat."

Belder ran a liver-spotted hand through his hair. "What Mr. Novac is suggesting is that whoever altered this virus was probably attempting to substantially reduce the incubation period . . . which is usually from seven to twenty days . . ."—he waved a hand—"to a matter of seconds . . . and what they unwittingly got in return was a drastic reduction in the life cycle as well."

"A virus that attacks immediately and then dies immediately," Colonel Himes added. "A tactical germ, as it were. Something that kills who you want, when you want, without rendering the terrain uninhabitable."

"Which means . . ." Ben Gardener began, "all the people we've got up at Harborview are going to be okay."

Belder smiled and bobbed his shaggy head. "Assuming both Mr. Novac and Mr. Walsdorf are correct, it most certainly does."

"And we can get started removing the remains from the tunnel," Sykes ventured.

"Absolutely."

A congratulatory sigh of relief was still being passed around when the door opened and Harry Dobson stepped back into the room. His face and his uniform were both a little the worse for wear, but the smile was brand-new.

"Homeland Security will have a team here this afternoon," Dobson said. "They're treating this as an act of international terrorism."

"Why international?" Ben Gardener wanted to know.

"Because we made the guy in the elevator," Dobson said.

"Already?" the mayor sounded surprised.

"From the coat we found in the mobile squad room. A fifty-six long. Custom-made by a company in New Jersey. Nine hundred bucks' worth of jacket. Sold in only one local outlet. A place down in the City Centre Building called Europa. We rousted the owner. Guy name of Boris Castellanos. Didn't even have to look at his records. Only jacket of that style and size he had custom-made was for a guy named Frank Corso."

"The writer?"

Dobson pulled a memo-sized piece of paper from

his coat pocket and held it at arm's length. "This is the guy who got fired by *The New York Times* for fabricating a story. Cost the paper a nine-million-dollar libel suit. Went to work for Natalie Van de Hoven over at the *Seattle Sun . . .*"

"The guy from the Himes case," Sykes said.

"Same guy," Dobson said. "Guy's got a jacket as thick as your wrist. A pair of felony convictions for assault and a misdemeanor interfering with a police officer in the performance of his duties. A very shadowy figure. Supposed to be some sort of recluse. Doesn't appear in public. Doesn't even sign the books he writes these days. Lives on a boat somewhere in Portage Bay."

"And they think this Corso guy could be the perp?" the mayor asked. "The one who set things off in the tunnel."

Dobson shrugged. "I mentioned his name to the feds, and all of a sudden they get real sticky on me. Said they've got a jacket on him too. Said he's got a connection to a terrorist organization. Said they'd bring it along and we could discuss the matter. Suggested it might be best if we told the press as little as possible."

"At least he's not a carrier," Dr. Stafford said.

"How do we know?"

Stafford laid it out for him.

"Then my officers . . ."

"Are gonna be just fine," she finished.

Dobson's joy was short-lived. His face clouded over again. "Except for the officer they found in the alley," he said quickly.

"What?"

Dobson's face darkened. "We had a sergeant posted

in the alley right next to the bus tunnel. We thought he might have had a heart attack, but the docs on the hill say they found a puncture wound on the back of his neck, like somebody stuck him with a needle or something." He took a moment to let his words sink in. "They're not having a lot of luck bringing him around."

"And you think this Corso fellow . . ." the mayor let it hang.

"Certainly explains how he got inside our cordon, now doesn't it?"

Nobody was prepared to argue the point.

"Speaking of the press . . ." Chief Dobson said.

"Harlan and his staff will give you everything you need," the mayor piped in. He looked at his watch. "By when do you think?" he asked Harlan Sykes, whose expression said this was all news to him.

"Say eleven," he answered uncertainly.

The mayor put on his handshaking face. "So . . . we keep a lid on this thing till eleven in the morning, then come out as a group." He drew quotation marks in the air with his fingers. "Terrorist act in the bus tunnel. So and so many dead."

"Let's try to get the number right the first time," Sykes added solemnly.

"Anyway," the mayor went on, "initial fears of possible contamination led authorities to seal the area . . ."—he waved a hand—"yadda, yadda."

Sykes squared his shoulders. "We'll get you a packet."

The phone rang. Ben Gardener picked it up, put the receiver to his ear and listened. Slowly, almost imperceptibly, his body began to stiffen. The fatigue-induced slump in his shoulders began to disappear, as he rose to his full height.

"I understand." He flicked his eyes over at Harry Dobson and then pulled them back onto the desk in front of him, as he continued to listen. "Those were the exact words?" he asked. "Thank you," and hung up.

When he lifted his eyes, the room was looking his way. "We've got a threat."

"Who's we?" Dobson demanded.

"All three newspapers. All three TV stations."

"When?"

"Ten minutes ago."

"Saying what?"

"Yesterday was the beginning. Sunday is the end."

"That's it?"

"That's it."

Fear is the first motivation. Fear if you do. Fear if you don't. Fear if you can't make up your mind. Fear that somewhere out there in the great beyond your golden moment has already happened and you never even heard the whisper of its passing.

Jim Sexton's greatest fear was that one of these days he was going to lose it. Going to let some silly slight or ignorant injustice push him over the edge, where he was going to come unglued on some pissant Johnny-come-lately like Robert Tilden and let loose with an invective-filled monologue . . . a tirade of such power . . . a rant whose particulars were so pointed, whose obscenities so obnoxious that rumors of the moment would linger near the water cooler for years, preventing the sorry soul who had invoked his rage from ever showing his face on the premises again. At least, that's how the scene played out in his head, when he wasn't under pressure.

In real life . . . under pressure . . . at this very moment, for instance . . . he was forced to deal with the world through his wife's greatest fear, which consisted of Jim losing his job at the station, beginning what she invariably envisioned as a downward socioeconomic slide to oblivion, to a two-bedroom subsidized firetrap down in the Rainier Valley someplace, to an inner-city school district where her girls would not only become objects of derision and scorn but would instantly morph into drug-sniffing unwed mothers whose multiracial special education spawn would summarily be dumped on Jim and Beth ensuring their much anticipated golden years would be fabricated of far baser material indeed.

So, with Robert Tilden all up in his face . . . first damn thing in the morning . . . right in front of God and everybody . . . Jim Sexton did what he always did. He ate shit.

"There you go with that attitude again," Robert was saying. "That self-defeating stuff isn't going to make it here, Jimbo."

"There was nothing going on, Robert. In case you didn't notice they imposed a complete news blackout on the scene."

"Now . . . now, let's watch that tone," Tilden chided.

"Have you got anything yet?"

"Sammy's on the—"

"Has he *gotten* anything?"

"I don't think I like that—"

And the words froze in his mouth. His eyes moved out over Jim's shoulder, sweeping the room like a prison break was in progress. Jim peeked over his shoulder just in time to see Senior News Editor Albert Lehane storming across the newsroom floor like a tornado. "Tilden," he called from across the room.

Robert opened his mouth to reply, but nothing came out. He coughed into his hand in an attempt to clear his throat, but by that time, Big Al, as he was known to his friends and close associates, was already at his side. "We need a remote," he said.

"I've got . . ." Robert croaked.

Lehane turned to Jim. "Jim," he said, "get your crew and hustle over to Harborview. I want you to camp out at the coroner's office."

"I've got Sammy Anacosta down at . . ." Robert tried.

Lehane waved him off. "He's just a kid," he scoffed. "We've had a threat," Lehane said. He pulled a piece of paper from his pants pocket. Read it. "The dead are just a reminder. Today is the beginning. Sunday is the end."

"Has somebody issued a statement?" Jim asked.

"Just what they said last night."

"The mayor's press conference is at the Olympic at eleven o'clock. I've got Kittie on the way with the number one unit," he said, referring to Kathy Greby, the station's long-standing female news anchor.

Lehane was still rambling. "If there's dead, there's bodies. Bodies eventually end up at Harborview 'cause that's where the coroner is."

"Mr. Lehane . . ." Robert Tilden began. "I could send . . ."

Lehane wasn't listening. "Let's go, Jim," he said. "Hustle it up to Harborview."

20

Detective Sergeant Charly Hart was not, by nature, a happy man. In the best of times, the most charitable description of his demeanor was reckoned to be somewhere in the immediate vicinity of morose. That he'd spent the past three hours with a nearly decapitated corpse and hadn't been to bed for a day and a half merely served to deepen the sense of gloom that followed Charly Hart around like a flock of starving pigeons.

That said, Charly Hart found himself intrigued by the young woman in the chair. Most murders were strictly mom-and-pop. Once in a while somebody got tricky and threw them a curve, but, for the most part, after nearly thirty years on the job, he could walk in the door of a crime scene and pretty much see what had come down. This one though . . .

Something about this one didn't feel right. His partner Reuben Gutierrez had picked up on it too. Instead of throwing smooth all over her like he usually did, Reuben the Cuban was over by the door, leaning against the wall, picking his gold front teeth with a matchbook cover, waiting for something to lend a little clarification before he picked up the ball. Reuben hated to be wrong.

"Paperwork in his pocket says his name's Martin Magnusen. From Toronto, Canada," Detective Hart said.

"His name is Brian Bohannon," she said again. "He's wanted on felony assault charges. He's been living in Europe for the past five or six years."

"The ID's legit," Reuben said.

"His name's Brian Bohannon," she said stubbornly.

Reuben sucked his teeth and then spit something small and white onto the floor. He was digging for another morsel when the squeak of shoes drew his liquid brown eyes toward the hall, where they followed an indistinct form as it passed by the wavy glass window and came to stop at the door of Interrogation Room Number Four. Reuben used his handkerchief to shield his hand from the doorknob. Pulled it open, stuck his other hand out into the hall, came back with a thick black folder.

Meg Dougherty and Charly Hart looked on in silence as Reuben used a well-buffed fingernail to pry open the folder. Several photographs were paperclipped to the inside cover. His facial expression said nothing at all.

He crossed the room, keeping his body between Dougherty and the folder as he made his way to his partner's side. He held the open file in front of Hart's face.

"Look like him to you?" he asked.

Hart thought it over. "Could be, I suppose."

"Hair's different."

Detective Hart's eyes moved to the bottom of the page. "Height and weight are about right," he said.

Reuben dropped the case file onto the scarred desk and leaned down into the woman's face. "So . . . let's go over this again."

Dougherty rearranged herself in the chair. Looked him right in the eye. "I had a show tonight . . ." she began. Waved a hand. "Last night."

"You're a photographer."

". . . at the Cecil Taylor Gallery on Occidental."

"Which ended when?" Reuben asked.

"It ended about nine o'clock when the cops came and told us we had to evacuate the area."

"So you what?"

"So I . . . we headed down to the stadiums to get a cab."

"We who?"

Charly Hart watched the waver in her eyes and, for the first time, thought she might be about to lie. "A friend of mine and me."

"You didn't mention a friend before," Reuben complained.

"I was making a long story short," she said.

"What's this friend's name?" Charly Hart inquired.

She hesitated. "Frank Corso," she said finally.

Charly Hart wrote it down. Reuben began to pace back and forth behind her chair.

"This Frank Corso . . ." Reuben said. "He your lover?"

She looked over at Charly Hart as if to question what this had to do with the subject at hand. Hart slipped his notebook into his jacket pocket and met her gaze. "We're gonna have to check this out with Mr. Corso," he said. "The nature of the relationship . . . between you two . . ." He waggled a hand. "I'm sure you understand."

She surrendered a grudging nod. "No . . ." she said. "Not anymore."

"But you used to be," Reuben pressed.

"Yes." She squeezed the word through her teeth.

"And you two were alone."

She started to say something and then stopped. Raised a finger. "We walked the last part with another guy." Reuben stopped pacing. She anticipated the next question. "I don't know his name, but he said he was the maintenance supervisor for the Smith Tower."

Reuben flipped Charly a quick glance. "So you get down to the stadiums," Charly prompted.

"It's a zoo down there," she said. "But I get a cab."

"What about this Corso guy?" Charly asked.

When her eyes flickered a second time, they knew they'd touched a nerve.

"He went his way and I went mine."

"What was his way?"

She shrugged. "Back to his boat, I guess."

"And where's that?"

"I don't know. He moves it around from marina to marina."

When neither cop said anything, she went on. "He's sort of a recluse. He doesn't like to be bothered."

"So you took a cab home," Charly Hart said.

She laid it out for them. For the third time. They had a few questions along the way, but mostly they just let her talk. When she finished, Charly Hart excused himself and left the room. Reuben Gutierrez waited for a moment and then picked up the case file from the table and began to leaf through it. Near the middle, he came to another set of photographs. Of Dougherty this time. She'd seen the look before. That odd amalgam of pity and lust that men experienced when looking at her tattoos.

She heard the involuntary rush of breath. When she looked up, he was looking her over with renewed interest. "Nobody'd blame you," he said in a soft voice. He looked down at the folder again. Shook his head. "What he did to you. Nobody'd blame you if you offed the guy. You come home. You're big-time stressed out and there's this guy who . . ." He flicked the folder with his fingernails. "Who wouldn't?" he asked sympathetically. Shook his head again, as if to say he was at a loss for words. "All those years . . . All that anger built up inside."

"I didn't kill him," she said. "I found him there on the floor."

Reuben stayed at it for another ten minutes. All kindness and understanding. Fishing for admission, he liked to call it. Dougherty sat there staring at the wall, occasionally issuing a denial, but otherwise refusing to play the game, until suddenly, the hall was full of voices and then people.

First in the door was Charly Hart, his hands thrown out at his sides as he backpedaled into the room, rightfully indignant that anyone would violate the sanctity of the interrogation process, negate the sense of isolation that skilled interrogators instilled in a suspect until finally it seemed as if the only people who existed were right there in that room and the only hope of salvation was to give it up and come clean.

"We got a murder investigation going on here," he bawled. "Who the hell are these yahoos to say they're gonna walk with one of our . . ."

A trio of suits followed him into the room. Mid-thirties. Clean-shaven. Looked like they had a mold somewhere out back and these guys were fresh off the assembly line. The guy in the middle cocked an eyebrow and pointed at Dougherty. "Margaret Dougherty?"

He didn't wait for an answer. Before anyone could respond, the other two stepped forward, took her by the elbows and helped her from the chair.

"What's—" she sputtered.

"FBI," said the center suit. "We'll be needing Ms. Dougherty here." He pulled out a black leather ID case and waved it around the room like he was dispensing holy water.

"No fucking way," Reuben said evenly. "You think you walking out of here wid . . ."

Center fed stuck out an arm as if to ward Reuben off only to have it brushed aside like a twig. "You're interfering with a—" the fed mewed, rubbing his elbow.

"Fuck you," Reuben spat. "You gonna take somebody in our custody, you damn well better—"

That was as far as he got. The doorway filled again. Everybody stood still.

"Detective," Harry Dobson said.

Reuben straightened his shoulders and stood at attention. In his peripheral vision he could see Charly Hart doing the same thing. Life without a pension was the first thought to cross his mind. "Yeah . . . ah . . . Chief," he mumbled.

"I appreciate your dedication to the job," the chief began. "But we've got an extraordinary situation going on here. These gentlemen are going to need to borrow Ms. Dougherty for the foreseeable future."

"Yessir," the two detectives said in unison. "But listen, Chief, we got a—"

Dobson waved them off. "One of you just make a file request on a Frank Corso?"

Charly Hart raised a tentative hand. "He's her alibi," he said.

Dobson nodded. "He's also involved in a terrorist act."

"No way," Dougherty said.

Dobson's eyes were hard as rivets. "We've got a hundred sixteen dead citizens," he said. "And this guy Corso is the closest thing we've got to a suspect."

"Frank would never . . ." Dougherty began. But, by then, it was too late. Her feet barely touched the floor as the G-men hustled her out the door.

Detectives Charly Hart and Reuben Gutierrez stood silent as the sound of scuffling feet faded from hearing. Chief Dobson heaved a sigh. "Get some sleep," he said. "Then report to your lieutenant for reassignment."

"We really got a hundred dead citizens?" Charly wanted to know.

"A buck sixteen," the chief confirmed. "And a viable terrorist threat for Sunday sometime."

Reuben swallowed hard. "This is the real deal then," he said.

"The President has been notified," Dobson said and walked away.

21

Shauna Collins caught sight of them the minute she turned the corner. The one in the Mariners cap . . . must be the cameraman . . . screwing some kind of aluminum tripod together over in the corner. The newscaster guy . . . the one with the red hair . . . the ski report guy . . . was leaning on the reception desk, smiling, trying to draw Laura's attention from the paperwork in front of her. Shauna thought about turning around and scurrying back down the hall to the cafeteria where the impromptu staff meeting had just been held, but instead took a deep breath and walked faster, her rubber-soled shoes squeaking on the clean tile floor as she hustled along.

She kept her eyes on the door at the far end of the reception area. The one marked NO ADMITTANCE—STAFF ONLY, hoping that if she didn't acknowledge the newshound, maybe he wouldn't acknowledge her. No such luck.

Three squeaks in, he lifted his eyes from Laura's desk, swallowed the grin and started her way. "Hi there," he said. "I was hoping you could help me . . ."

She waved him off. "Information is released through

the Public Affairs Office," she said, picking up her gait until it amounted to a brisk trot.

He was at her left shoulder now, keeping pace as she hurried along. "You're a pathologist, right?"

She didn't answer, just kept making a beeline for the door. "All information is released through the Public Affairs Office," she said again. He hurried over to the door, and while not exactly blocking the way, made his presence conspicuous.

Shauna Collins moved him aside with a swimming motion, belly-bumped the swinging door open and started down the hall toward the autopsy room. He was still throwing questions her way when she turned hard left and let herself into the room.

She pushed a long breath of air out through her generous lips, grabbed a fresh pair of latex gloves from the box on the wall and began to pull them on over her chubby hands.

"Let's clean this up and then get that last one outa here, George. That way we'll have the decks clear when they start coming down from upstairs."

"Comin' right up." George Bell announced it like it was an order for chili con carne. Sixteen years of dancing with the dead had taught George the value of a positive outlook. Early on, he'd come to realize that survival as a coroner's assistant was entirely contingent upon the manner in which one approached one's job. Although he'd begun his tenure as a full-fledged adult—thirty-four to be exact—long past starry-eyed illusions regarding the goodness of man and the sanctity of life, the true nature of the urban slaughterhouse had not become apparent to him until he'd spent sufficient time on the job to see, firsthand, the array of violence, casual and otherwise, which members of the species were prepared to visit upon one another on a daily basis.

So it was with a cheerful whistle that George Bell wheeled the silver table to the middle of the room and began to hose it down. When the trickle of murky water got too loud, he switched to humming while he worked. Somewhere among the whistles and the hums and the slap of water, "When You Wish Upon a Star" found its way along the tile walls. He'd been humming the tune for the better part of three days now. He was like that. Something caught his ear and, sure enough, he was stuck with it until another tune came along to take its place. The Jiminy Cricket thing was wearing thin on him. He was ready for something new.

"They tell you what they got going on up there?" he asked as he worked.

When he looked up, her round face was grim. "Just that we've had an act of terrorism," she said. "The figure I heard was in the low hundreds. Hundred ten . . . hundred twenty dead. Something like that."

George shook his head sadly. "What are we comin' to around here? What those Al Queda people got with us make 'em do something like that?"

"They think we're the devil. And let's not jump to any conclusions here. We don't know for sure who did it," she chided.

"Who else it gonna be?" George demanded. "Who else crazy enough to do something like that 'cept that Osama Ben Saddam fella." He placed the power washer on the cart. "Somethin wrong wid those damn people. Might better we just took out that whole section of the world and be done wid it . . . once and for all." He made a chopping motion with his free arm. "Good-bye."

She said, "I don't think we can do that, George," which, not surprisingly, did little to soothe his wrath. He continued to rave about world politics as he worked to remove every last scrap of blood and tissue from the smooth stainless steel surface.

"What kinda crazy son of a bitch gonna strap fifty pounds of dynamite to his ass and then set the damn thing off?" He made another chopping motion with his arm. "How crazy you gotta be? Wanna die that damn bad. Suicide bomber my ass. They wanna die that damn bad, we ought to help their ass out. If it was me . . ."

George ran out of gas by the time he was satisfied with the table and had rolled it to the far side of the room. Dr. Collins had replaced the cassette in her tape recorder and was about ready to go. Collins was all right. Not too cheery, not too grim. Got her business done and got the hell out of there . . . just the way George liked it. Not like that damn Dr. Chiarchiaro. Always playing that loud rock music and singing while he worked. Or that Petersen woman with her jokes and disrespectful talk about the dead. No. Far as George was concerned, Dr. Collins was just right.

"He's in eleven," she said as George pushed the cart across the room to the bank of refrigerated storage bins covering the north wall. He twisted the handle and eased the rollers outward until the entire body came into view beneath the harsh overhead lights.

The victim lay on his back, hands neatly folded across his chest. Drained of blood, the cadaver seemed to have absorbed the unnatural purple hue of the over-head lights. This one was easy. What the doctors called a slam dunk. Somebody damn near cut the boy's head clean off. Nothing but a little flap of neck muscle holding the head on at all.

George moved his eyes downward. Guy was covered with tattoos. At least a dozen. Some of it . . . like the dragon on his chest . . . was really nice work. Some of the rest was blurry and indistinct. Strictly amateur stuff.

This kind was easy. Like the car wrecks and the knife killings and the baseball bat beatings . . . you didn't have to wonder what had come down. The worst mankind had to offer was right there in front of your face and what was left was no longer worth keeping.

The ones that bothered George were the ones without a mark on them. Perfect in every way except for the purple hue around the lips. Looked like maybe they were just sleeping there on the cold hard metal. Like they were gonna get up later and go out for dinner. They were the ones reminded him how fragile and elusive the spark of life could be and how close to the line we all walk every day.

George raised the table to the same level as the cadaver. He started to slide the body his way and then stopped. The head had stuck to the table and was not coming along for the ride. If he wasn't careful, the guy's noggin was gonna end up swinging around in the air, or, worse yet, gonna fall on the floor and roll around. Couldn't let that happen neither. The man had a right to his dignity. Bad enough to be laying around stark naked, with your throat cut and your dick all shriveled up. No need for any of that head-rollin' stuff. None at all.

"Think maybe I'm gonna need a little help," he said.

Dr. Collins crossed the room to George's side and stood for a moment looking down at the corpse. "Clean," she said.

"Excuse?"

She poked a gloved finger into the wound. "A clean cut," she said, lifting the victim's chin to expose the gaping maw that was now his throat. "One clean stroke. No hesitations . . . no sawing . . . no nothing. Something real sharp used by someone real strong," she said. "Somebody without the slightest hesitation about what he was doing."

She lifted the shoulders, slipped her arm under the upper torso and then used her other hand to push the head back into place.

"You ready?"

George said he was and, on the count of three, they slid the body, head and all, onto the table. As Dr. Collins wheeled the cadaver over to the autopsy station and used her foot to lock the wheels, George reached into the bin and came out with a green plastic bag. He untied the rough knot and looked inside. The victim's stuff. Cops had already been through it for anything they might want. The rest they left for the coroner, in case something might shed some light on the victim's last moments. Later on, they'd send whatever was left over to the evidence room to be cataloged.

George shook the contents out onto the tray. The short leather jacket was still in pretty good shape. Other than a couple of bloodstains along the inside edge of the zipper, the garment seemed little the worse for wear. George was careful as he went through the pockets. Never knew when you were gonna come across a needle or something like that.

Across the room, Dr. Collins had adjusted her minimic and begun her monologue. *"Subject is a white male. Thirty to thirty-five. Brown hair, blue eyes. Approximately a hundred and ninety pounds. Severe frontal laceration to the . . ."*

From the inside pocket of the jacket George extracted a fresh pack of cigarettes, an old-fashioned silver Zippo lighter and a plastic credit card type thing. Had an arrow on it. Looked like it might be one of those electronic keys to something. The rest of the pockets were empty. The shirt was a wadded-up mess. Barely tell it had once been brown. George used the tips of his gloved fingers to pry the blood-soaked folds apart, smoothing and separating the stiff fabric until he had the shirt laid out on the table before him. He patted it down for evidence, but found nothing. By the time he'd finished, the rusty-iron smell of blood wafted its way to his nostrils causing him to turn his head to the side for a couple of quick breaths before continuing.

Dr. Collins used a metal caliper to measure the depth and width of the wound and then set the tool aside as she circled the body, lifting it here and there, poking this and prodding that. *"Contusions on the upper arms and neck suggest the victim was in a struggle at some time immediately prior to the fatal wound. The amount of residual bleeding suggests less than an hour passed between the struggle and the moment of death. Victim was, in all probability . . ."*

The black parachute pants were stiff with dried blood, making it difficult for George to go through the maze of pockets and compartments, zippered and snapped and Velcroed and buttoned, that made up the design. He could feel something inside the rough material but couldn't figure out which of the many pockets it was in. He narrowed his search to the right leg and began a systematic search, top to bottom, until, finally, he pulled aside a small silver zipper and extracted a glass vial from a little compartment along the outside of the thigh. A black rubber stopper filled the top of the vial. He held the glass tube up to the light. Inside, a fine white powder filled the vial nearly three quarters full. George shook it and was amazed at how completely it filled the void . . . whatever the stuff was floated around inside like one of those Christmas paperweights. He stood openmouthed, waiting for the material to settle back into place, but it didn't. It was like the stuff had some kind of motor that kept it aloft. Weird.

He shifted his gaze to Dr. Collins who was about to make the central incision in the cadaver, the T-shaped cut they used to take the organs out, so they could check for damage and then weigh them one by one. The doctors didn't like being bothered when they were doing that, so George returned his eyes to the vial, where the powder was still roiling around inside like a blizzard of artificial snow.

"Whatcha got there?" Collins wanted to know.

"Maybe some new kinda club drug or something," he said.

"Save it for the boys in blue," she said, as she folded back the abdomen walls to expose the dark shimmering mass of internal organs. "Probably got something to do with how he got this way."

Wasn't like he thought about it. Somehow or other . . . no tellin' why . . . just seemed to be the thing to do . . . George pushed at the stopper with his thumb. Turned the vial and worked it from the other side. Then again. Nothing. Damn thing was jammed in there tight as hell. He thumbed it again, and again failed to budge the rubber.

Being careful not to squeeze the glass vial too tightly, he grasped the stopper with his thumb and forefinger and gave a twist. The plug squeaked as it turned. He applied upward pressure and finally the plug began to move. A third of the way out, it bound and wouldn't move again. Frustrated, he jerked hard. The stopper came out in a hurry, eluded his twitching fingers and fell to the floor.

George watched the stopper bounce twice and finally come to a jerky rest on the tile. Just then, his vision wavered. He blinked his eyes, trying to maintain his focus. His head had suddenly begun to throb, as if an animal were trying to claw its way out from inside his skull. Seemed like the air around him was filled with tiny white particles. Seemed like he weighed a thousand pounds and that his legs just couldn't carry the load.

Wasn't till he heard the clink of the vial on the floor that he realized he'd gone down. "George," he heard Dr. Collins call.

His chest felt like it was full of water. He listened to the shuffle of her feet and felt his bowels empty themselves down his pant legs and onto the floor. He opened his mouth to apologize but could manage only a wet gargle. And then she was kneeling at his side. Blue eyes wide behind the rimless lenses. And he watched as a red flower bloomed on her white surgical mask. Watched as it grew from a tiny dot in the middle of the mask to a spreading tulip of crimson that rolled down over her chin in the last moment before she collapsed on the floor beside him. He sought for a phrase. An epithet perhaps. But nothing came to mind. Only the roaring in his head and the sound of waves lapping on a distant shore.

22

Pitch black. Corso hurried now. Running quietly on the balls of his feet for just a few strides before losing patience and stretching his long legs into a full sprint, his headlong soles slapping the street as he covered the distance to the corner only to find her gone again . . . He . . .

. . . sat up with a start and looked around. The sound of halyards clanking against masts told him where he was and that the overnight wind had risen. *Saltheart* rocked gently in the slip. He pulled aside the curtain and peered out into a steel gray morning and then flopped back into the bed. He closed his eyes, tried to sleep for a moment and then gave it up, sliding his legs over the edge of the berth and down onto the floor.

He looked around for his clothes only to discover he was wearing them, then levered himself off the bed . . . groaning at the effort as he shuffled around the corner into the head. The ache in his feet reminded him that he'd walked home. Better part of four or five miles he'd estimated. He ran his hands over his stubbly face and shuddered. Remembering how cold he'd been at the end and wishing he hadn't been forced to leave his jacket behind.

He used the teak handrails to help himself up the three steps into the galley, where he put together a pot of coffee before stepping out on deck. The air was thick and wet. A glance at the brass clock on the galley wall said it was seven-forty . . . full-bore rush hour. Overhead, the swoosh of cars on the freeway bridge seemed somehow slower and more ponderous than usual.

Across the lake, the rusting carcass of the ferry *Kalakala* sank slowly into the sand, its peeling art deco dome a sad reminder of better times with higher hopes and brighter dreams. A Coast Guard patrol boat cruised slowly along the far bank, its black machine gun mount ominous on the foredeck.

He closed his eyes for a moment and saw what he knew he would—the bodies strewn about the bus tunnel . . . the pools of blood and effluent . . . the final odd angles of the limbs . . . the horrified looks on their faces . . . the—he blinked a couple of times, swallowed hard and looked up into the slate sky.

He could feel the change. The uncertainty in the air and how Seattle was now a completely different place than it was this time yesterday morning. He watched the early morning boat traffic on Lake Union for a while and then stepped back inside the galley.

The coffee gave a last, rapid-fire series of gurgles and then went silent. He poured himself a cup and doctored it to his liking. Cream and sugar. New York regular. He held the cup in both hands and sipped at it tentatively as he made his way aft into the salon. Setting the coffee behind the pin rail, he reached up and unfastened the latch holding the thirty-six-inch flat screen TV pressed tight against the ceiling. He eased the screen down and looked around for the remote. He felt like a gawker at a freeway wreck, at once horrified by the twisted steel mayhem and at the same time, inexplicably drawn to leer at the carnage like a peeper at a bathroom window.

The screen lit up, and there it was. The nightmare. Right there in front of his face. CNN. Talking head and a stock picture of Yesler Street. He pushed the volume button. An electronic voice-over filled the air. "Homeland Security confirms an unspecified number of casualties from an unspecified biological agent." Another ten seconds of noninformation and the picture cut to Harry Dobson, Seattle's chief of police, standing behind a forest of microphones looking old and haggard. "We aren't releasing any further information pending the notification of kin. We are . . ." He stopped talking and strained to hear a question shouted from the throng of reporters.

His face darkened. "The investigation is no longer in the hands of the Seattle Police Department." He waved off a shouted question. "It's business as usual," he said, then caught himself and went into his canned spiel. "Excepting, of course, the tragic plight of the victims and their families." Another question was flung his way. "Several federal agencies," he said. "The FBI, the CIA, the Homeland Security people, the Centers for Disease Control . . ." He spread his hands in resignation. "Your guess is as good as mine," he said finally. He listened again. "No," he said emphatically. "To my knowledge, the threats delivered to the media were not attributed to any particular group . . . Arab or otherwise. Let me say . . ." he began, before his words were swept away by a torrent of shouted questions.

Corso changed the channel. MSNBC running a canned compilation of terrorist activities. September eleventh. Pictures of Osama bin Laden, Saddam Hussein and a bevy of other Arab terrorists. He pushed the channel button again.

Channel Five. Local news. Old guy with flyaway hair standing at a dais like he was accustomed to it. Caption identified him as Dr. Hans Belder. "I have seen the pictures . . ." he was saying. He used a knarled hand to sweep over the collection of two dozen serious-looking souls who stood behind him on the dais. "Many of my colleagues have also seen the pictures. There can be no doubt. What we have here is a genetically altered form of hemorrhagic fever."

As he spoke, the camera panned again, sliding over the somber group from end to end. At the far right of the screen, a familiar face peeked out from the forest of shoulders. Corso had to bring his other hand to bear on the coffee or he would surely have dropped it onto his shoes. It was her. The woman from the bus tunnel. He was sure of it. The short blonde hair. That competent . . . almost arrogant . . . look in her eyes. A shiver ran down his spine like a frozen ball bearing.

"Go back," he shouted at the screen, which instead segued to a shot of Mayor Gary Dean holding a pile of note cards. Corso growled, grabbed the remote and began furiously pushing the channel button. He kept at it until he was satisfied that nobody else was running the Belder interview and then, with a shouted curse, switched back to the mayor.

"The situation is completely contained," he said. "We are assured that there is absolutely no danger of further contamination." He shook his head.

"No," he said. "Other than the fact that Providence

Hospital will take over the role of Regional Trauma Center for the next several days . . . and that the bus tunnel will remain closed . . ." He waved a blasé hand. "Other than that . . . we want to encourage Seattleites to go about their business." He looked narrowly into the camera. "It's important that we don't allow these people to affect our daily lives. That we show these people that we will not be intimidated by a bunch of—"

Corso changed the channel. More talking heads. More stock terrorist footage. Then the President, with the word *LIVE* displayed in the lower left-hand corner of the screen.

He and the mayor must have shared the same speechwriter. Same call for calm. Same antiterrorist rhetoric. The usual steely-eyed Baptist assurances that the perpetrators would be brought to heel and punished in a way only Americans had the stomach for.

Corso pushed POWER and threw the remote onto the settee, where it bounced twice before coming to rest. He started for the galley to refresh his coffee, when a movement in his peripheral vision stopped him cold.

You don't see a lot of suits on a dock. Living on a boat not only means you have virtually no closet space, but that whatever you do own, whether from Sears or Armani, is destined, in very short order, to smell like diesel fuel. So the sight of old man Gentry letting a trio of suits through the security gate at the far end of the dock was reason to be concerned.

Corso set the coffee on the counter, turned on his heel and walked quickly toward the stern. He had no doubt. They'd traced the jacket already and were coming for him.

He moved through the boat at a lope, threw open the sliding doors and stepped out onto the stern. In one smooth motion, he untied the dinghy line, stepped up over the transom rail and climbed down onto the swim step before stepping into the inflatable and pushing off.

Through the pea-soup air, he could hear old man Gentry bawling something about "infringing his rights." He reached behind himself and pulled out the choke on the thirty-horse Evinrude. A push of the START button and the engine was purring. He goosed it a couple of times and then pushed the choke back in. Above the purr of the engine, he could hear the hard sound of heels on the ancient wooden dock. They were running now. Old man Gentry was still yelling at them. "Assholes" something.

He jacked the wheel hard to starboard and gave the little boat way more gas than was polite inside the marina. The propeller sucked itself down into the water. The bow began to rise. He slammed the throttle forward and bent low over the wheel. Looking back under his arm, he caught sight of the trio as they skidded to a stop at the rear of his boat. Corso winced as the one on the right reached toward his belt. Crazy bastard was going to shoot. Right here in the middle of the marina. He bent lower, waiting for the whistle of gunfire as he slalomed the boat sideways around the corner, past the big Tolly moored at the end, and went ripping out into the lake.

A smile spread halfway across his lips before the deep rumble of another engine wiped it from his face. He snapped his head around. The Coast Guard patrol boat bounced on the chop. The machine gun was manned.

Corso cut the throttle. Pulled the lever back into neutral and raised his hands above his head. The little aluminum cruiser began to rumble his way. The guy on the sixty-caliber couldn't have been older than twenty-five. Standard issue Coast Guard blues, orange life jacket, baseball cap turned around backward so as not to interfere with his aim. He was sighting down the barrel at Corso, who raised his hands higher into the air and stood up.

"No problem," he shouted.

The kid smiled. He had braces, for christ sakes. Corso watched in horror as the kid's finger tightened around the trigger. Corso closed his eyes. The static clack of gunfire filled the early morning air. The power of the reports shook the little boat, nearly causing his knees to buckle.

Corso held his breath and waited for the huge slugs to tear off one of his arms, to grind his torso in two . . . to . . .

His feet were suddenly cold and wet. He frowned and opened his eyes. The front half of the boat was gone. The weight of the engine was rapidly pulling the remaining rig under the water. The kid's metallic grin was bigger than ever. He let go with a whoop, like he'd just won a kewpie doll at the state fair. Corso was wet to the armpits now, and then, with a single hiss, the dinghy slid into the darkness below.

Corso began to tread water.

23

They had always known each other. That's how it was in the towns. Everybody knew everybody else forever. If you were not related to them, you knew someone who was. Or at least someone who came from that same town and recognized the family name.

They had new names now. Names they had learned together. Learned to answer to without thinking of who they used to be, or what the new names meant. The kind of names that fell easily from the American tongue. Way back when, he'd had another name. The one his parents gave him, so many years ago. Parag Dubey. After his grandfather. But that was then, and this was now. Now he was called Bobby Darling. He was a boyish, gangly twenty-eight. Narrow-faced, with a sheaf of straight black hair that tended to fall across his damaged left eye. Hair the color of obsidian, his mama used to say.

Bobby Darling had known Vijay Kumar for as long as he could remember. When the doctor peeled the stiff bandage from his eye, Vijay Kumar had been the first thing he'd seen, standing there next to his dirty cot, hopping from one foot to the other like a monkey.

These days Vijay called himself Nathan Kimberly. Like the spawn of one of those families who took on the surnames of their oppressors. As an act of respect, they said at the time.

Nathan paced back and forth across the dusty front room like a caged tiger. He'd always been nervous and quick with his hands, but the excitement of approaching events had lent an even more manic quality to his birdlike movements.

"Martin's been gone too long. Something's not right here," Nathan said.

"Not much gets by you does it?" Bobby snapped.

If Nathan picked up on the sarcasm, he didn't let on. "What did Mr. Holmes say when you told him that Martin had broken ranks?"

"He said he'd take care of it."

"What if Martin's gone to the authorities?" Nathan wanted to know.

"If he'd gone to the authorities, they'd be here by now. Besides . . ." Bobby hesitated. "I'd be willing to bet he's in no position to be dealing with the authorities." He threw a grin around the room. "Just like everybody else in this house. Huh?"

Nobody bothered to argue.

"His real name's Brian," Madhu Verma said out of the blue. "He used to live around here. That's why they brought him along." Nathan scrunched his features and did his "I'm offended" face, the one Bobby wanted to pound to jelly with an iron rod.

"His safety depends on anonymity," Nathan chastised. "If he really told you—"

Madhu laughed in his face. "Fucking amateurs," he spat.

Madhu Verma was now known as Wesley Singh and

was, without doubt, the angriest human being Bobby Darling had ever encountered. When they were children together, Madhu had tortured small animals until their anguished cries had filled the air like funeral smoke. To see him there, sitting on the couch cleaning the nine-millimeter for the millionth time, stroking the weapon like it was his private part, sent a shiver down Bobby Darling's spine. This was the person Bobby wanted to keep in front of him at all costs. He had no doubt that, if pressed, Wesley would murder any one of them in a heartbeat.

Parul Rishi and Suprava Remar were cousins. With Parul it had been easy. They'd taken out the *r*, made his first name into Paul. Left the last name alone. Suprava had become Samuel Singleton. Depending upon how one looked at it, it could be said that Paul and Samuel had suffered the worst luck of all of them. They had merely been visiting when the disaster struck. On any other day, at any other time, they would have been safe in faraway West Nimar where they had lived. As fate would have it, however, their entire families had journeyed north to attend the wedding of yet another cousin, and thus had suffered the same fate as the locals.

The doorbell rang, sending the room into a state of suspended animation. Nobody moved except Bobby, who pushed himself off the couch and ambled over to the door. It was the old lady from the house next door. Bobby made sure Wesley had lost the automatic before he pulled open the door. She was short. No more than five feet tall. Hair all piled up on top of her head in a grandmotherly way. Long beaded chain looped around her neck with her glasses dangling from the ends. She was angry.

"This has got to stop. I've called the paper. They're sending a man out."

Bobby gave her his boyish puzzlement face. "Excuse please?"

"My newspaper," the old woman said. "It's gone again."

Bobby kept his face in concerned mode. He looked back over his shoulder. Surveyed the room. "Any of you know anything about this lady's newspaper?" he inquired. He waited for the grunts of ignorance to settle and then turned his attention back to the woman. "I'm sure it's nobody here," he said.

She tapped the screen door with her finger. Bobby thought about severing the finger with his Buck knife. Maybe sticking it up her ass. Maybe sticking it up her ass without cutting it off. Decisions. Decisions.

"Ever since you guys moved in here, three mornings in a row now it's the same thing. I go out and the paper's gone."

"Must be somebody else," Bobby tried.

"Somebody else my butt," she spit. She wagged a bony finger in his face. He could feel the blood rising in his chest like a wave. "It better stop, sonny," she said. "I'm telling you . . . it better darn well stop."

With that, she turned on her heel and waddled off down the brick walk. Bobby parted the dusty curtains and watched as she skirted the separating hedge and then cut across her own front lawn on her way home.

"Bitch," he said.

When he turned back toward the room, Wesley was smirking as he pulled the folded newspaper out from under the sofa cushions. "I like to watch her scratch around for it," Wesley said. "Like a chicken after you cut off one of the legs."

Killing a chicken for dinner had never been enough for Wesley. No . . . he had to make it into a spectator sport . . . something that satisfied that bottomless thirst for pain and suffering he carried around inside himself.

Bobby opened his mouth to protest, even though he already knew the answer. He wanted to ask what kind of person steals a paper he doesn't even read, at a time like this, when they're this close to having their revenge. But a sudden movement in his peripheral vision pulled his attention to the street in front of the house.

Holmes . . . driving by slowly with the window down. Driving a dark blue van just like the gray one Martin had left in. Holmes. The man who had come to help them and, for his trouble, had lost everything in the world he valued. The man who'd picked them from the garbage and brought them together for this moment.

He watched as Holmes cruised by. Then stepped out onto the porch and kept his eye on the van until it turned left into the Safeway parking lot and disappeared. Four minutes later, Holmes strode into view.

Holmes nodded at Bobby on his way up the stairs.

"Where's Martin?" Bobby asked.

"Elsewhere," was the terse reply.

"Is he going to be a problem?"

Holmes shook his big square head. "Not in this world. Perhaps in the next."

24

The first thing he noticed was the red emergency light over the door. Inside its little metal cage, it had begun to blink, silently, on and off in a rapid cadence. Jim Sexton looked over at Pete Carrol, who was filling time picking lint from his baseball cap. Pete didn't look up, just kept picking away. Then the door banged open and a pathologist in a green scrub suit came through at a dead run, surgical mask hanging down over his chest, mouth gasping for air as he sprinted across the reception area and disappeared down the far hall, gone only long enough for Jim and Pete to exchange glances before the buzzer began to scream, its hoarse electronic bleat bouncing off the walls and ceiling like a fire drill at school.

And then the reception area was full of people. Ten . . . a dozen . . . doctors, lab types in white coats, security guys, a pair of secretaries, a guy in a suit . . . all hurrying across the brown tile floor toward the blinking light and the screaming buzzer.

Pete bounced off the wall and reached for the camera. Jim made eye contact, shook his head, and then, while Pete was still collecting his jaw, he fell in with the shuffling pack of humanity as it squeezed through the NO ADMITTANCE door and hastened down the long polished hall. His presence was lost in the gravity of the situation. Before he got to the viewing window, he heard a sob and then the sound of tears. "Oh God . . . Shauna," someone said. Someone wept out loud.

One of the suits turned to the nearest security guard. "We've got a Phase Four emergency here, Phillip. We need a fire department hazardous materials team here as quickly as possible. We're going into isolation mode. Nobody goes in. Nobody goes out." Phillip pulled a handful of keys from his belt and began to jog up the corridor.

"Oh God, God, God," somebody sobbed.

Assistant Fire Chief Ben Gardener slipped into the Critical Incident Room unnoticed . . . no easy feat for a man six and a half feet tall bearing disturbing news. As he closed the soundproof door, the intense buzz of conversation piqued the skin on his face in much the same manner as cannon fire flattens the cheeks of those standing close by. The feds had moved everything. Brought in more tables to accommodate the brigade of federal agencies which had been brought to bear on the situation. Wired the place for what must have been a hundred different phone lines, twisting miles of thick braided cables that ran along the baseboards like the roots of some newly discovered tree.

Gardener's eyes swept the space. The Homeland Security Agency had taken over the entire north wall of the room. Half a dozen agents whispered into plastic mouthpieces, while another trio fed documents into fax machines. The U.S. Army Medical Research Institute of Infectious Diseases shared the south wall with an unnamed agency whose role was apparently so sensitive they had declined to identify themselves. Braced as to their bona fides by Frank Thome, the State Department's coordinator for counterterrorism, they were rumored to have produced a document whose mysterious contents had very nearly reduced the coordinator to genuflection.

For obvious reasons, the Centers for Disease Control had set up shop at Harborview Medical Center, while both the FBI and the CIA had commandeered entire floors of luxury hotels for use as command posts. Between the three agencies, more than a hundred federal operatives presently roamed the city, while a hundred more were being held in reserve.

Out in the center of the room, Harry Dobson was making measured conversation with that same smarmy bastard from the State Department who'd thanked them both for their departments' efforts and then informed them that neither department would henceforth be required.

He raised a hand and ran his fingers through his thick hair. The movement caught Harry Dobson's eye. Ben Gardener inclined his head no more than an inch and then turned and exited the room in three long strides.

Two minutes passed before the door opened again and Harry Dobson stepped out into the hall. Ben Gardener didn't say a word. Instead, he turned his back on Dobson and strode quickly down the hall. Dobson followed along in silence. All the way to the elevator. Down fifteen floors to ground level and then out onto Third Avenue, where Gardener walked half a block from the entrance before coming to a halt next to a forest of newspaper dispensers. "EBOLI," one headline shrieked. "JIHAD VIRUS," trumpeted the other.

Again Gardener used his head to motion. This time back at the Public Safety Building. "Those guys make me nervous," he said by way of explanation. Dobson nodded his wholehearted agreement. Ben Gardener checked the street before he went on. "We've had another incident," he said.

Dobson blanched. Held his breath. Gardener went on. "Two dead. A forensic pathologist named Shauna Collins and a coroner's assistant named George Bell."

Harry Dobson exhaled with a rush. "Only two?"

"Yes."

"At the morgue?"

"Yes."

"Tell me about it."

"One of my teams responded to the call," Gardener began. "Same thing. Dead people . . . dead virus."

"The CDC do the tests?"

"They trained all our people this morning. We did them ourselves. Why?"

"Go on."

Harry Dobson listened in silence. By the time Gardener was finished speaking, Dobson's forehead was a washboard of furrows. "What was the vic's name again?" he asked.

"Shauna Collins—"

"Not them. The corpse they were working on," Dobson interrupted.

"Martin Magnusen," Gardener said. "A Canadian citizen."

"This is the guy with his throat cut?"

"Ear to ear from what I hear."

Dobson smiled at the rhyme and thought it over.

"A glass vial?"

"Just like the bus tunnel."

"And your boys think it came out of the vic's pockets."

"That's sure how it looked."

Again Harry Dobson paused to reflect. "The feds know about this?"

"Not yet."

"Why don't we keep it that way?"

Gardener raised an eyebrow. "Any particular reason?"

"They're sure as hell not telling us anything."

Gardener shrugged. "They never do."

"Unless the investigation goes in the Dumpster, in which case they'll disappear like a cool breeze and we'll be left holding the bag."

"That's how they operate."

"So what say we keep this little tidbit under our collective hats . . ."—he waggled a hand—"for the time being at least."

Gardener made a doubtful face. "Counting people like dispatchers and morgue personnel, probably a dozen people already know about it."

"See what you can do to keep it quiet."

"That kind of thing usually doesn't work out too well for anybody."

Dobson nodded his agreement. "Give it a try. Anything happens, I'll take the heat." This time it was Ben Gardener who took his time answering. From nearly anyone else in state or city government, such a statement would have to be considered pure unadulterated bullshit. From Harry Dobson, however, the promise was another matter.

"You want to give me a hint here, Harry?" Gardener said.

"Things get ugly, might be better you didn't know."

"I'll take my chances."

Dobson ran both hands over his face. "Okay . . . so . . ."—he waved a hand—"I'm not sure exactly what time, but sometime last night the East Precinct gets a nine-one-one call about a possible homicide up on Capitol Hill. What we got is a guy in his mid-thirties with his throat cut. He's kneeling on some woman's kitchen floor with his head just about cut off, and she claims she doesn't know a thing about it. She claims she found him that way when she got home. No idea how he got in the house or who might want to do something like that to him." He paused. "Other than her, of course."

"She knows him?"

"Used to. According to her he's been living out of the country for the past six years or so . . . dodging an assault beef." Gardener opened his mouth to speak, but Dobson waved him off with a finger. "An assault beef for tattooing this same woman from head to toe against her will."

"This the woman who woke up and found herself decorated with all kinda . . ."

"That's the one."

"And she claims she just found him there on her floor? After all these years? He just shows up dead on her floor."

"That's what she says."

"Strange."

"We haven't gotten to the strange part yet."

"Oh?"

"She says his name's not Magnusen. She claims he's some guy named Bohannon. Says she spotted him in the street outside her house and then she and some cabdriver spent most of the evening following him around the city, until she finally lost him, at which point she goes home and finds the guy bleeding all over her kitchen."

"You look into this?"

"We never got the chance. I had a couple of gold shields questioning her about the murder when, all of a sudden, the feds show up and snatch her from us."

"Over what?"

This time, it was Dobson who checked the street. "Here's where it gets interesting. The feds want her because she spent the early part of last night with none other than our friend Frank Corso."

"The guy from the bus tunnel?"

"Seems they used to be an item."

"You're kidding."

"What's even more interesting is that my detectives felt pretty certain she was telling the truth about just finding him there on the floor . . . and these are experienced men I'm talking about here. Twenty years plus . . . both of them."

"You thinking this Bohannon guy is somehow connected to whoever did the bus tunnel job?"

"That's exactly what I'm thinking."

"Which means the girl is probably telling the truth."

"Yes . . . it does."

A smile threatened to break out on Ben Gardener's lips. "The feds are looking for Arabs," he said.

"Yes . . . they are."

"Maybe this Bohannon guy is like a John Walker character or something."

"Maybe."

"But you don't think so."

"No."

"What?"

"I don't know."

"But you want me to try to put a lid on the morgue incident."

"Do the best you can."

"And you're going to do what?"

"I'm going to put some people on it."

"The feds are gonna hate it."

Dobson threw an exasperated hand at the Public Safety Building.

"They're all carving out kingdoms up there, Ben. Spend an hour in the room. You'll see. Nobody's co-operating with anybody else. One hand doesn't have a clue about what the other is doing. They're scrimmaging for next year's budget appropriation."

Gardener rolled his eyes. "Just like us," the expression said.

25

"I want to call my attorney."

"You're starting to get repetitive, Mr. Corso."

"Maybe I ought to say it slower."

"Maybe you ought to wise up," said the hatchet-faced guy. The one leaning against the wall with his hands thrust deep in his pockets. He hadn't uttered a word for over an hour. Not since being restrained after nearly losing it on Corso. "I'm going to tell you one more time . . ."—he held up a stiff finger—"we consider this to be a matter of national security. For the time being you don't have constitutional rights of any kind. Under the provisions of the Homeland Security Act, there are no limits on how long we can keep you." He put his face right in Corso's. His breath mints had worn off. "Do you understand what I'm saying here, Mr. Corso?"

"You're saying we just turned into Iraq."

The two feds passed one of those looks that told Corso they didn't normally work together. Probably weren't even employed by the same agency. As neither man had bothered to identify himself, Corso had come to assume his primary tormenter was from the FBI. He was all-around slick. A good-looking guy. Maybe forty years old in a nice gray Italian suit and a pair of Vittorio Virgili loafers that must have cost him three bills. Knew what he was doing, too. One of those Quantico-trained interrogators whose questions loop around one another like threads in a tapestry. Didn't take it personally that Corso wouldn't so much as admit to his name . . . just kept at it like a pro.

The other guy was another matter. A much looser cannon. More likely from the CIA. Way more used to getting what he wanted right away. More pissed off when he didn't. The kind of guy who wasn't above pumping you full of drugs or hooking your privates up to a field telephone. Whatever it took.

Corso held no heroic illusions. He'd been questioned by experts and tortured by amateurs and knew, beyond all doubt, that, left in the hands of either of them for long enough, he'd eventually confess to whatever they had in mind.

"So . . . what's it gonna be, fellas?" Corso asked, looking from one to the other. "You gonna put my head in a black bag and fly me down to Cuba? Put me in Guantánamo with the rest of those poor bastards you've got sitting around in the sun?" When they didn't respond, he went on. "Or maybe you could put me in the cell next to that poor Walker kid. The one doing twenty years for being a truth seeker."

CIA flushed slightly. "John Walker was a traitor to his—"

Corso cut him off. "John Walker was a dope. A scapegoat. A young, stupid kid fighting in the Afghani civil war whose biggest mistake was being in the wrong place at the wrong time, right when Uncle Bush just happened to need a symbol."

FBI gave Corso a wink. "Then you must be aware of the kinds of miscarriges of justice that can happen in times of great national distress," he said pleasantly.

"Is that a threat?"

"It's a possible scenario."

"We have met the enemy and he is us," Corso said.

CIA waved that finger again. "I'd be careful with that kind of talk, Mr. Corso. I think you'll find that precious few of your fellow citizens agree with you."

"Are we talking about the same people who don't seem to mind that there weren't any weapons of mass destruction found in Iraq? That their President went on national TV and lied to them? Those fellow citizens?"

"It must be hard always holding the moral high ground," FBI commented.

Corso nodded gravely. "It's quite a cross to bear."

Corso watched in silence as FBI moseyed around the table and sat down next to him. "We gonna hold hands now?" Corso asked.

"You know, Mr. Corso . . . if you could maybe manage to stop being such a hard-ass . . ."—he held his thumb and forefinger about an inch apart—"for just the littlest bit, we might be able to resolve this matter and let you back on with your life."

Corso brought a hand to his throat. "Gee . . . I feel all warm and fuzzy now."

A moment of strained silence passed before FBI pushed back his chair and got to his feet. "It doesn't matter, Mr. Corso. Your girlfriend is singing like a bird. Anything we really need to know about you we can get from Ms. Dougherty."

Corso broke into a smile. "Yeah . . . sure she is."

CIA wasn't ready to let it go. "Why don't you tell us what you know about Melissa-D?"

Again Corso laughed and made a disgusted face. "Not that tired old shit again."

"Our information . . . reliable information . . . says that you're a major player in a terrorist organization which has hacked into nearly every computer system worldwide. Your Interpol file says you're one of their major customers. Why don't you just—"

Corso cut him off. "Melissa-D is an urban legend. It's something reporters talk about when they've had too much to drink . . . which is mostly. There's no such thing."

"Is it true that—"

"I want to call my attorney."

"I don't think he's been listening," CIA said.

"I want to call my attorney," Corso repeated.

FBI went for reasonable. "You're already on the hook for the bus tunnel massacre. Correct me if I'm wrong here, Mr. Corso, but it seems to me you don't have a heck of a lot to lose here. One way or the other, you're going down here. You might as well—"

"You think I killed those folks in the tunnel?"

"Perhaps not you personally," he said. "But certainly someone known to you." He read the surprise in Corso's expression. "I've seen the tape, Mr. Corso. And you see . . ."—he spread his hands—"until you manage to explain to me how you knew it was safe to take off your breathing device in that tunnel, I'm going to have to assume that you had prior knowledge."

"I want to call my attorney."

CIA pushed a big breath of air out through his pursed lips, then stepped out into the hall for a second before returning with a couple more field agents. Older guys. A little more shopworn. No longer fit for the field. Relegated to guard duty.

"Get him the hell out of here," CIA said. He looked over at Corso. "We're gonna bury you so deep not even your lawyer's gonna find your ass, Mr. Corso. About the time people start to forget your name, we'll see if you're still such a first-class smart-ass." He gestured violently with his arm. "Get him the hell out of here."

26

He'd told her to hold all his calls, so the incessant buzzing emanating from his phone was even more annoying than usual. He stifled a growl as he picked it up.

"It's Sheriff Reinhart, Chief," Margy said.

Harry Dobson swallowed his anger, pushed the blinking red button and spoke into the mouthpiece.

"Dan," was all he said.

"We got those bodies you were looking for, Harry."

"Really."

"Big guy with a bad attitude."

"He got a name?"

"Not on the warrant. Strictly a John Doe."

"And he's not talking."

"I hear he's mostly yelling."

"About what?"

"The usual. His constitutional rights. Nazi motherfuckers. What the country's coming to. Wants to call Abrams and Stone, so, whoever the hell he is, he must have access to some serious money. Those guys won't piss on you for under ten grand."

"What about the woman?"

"She wouldn't talk to the feds, and she's not talking to us."

"That so?"

"I was about to transfer her over to the city lockup. I've got people sleeping on the floor. Besides . . . her paperwork says she was in your custody when the feds borrowed her."

"I've got an idea," Dobson said.

"What's that?"

"Why don't you transfer both of them over to the city lockup?"

Before Reinhart could answer, he went on. "Strictly a matter of space. You were full. We weren't. As simple as that."

Another airy pause. "Not a good idea to screw with those people, Harry."

"Let me worry about that. Space transfers are strictly business as usual. We do it every day of the year." An exaggeration, but not by much.

Reinhart thought it over. "When did you have in mind?"

"Right now."

"It'll look better that way."

"Yes, it will."

"This gonna get all sticky?"

"Not on you."

"It's an election year."

"I know."

Long pause. "They're on the way."

Dobson replaced the phone only to have it buzz again.

"Sorry, Chief." Margy's voice again, not sounding in the least bit sorry. "I've got two detectives from the East Precinct out here. They say they were ordered to show up here posthaste."

"Send 'em in," hc said. "And Margy . . ."

"Yes, Chief."

He used his nicest voice. "Hold all my calls, please."

"As always, Chief."

They came through the door walking sideways. Neither had ever been here before. Hadda figure they were in deep shit over something. Guy gets called to the police chief's office, it's usually the last call he responds to.

Dobson got to his feet. Nodded at each of them but didn't offer his hand.

"Gentlemen," he said, "have a seat."

He remained standing as they sorted out a pair of black leather chairs and sat down. He looked from one to the other. "At the risk of being accused of racial profiling, which I'm sure you detectives know is a rather sore issue around here these days . . ."—he nodded first at Reuben the Cuban and then at Charly Hart—"I'm assuming you're Gutierrez and you're Hart." Pause. "Right?" He waited for a reply and got one.

Harry Dobson eased himself into his chair. "Relax," he said out over the polished expanse of his desk. "I've got no beef with either of you."

He watched air pressure drain from the men as if somebody'd pulled the plug. "It's about the young woman who phoned in that homicide last night."

"What about it?" Charly Hart asked. He leaned forward, resting his bony elbows on his equally bony knees. The guy was all angles. Tall and skinny as a coat hanger, his long-limbed joints seemed to operate independently of one another, allowing him to fold himself into awkward-looking positions, seemingly with little or no effort. He used a big round pair of black glasses to add some width to his razor face. His thinning white hair was cut short and combed forward. Around the station house, it had occasionally been noted that he looked a lot like a boiled owl.

Gutierrez was another matter. Whatever hair he had left was buzzed all the way down to the bone. When he moved his head, the muscles in his neck looked like knotted rope. The guy was burly. A thousand crimped and twisted muscle fibers hiding under a nice Italian suit. And the two gold front teeth. They were like . . . halogen.

"You have your notes? From when you questioned her?"

Charly Hart did what all good cops do at a moment like that. He looked to his partner. Nobody was going to embarrass anybody else here. Gutierrez picked up on whatever message his partner was sending. "Charly took the notes."

As if by magic, a shiny black notebook appeared in Charly Hart's hand. He started to leaf through the pages.

Dobson stopped him. "Before we get specific here, I want to get your impressions." He looked from one detective to the other. "How'd you guys read it? You make her for the perp?"

"No way," Reuben said.

"Me neither," chimed Charly.

Harry Dobson processed the information behind hooded eyes. "Gimme an alternate scenario," he said after a minute.

"Somebody real strong," Gutierrez said immediately.

"Real sure," Charly added. "No other lacerations of any kind on the vic."

"Cuts the kid's throat." Reuben used his forefinger to demonstrate. "Bleeds him out right there on the floor."

"Then picks him up, forces the body into the kneeling position and flops his head over onto his back so that whoever walks in gets the fifty-cent show," Charly added.

"Good technique. Bad sense of humor," Gutierrez said.

"What's the autopsy report say?" Charly Hart asked.

When Dobson was not forthcoming with an answer of any kind, the detectives passed a quick look and then, as the silence lengthened, began to fidget.

The chief pinned them in place with a broken glass glare. "What I'm about to tell you two is for your ears only." They nodded in unison. "It doesn't leave this room." Another round of steel-jawed assurances.

"The vic . . ." he began, "I've got reason to believe he may in some way be directly connected to whoever committed the crime at the bus station." He paused. Both detectives started to come out of their chairs. Dobson waved them back down. "Or . . ." He seemed to debate with himself. "Or . . . more likely . . . he may be the actual perpetrator of the crime."

"We got something hard that points that way?" Reuben asked.

Dobson told them everything he knew. They listened without comment. Halfway through, Charly Hart began to take notes. Chief Dobson shook his head and kept on talking. Charly dropped the pencil into his side pocket and sat back in the chair.

"The feds know this?" Reuben asked about three seconds after Chief Dobson finished talking.

"Not yet," Dobson answered.

"But they're gonna," Charly filled.

"Chances are," the chief said.

"But . . . in the meantime . . ." Reuben looked over at

Charly Hart. "The girl's story about how she followed him all over all night might bear a little checking."

"Exactly," said the chief.

"We're gonna need to interview her again," Charly said. He waggled the black leather notebook. "Stuff we got is pretty vague."

The chief nodded. "I've managed to pry her away from the feds."

Charly Hart cocked an eyebrow. "Feds know she's gone?"

"Not yet," Harry Dobson said again.

Detective Gutierrez whistled through his teeth.

"Is there a problem, Detective?"

Gutierrez shook his head. "No sir," he said emphatically. "Just a concern." He looked over at his partner. "You know . . . this whole terror thing . . . it's uncharted territory . . . I'm just worried . . . you know . . . not playing it altogether straight with the feds . . ." He spread his hands. "I mean . . . what if ?"

"What we need to know is whether anything Mr. Bohannon did in the hours that Miss . . ."

"Dougherty," Charly Hart supplied.

". . . whether anything he did in those hours could possibly lead us to the people who murdered those poor souls in the bus tunnel." He dropped his hands on the desk. "You think the feds are better prepared to follow up on Mr. Bohannon's activities than we are?"

"No way," said Reuben Gutierrez.

"Then we better get to work."

Jim Sexton stepped into the toilet stall and pulled the door closed behind him. Three stalls down somebody was puking into the commode, retching up breakfast in a series of grunts and hawks that seemed to ooze from the very walls. Jim pulled the cell phone from his pocket. Dialed the station.

"Gimme Tilden," he whispered.

Waited. "Robert Tilden. Associate—"

"It's Jim," he said quickly. "We've got a pathologist and her assistant dead in one of the autopsy galleries. Blood all over the place. The whole area of the coroner's office has been sealed off. Nobody comes in, nobody goes out. They've called for a haz-mat team. They've—"

"You've got film?" Tilden interrupted.

"Not yet." He could feel the blood rising to his cheeks. "I'm not even supposed to be here, man. Are you listening to me? I've got a—"

"Call me when you've got some film, Jimbo. In case you haven't noticed, this is a TV station."

The line went dead. The retching went on.

27

He gave them ten minutes to swap stories. Gutierrez and Hart stood nearby as Harry Dobson studied the pair through the one-way viewing panel of Interrogation Room Number Four. He'd hoped that seeing Corso might loosen her tongue, create some discrepancies in the story she'd told his detectives last night. No such luck. When he looked over at Gutierrez and Hart, they merely shrugged.

"Same story," Charly Hart said.

"Let's go," Dobson said finally. Charly Hart held the door as the chief of police strode into the interrogation room and walked over to the phone on the far end of the table. "Get me a couple jail personnel," he said. "Number four."

The chief replaced the receiver, then walked over and stood in front of Dougherty. Gutierrez and Hart circled the room, taking up positions along the far wall, behind Corso and Dougherty, arms folded across their respective chests.

"I need your help," Harry Dobson announced.

"My help?" Dougherty repeated.

Before Dobson could respond, a pair of burly jailers

in two-tone brown uniforms pushed into the room. "Take Mr. Corso here back to his cell," the chief said.

The nearest jailer was reaching for a pair of handcuffs when Dougherty stepped forward, close enough to the chief to nearly put her nose on his. "You need my help, maybe we better keep Frank around."

"Mr. Corso has several charges pending," Dobson said.

"I really don't give a damn," she said.

They stood for a moment, gazes locked on one another, until the chief broke it off. He turned to the jailers. "Wait in the hall," he said.

Harry Dobson watched the pair leave the room, then stepped around Dougherty. He walked over to Corso and stood looking up at Corso's face.

"I've got an officer down." He waited a moment, checking out Corso's reaction. "In the alley closest to the bus tunnel," he went on. "Somebody stuck a needle in him. Whatever it was . . . it's nothing the doctors up at Harborview have ever seen before. They're having a hell of a time bringing him around."

"What's that got to do with me?"

"That's the question."

"You asking me if I did it?"

"Yes . . . I am."

Corso met his gaze. "I didn't," he said.

"Know nothing about it?"

"I didn't say that."

"If you have knowledge—"

"I don't know anything for sure," Corso interrupted. "I didn't see it happen, if that's what you're asking."

"But?"

Corso chose his words carefully. "But . . . I was probably somewhere in the immediate vicinity when it came down."

"Which means what?"

"Which means I answered your question."

Dobson flattened his lips and rocked on the balls of his feet. "You want to tell me how you knew it was safe to take off your breathing device down there in the tunnel?"

"Not particularly."

Dobson tilted his head toward the door. "You of all people, Mr. Corso, are aware of what's going on out there. We've got slightly less than a hundred twenty dead citizens. Murdered by a genetically altered hemorrhagic fever virus." He fixed Dougherty with a stare. "Ask your friend Mr. Corso here. It's not a pretty sight. He's seen it firsthand."

She flicked her eyes Corso's way. His face was hard as stone. She watched as he gathered himself to speak only to be cut off by the chief.

"We've got another threat. Worse. Bigger."

"They say when?" Corso asked.

"Sunday. Sunday is supposed to be *the end.*" He emphasized the final words. "That's what the message said."

"Why Sunday?" Corso asked.

"What do you mean, 'Why Sunday'?"

"If I was going to pull off some sort of terrorist act, I'd want the city full of people. I'd want to do as much damage as I could. Hurt as many people as possible. I sure as hell wouldn't pick the day when the city is the least populated."

"Unless the target is something that only happens on a Sunday," Dougherty said. "Like football or something."

Dobson shook his head. "We've been over this with the feds. Both the Huskies and the Seahawks are playing out of town. The only weekend events going on are the biotechnology symposium at the Westin and a quilting show at Seattle Center."

"The symposium would be the obvious target."

"That's what the feds think," said Corso.

"What if it's not?"

"Then we haven't got a clue."

A strained silence settled over the room.

"There was a woman," Corso said suddenly. "She came out of the alley." He looked over at the chief. "Same alley you say you had a man down in."

"When was this?"

"Right before they sent the robot inside."

"The alley closest to the entrance?"

"Right behind the Smith Tower," Corso said.

"Describe her."

Corso did so. In detail. Caucasian. Late thirties. Five seven or eight. Even features. No distinguishing marks. Short blonde hair. Athletic build.

"What then?" the chief asked quickly.

"She came out of the mouth of the alley, walked up to the entrance, pulled aside the plastic and went inside."

"Wearing no protection of any kind?"

"No mask, no nothing."

"Which you took to mean . . ."

"Which I took to mean she knew something I didn't."

"Would you recognize this person if you were to see her again?"

"I *have* seen her again."

Dobson recoiled slightly. "You have?"

"Twice."

The chief waited. Corso kept on.

"First time was down in the tunnel last night. When

I was in there with the firemen. She was standing up on the mezzanine. Watching us."

"And then?"

"On television this morning." Corso waved a hand. "They had all those scientists from the symposium on there . . . explaining hemorrhagic fever and all of that. She was standing at the back of the crowd."

"Do you recall what channel?"

"Five."

"You think maybe she's the one who killed those people in the tunnel?" Dougherty asked.

"No," the chief said. "As a matter of fact, we don't." He paused. "What would you say if I told you that we have reason to believe the bus tunnel incident was perpetrated by the man you knew as Brian Bohannon?"

"Reason to believe?" Corso repeated.

"Solid reason to believe," Dobson amended.

"I—I—don't . . ." Meg Dougherty stammered. Dobson laid it out for her. The dead pathologist and her assistant. The vial. All of it. She listened in silence as he told her everything he knew.

"So . . . you don't think I . . . I'm not a . . ."

"Suspect. No. You're not." He waited for it to sink in. "Our current assumption is that Mr. Bohannon's death was connected in some way to his terrorist activities and not in any way with you."

"Where would somebody like Brian Bohannon lay hands on a genetically altered strain of hemorrhagic fever?"

"That's the sixty-four-thousand-dollar question, now isn't it?"

"The feds are looking for Arabs," Corso said.

"Yes . . . they are." Dobson's voice was flat . . . emotionless.

"They know about your suspicions regarding Mr. Bohannon?"

"Not at this time." He sounded like a machine. The machine anticipated Corso's next question. "An army of federal agents is already stomping all over town, doing what they do best," he said. "Every phone call, every e-mail, every airplane and train reservation is being screened and monitored. They're talking about calling out the National Guard." He shrugged. "A couple cops one way or the other isn't going to make any damn difference." He gestured with his head, indicating the detectives leaning against the far wall. "I'm thinking . . . if there was anything in Mr. Bohannon's movements last night . . . anything that might lead us to the people threatening our safety . . . I figure my men are better prepared for the job. They know the neighborhoods. They know the people."

"And you want me to . . ." Dougherty let it hang.

"We want you to retrace your steps of the previous evening. We want you to take Detectives Hart and Gutierrez here to the exact places where you followed Mr. Bohannon. We want to start where you started and end where you ended." He shrugged. "Who knows . . . maybe we'll turn something." He moved his eyes to Charly Hart. "You get through to Canadian Immigration?"

Charly straightened up. "Yes sir. Blaine's going over their records for the past week. Same MO as Magnusen-slash-Bohannon. Canadian passport. Traveling alone. Somebody whose present whereabouts we can't verify."

"They give us any ideas on a time line?"

"Midafternoon."

The chief sighed. "All right then . . . Let's get Miss Dougherty—"

Meg interrupted. "I'll be needing Frank." She gave the chief a faraway smile. "For emotional support."

The chief shrugged in resignation. "Take them both," he said, before striding quickly across the room. Then he stopped and walked back to the table, reached into his jacket pocket and pulled out a pair of identical cell phones, which he slid onto the tabletop. "I want to be kept strictly in the loop," he said. "Use the walkie-talkie button on these things. They're connected directly to mine. Don't use the radio. Maybe we can keep the newshounds from breathing down our necks this way. God knows they're going to be all over the airwaves."

Gutierrez and Hart pocketed the phones and assured their boss that he'd be informed of the slightest development.

"My ass is on the line here," he reminded them and then headed for the door. The phone rang. The chief stopped. Charly Hart picked it up. He listened briefly and then held the phone against his bony chest.

"For you, Chief," he said.

The chief winced. His secretary was the only person on earth who knew where he was, and, after seventeen years on the job, she knew better than to interrupt an interrogation for anything short of nuclear war. Whatever this was, wasn't good. He handled the receiver gingerly, as if it were radioactive, using only his thumb and forefinger to hold the phone an inch away from his ear.

For thirty seconds, the chief of police listened without comment. Only his eyes moved, twitching here and there as he concentrated on what was being said. "Send them down here," he said finally. "Interrogation Room Number Four."

He replaced the receiver and turned his attention to Hart and Gutierrez. "Take these two next door," he said. "Make sure the door's locked."

When nobody moved, the chief jerked his thumb toward the door. "Hurry up," he said. "We're about to get some company."

Charly Hart started for the door. Dougherty and Corso were close behind, with Gutierrez bringing up the rear as they hurried down the hall, took a left past the Coke machine, then another left right after the ladies' restroom.

The room was narrow. More like an enclosed hall really. No chairs. No nothing. Just the lingering odor of long-ago cigarettes and fresh sweat. A five-foot-wide viewing area where whoever was on this side of the window could look out across the proceedings in Interrogation Room Number Four. The chief was on the phone again. His voice crackled through a pair of speakers in the ceiling. "Have him call me on my cell phone," he said.

"Can they hear us in there?" Dougherty asked from the other side of the black glass.

"Not unless you start banging on the window," Detective Gutierrez said.

"All you gotta do is keep your hands in your pockets and stand still. You get to movin' around a lot and they can sometimes sense movement."

Charly Hart had his owl eyes locked on Corso. "You were down there," he said. Failing to elicit a response, he clarified. "In the tunnel."

Corso looked at the speakers in the ceiling. "Yeah."

"It's like they say?" Gutierrez asked. "Some kinda virus thing in the air? Just knocks you down and kills your ass right in your tracks?"

"Your blood vessels explode. You bleed out, right there on the spot," Corso said. What he didn't mention was the look of recognition on most of the victims' faces. The horror of suddenly knowing, with absolute certainty, that the end was near. Must be what swimmers felt in those last instants before a shark bite, he thought to himself. That nanosecond when the word *shark* etches itself in neon on the mind and the world is, once and for all, reduced to nothing more than the scrape of tooth on gristle.

"Jesus," Charly Hart muttered. "What if they sprayed that stuff from a plane?" he mused. "They could kill everybody."

"I gotta call my wife," Gutierrez said. He looked over at his partner. "Duty is one thing, man . . . but this kind of shit . . . I don't know. Get offed by something you can't even see." He shook his head. "I don't know, man."

On the other side of the viewing panel, the door to Interrogation Room Number Four burst open. The chief folded up his phone and stowed it in his jacket pocket.

"FBI," Meg Dougherty muttered. "Same guys they sent after me." They watched a strained round of introductions and ID ogling.

"The one in charge calls himself Payton. Special Agent Payton," she said.

Payton wasted no time. He reached into the inside pocket of his suit jacket and pulled out a thick envelope. The jagged edges along the top attested to the fact that the package had already been opened at least once. Payton proffered the pages. "We'll be requiring some assistance," he said.

The chief kept his face as bland and emotionless as

a cabbage as he looked the other man up and down, before reaching out and taking possession of the envelope. He removed the contents, dropped the torn envelope onto the tabletop. Looked to be about five pages. Single-spaced names and addresses. He gave the printed matter a quick perusal and then focused on Agent Payton.

"What kind of assistance would that be?" he inquired.

"We need you to pick up these people," Payton said.

"Pick them up?"

"Take them into custody."

"For what?"

"For questioning."

"On what charges?"

"Under the provisions of the Patriot Act . . ." Payton began.

"These people are citizens of the State of Washington. Residents of the City of Seattle. I've sworn to protect and serve these people."

"As I said . . . the Patriot Act allows us to—"

"Then do it yourself," Dobson snapped. "No member of my department will take anyone into custody without due process. Not now. Not ever."

"We have other resources," Payton said evenly.

"Then bring them to bear," Dobson said.

"Be assured that we will."

The agents passed a glance. Harry Dobson took a chance. "You've already been to the county . . . haven't you?" A slight twitch in the nearest agent's cheek told him he was on the money. "Dan Reinhart wouldn't do it either . . . would he?" No response. When they continued to stonewall, the chief dropped the list of names onto the battered table.

"Unless and until these people are charged with a crime of some sort, I'm not picking any of them up." He cut the air with the flat of his hand. "Period." He looked around the room. "Am I making myself clear to you gentlemen?"

His final phrase was wasted on their backs as they slid out the door like nickels down a slot. The chief turned toward the black glass panel. Toward Charly Hart and Reuben the Cuban, Corso and Dougherty. "Go," he mouthed.

28

They were lined up like so many schoolboys. Standing at attention in their new clothes, still and silent, as Holmes moved around them, inspecting the young men from every angle. Not surprising really. He had, after all, once been a policeman, accustomed to rank and file, to inspections and the chain of command. Their acquiescence was a show of respect from those who had long ago ceased to believe in such inanities as right and wrong, or good and evil . . . an assemblage who had tasted the bitter backwash of despair in their mouths for so long they had come to imagine it to be nourishment.

In a way, it was worse for Holmes. He wasn't so much a victim as an unwilling accomplice. While the five young men standing before him had been purely the victims of circumstance, Holmes had played an unwitting part in his own personal doom and thus was as much a victim of himself as of the pack of dogs who had torn their lives to pieces.

Bobby remembered him from way back when Holmes was trying to restore order from chaos. Back when he still believed in something. Back before

Bobby learned to make a life on the streets, hustling a living from garbage bins and gutters and before even Holmes learned that certain circumstances required redress regardless of the human toll.

Then he didn't see him for a long time. Not until he heard someone calling his old name in the street. *"Parag,"* the voice called. *"Parag Dubey."*

He recognized the man right away. "Do you remember me?" the man asked.

"The policeman," Parag said.

The man looked him over. His sad liquid eyes flowed over the boy's gaunt frame, to the unkempt mop of hair, over the greasy assemblage of rags that passed for clothes, down to the hard calloused feet that clicked on the pavement like the talons of a bird.

"Do you remember what happened? What came to pass that sent you out here to live this life you are living?"

Parag had never thought of it in those terms. For him, it had seemed a gradual decline. From the hospital and his awful eye, to his ancient uncle in Sanchi. And then his uncle had passed away and he had been on his own, driven from the neighborhood for his insistent begging. Moving from one street to another. Learning to take advantage of his deformity. It was not a single event, it was . . . a series of unfortunate . . . And then, for an instant, in his mind's eye, Parag could see the beasts lying still in the watery fields in the moonlight. He could hear the wailing of the voices wafting above the warm breeze. Feel the awful burning in his eye. Without willing it so, he brought his hand to the fetid crust that had, for the past twelve years, habitually surrounded his left eye.

"I remember," he had said. "Yes, I remember."

"Do you know of any other boys? Boys who lost their families as you did and are now forced to fend for themselves?" He stared directly at Parag's left eye. "Who themselves perhaps were injured at the same time?"

"Some," he had answered, in what he imagined to be a noncommittal response, and yet, with that single word, in an odd, roundabout manner far too complicated to describe, this present moment in Seattle had begun to take shape.

Holmes stepped back a pace and looked them over. *Satisfied* would be far too strong a word to describe his feelings. No . . . this crew was far too motley for a word as strong as that. *Hopeful* was the best he could manage. Hopeful they could keep themselves together for long enough to get the job done. Hopeful their former lives burned in their chests like embers. Embers they could fan into enough of a fire to take their places among the pantheon of heroes. Or, failing that, into the ground with their brothers and sisters and mothers and fathers and all who had come before.

"Your identification cards are legitimate," he said. "Your names appear on company rolls. You have actually been hired by the companies involved in the service." He waited a moment for his words to sink in. "There will be no problem with your bona fides. The only trick will be to substitute your canisters for the ones you will be given."

He pointed. "Wesley and Nathan will take the van." They both nodded solemnly. "Nathan will drive. Your crew assembles at eight-thirty sharp. I have left directions from the hotel to the lot where you are expected to park. They're on the same street."

He now turned his attention to Samuel and Paul. He

walked to the window. "Come here," he said. They walked quickly to his side. He pulled back the curtains and pointed out into the street. "You see the red Subaru?" He didn't wait for a reply. "That is for you. Samuel is to drive." Since the plan had first been outlined, the cousins had good-naturedly argued about who was going to be what Paul liked to call "the wheelman." The matter was now settled. Paul cast a disgusted look his partner's way. "The registration and insurance cards are in the compartment. Your crew assembles at ten o'clock."

"What about Martin?" Wesley asked. "Bobby can't drive. How's he going to get—"

"I will be Bobby's new partner," Holmes said quickly. "The company has been notified that Martin will not be showing up for work. They are expecting me instead."

He crooked a finger at the group. "Remember . . . there is no reason to hurry. The crews are working into the early afternoon. Be circumspect. Try to do your work on common areas rather than individual spaces. Wear your breathing devices at all times. Take your time. What you will be spraying will not become active and contagious for thirty hours. So long as you don't breathe any of it, you will have plenty of time to do your work, decontaminate one another and be on your way."

He looked at each of them . . . one after the other. "If they put you together . . . that's good. If they assign you a more experienced partner . . . if the partner is in the way . . . you do whatever it takes." A rustle of understanding passed among them. "We have practiced over and over. You have been well trained. All you need to do is what you have been trained to do . . ."—

he aimed his palms at the ceiling—". . . and you will . . ."—he stopped himself. "You will finally have your moment."

"And you yours," Wesley pointed out.

Holmes straightened his spine and squared his shoulders. "I have lived a dozen years of my life, only for this moment. I have searched my soul. I can safely say I am willing to die for this to happen." He said it with enough conviction to surprise himself. "Not anxious, but willing," he added with a small smile. A ripple of nervous laughter rolled through the line of young men.

Holmes waved himself off. "Listen to me," he scoffed. "Lecturing to you. You who have fallen through the cracks of the cracks and survived." He nodded approvingly to each young man in turn. "They have enemies all over the world. They are looking over their shoulders for everyone but us. They have no idea we are coming. They—"

The doorbell rang.

29

Along the western horizon, a dark line of clouds rolled north like dirty boxcars. Below, a stiff southerly wind had churned the surface of Elliott Bay into an uneven washboard of whitecaps, swirling the black water in all directions at once, slamming the waves against one another in a disorganized maelstrom of foam and windblown water. Far out over the surface, halfway to Bainbridge Island, a solitary set of sails . . . reefed hard . . . straining . . . showed white against the dark surface of the Sound.

Corso gestured at the sails as he and Detective Gutierrez waited to cross East Republican Street. "Guy's got a lotta balls," he said. "It's blowing like hell out there today. You gotta know what you're doing to sail in this."

Gutierrez shook his head. "Never understood that sailing thing people got," he said. "Gotta be a better way to get from one place to another without freezing your ass off on the back of a boat." A huge green and white Bekins truck had run out of momentum at the apex of Republican Street and now sat with its cab nearly up on the flat and its load dangling precariously over the steepest part of the hill. Inside the cab, the driver and his partner were engaged in an animated discussion of what to do next.

Corso chuckled. "Sailing's hard to describe. There's a zen to it. Something about the feel of the wake behind the boat, the hum of the sails and the rigging." From the corner of his eye, Corso could see that Gutierrez wasn't buying any of it, so he shut up.

The moving van roared as the driver suddenly raced the engine, then shifted down to granny gear, slowly pulling the big truck upward out of the intersection, bringing Dougherty and Charly Hart into view, half a block down, standing on the sidewalk in front of her house, making conversation.

"Forensics went over this last night," Gutierrez said as they walked along scanning the sidewalk and the adjacent strip of grass. "Just want to be sure."

As the pair approached, Dougherty and Hart strolled across Thirteenth Street. Meg was talking and gesturing with her arms as she walked. Corso could make out the words above the rush of wind in the trees. "We were parked right here," she was saying. "Stevie and me." She looked over at Charly Hart, who stood at her side, notebook and pencil poised.

"This is Steveland Gerkey you're referring to?"

She nodded. "You know . . . it might help me remember if we had . . ."

The detective read her mind. "His landlady says he went to Las Vegas to see his kids. We've got a want in with the Vegas police for him."

Detective Gutierrez placed his pocket handkerchief on the sidewalk and rested one knee on the neatly folded square of black silk. He meticulously combed the semicircle of grass on the sidewalk side of a massive oak tree, using his fingers to pick through the rough tangle of autumn grass. After a few moments, he rose to his feet empty-handed.

He raised his voice, talking to Meg Dougherty across the street. "In your original statement, you told us you thought there might have been someone else on the street last night when you first spotted Mr. Bohannon."

Dougherty looked confused. Annoyed even. "Did I?" she wondered.

Charly Hart flipped through his notebook. He began to read. " 'It was like there was somebody over on the sidewalk. It was like this shadow went behind this big tree and never came out . . . and then like I recognized Brian . . . and you know forgot all about . . . ' What did you do then?" Charly Hart asked. "After you recognized Mr. Bohannon?"

She thought about it. "I told Stevie. I said, 'That's the guy—you know, the guy who did this to me.' I had to explain it to him. You know . . . about Brian and the tattoos and all that stuff."

Detective Gutierrez stood on the grass, with his back to the tree.

"And you and Mr. Gerkey were exactly where when all this was happening?" Charly Hart pressed. "You were both still sitting in the cab while you were explaining the situation to Mr. Gerkey?"

"Yes . . ." She caught her breath. Raised a long finger. "No. No we weren't. We were standing in the street. I'd gotten out of the car and so had he. I was about to pay him when I saw Brian start up the street." She pointed north.

"So then . . ." Corso began, "presuming you were right and there was somebody else in the street last night, it's safe to assume that whoever it was heard everything you said to Mr. Gerkey."

"Well . . . I don't know . . . I guess it's possible."

Detective Gutierrez stepped out from behind the oak tree. "I had no problem hearing everything you just said to Detective Hart," he said. "And at that time of the night there was probably less ambient noise than there is right now."

"So . . ." she began.

"That would explain a major portion of the mystery. The part about how a stranger would know where you lived and how they would know enough about the situation between you and Mr. Bohannon to consider leaving his body dead on your kitchen floor."

"But how would this person know I wasn't home? How would a stranger know I don't have a housekeeper and six kids?"

Gutierrez crossed the street now. "You told us you followed Mr. Bohannon."

"Yes . . . we did. Stevie and I."

"What if the stranger followed you?" Corso asked.

Her brow furrowed. "You mean while we were following Brian?"

"Yup."

Before she could respond, Charly Hart spoke. "So Mr. Bohannon leaves your house. What next?"

Again she pointed north. "He had a gray van parked up there."

"Let's go see," said Detective Gutierrez.

They walked the half a block. "Right here," she said, pointing to the first parking space on the east side of Thirteenth Street, a place currently occupied by a rusting Dodge Dart. Last car on the street anybody was going to steal had The Club locked across its steering wheel. "Guy leads a rich fantasy life," Charly Hart commented.

While the others milled around the sidewalk, Detective Gutierrez got down on one knee and examined the area adjacent to the parking space. Again he came up empty, dusting his hands against one another and shaking his head.

"So you follow him where from here?" he asked.

"To the U District," she said. "And then all the way back to this neighborhood again."

"Let's do the Broadway stop next," said Detective Gutierrez, "while we're in the neighborhood. Then we'll head for the U District."

On the way back to the car, the wind was full in their faces, tousling their hair and flapping their outer garments about them like spastic wings.

The steep face of Mercer Street had everybody hanging on. Seemed like it was almost straight down, as if the designers, in a fit of whimsy, had decided to add a little adrenaline to the otherwise unspectacular five-block jaunt to Broadway.

They parked the Ford Taurus illegally close to the corner of Broadway and Harrison. Just about the time Detective Gutierrez slipped the police department sign onto the dashboard and locked the doors, about the time everybody got their clothes straightened out, the ongoing chatter suddenly fell silent. Everyone looked around, scanning Broadway as if they'd dropped their wallets, looking for something unnamed but unquestionably missing. A "What's wrong with this picture?" kind of thing.

Dougherty broke the silence. "Dead," she said.

"Never seen it this quiet," Charley Hart agreed.

They were right. Broadway was usually the most insistently alive part of the city. Not so today. The usual river of pierced, painted, black-clad humanity that flowed down the sidewalks twenty hours a day had been reduced to a mere trickle. Not even a trickle really. More like languid pools of fools. Without options. The homeless. The runaways. Those too sick, too stupid or too far gone to be anyplace else but the streets. Maybe ten percent of the usual Saturday afternoon traffic lolled about.

The Four Horsemen Tattoo Parlor was located on the upper floor of an off-street shopping mall. Wedged between a sandwich shop and a design consulting firm, the sign featured a passable rendition of Dürer's famous pale riders and an offer to pierce any and all parts of your body.

Meg Dougherty stood on the sidewalk, hands thrust deep into her pockets, looking up, seemingly transfixed by the sight of the ghostly mounted riders.

Charly Hart broke the spell. "Anybody in there gonna recognize you?" he asked.

"Maybe," she said. "I used to know a lot of people in this neighborhood."

"Probably better you stay down here then."

She nodded and turned away from him, milling around the immediate area, taking in the bank of free publications lining the curb: help you find a car . . . help you find an apartment . . . help find you a lover . . . help find you that soul mate to play nude Yahtzee with.

Corso watched as the detectives disappeared inside. When he turned back to the street, Dougherty had wandered farther up the block toward the espresso stand and the outdoor café, rain or shine usually one of the major venues for the "see and be seen" crowd, nearly empty today. *USA Today* proclaimed, "DOOMSDAY IN SEATTLE."

He watched as she worked her way to the front of the line and ordered. She paid for the coffee and started back his way. Corso opened his mouth to speak.

She held up a palm. "Don't," she said. "I'm not in the mood for any of the usual juvenile banter."

"Juvenile?"

She took a deep breath and a sip of coffee. "I've had a tough night, Frank," she said. "I've watched my career go up in smoke. I found somebody I used to love dead on my kitchen floor. I've had some nut in a car try to run me down. I've witnessed a fistfight . . . seen somebody die of a heart attack. I've been arrested by the police, hijacked by the FBI, then rehijacked by the police . . . who are . . . who are making me relive the whole damn thing over again . . ."—she waved a disgusted hand—"so if you don't mind, just leave me alone. I did my duty. I kept them from putting you back in jail. From here on in, you're on your own." She turned her back and wandered farther up the street.

Corso leaned against a parked car. Watched her slowly window-shopping her way back in his direction, when Hart and Gutierrez reappeared on the sidewalk.

Gutierrez was the first to speak. "He stopped in to see a guy he used to work with . . ."

Charly Hart checked his notes. "Back in ninety-seven, ninety-eight. Yushi Takei is his name. Another tattoo artist. He says Bohannon stopped in out of the blue last night. Says he hasn't seen him in years. Says Bohannon just wanted to shoot the breeze about old times and such, but Takei was working on a customer and couldn't do a whole lot of talking, so Bohannon stayed about five minutes and then hit the bricks." He looked over at Dougherty. "That square with how long you remember Mr. Bohannon being inside?"

She nodded, said, "Yeah," and went back to sipping her coffee.

"Interesting though . . ." Detective Gutierrez began. "Mr. Takei says he's gotten a couple of postcards from Mr. Bohannon in the past couple of years. Says they weren't from France either. Says they were from somewhere in India. Says Bohannon's family imports a bunch of stuff from India for their business. Says Bohannon's been hanging out there for the past couple of years. Waiting for things to die down so's he could maybe come back to the States."

"Says he knows you," Charly Hart said.

Again Dougherty nodded. "Yushi's real good," she said. "Been around a long time. Booked up months in advance. Does a lot of traditional Japanese work."

Gutierrez looked around the half-deserted street. "I think I like it better when the slimeballs are out in force," he said. Charly Hart agreed and then turned to Dougherty.

"Where to?"

She dropped the remains of her coffee into a trash can. Wiped her hands on the paper napkin and then threw it in too. "U District," she said.

30

Governor James Doss unfurrowed his brow just long enough to allow the chubby woman in the blue smock to dab makeup onto his forehead with a small triangular sponge. The sight of Seattle Police Chief Harry Dobson and King County Sheriff Dan Reinhart approaching the makeshift dais in tandem brought the furrows back . . . harder . . . deeper than before. "Nice touch," he thought to himself. "Showing up together . . . shoulder to shoulder. Nice show of solidarity."

When she reached out with the sponge again, he pulled his head back. "That's enough, Ruth," he said. "Time for me to go to work."

Without a word, she pocketed the sponge and waddled down the stairs, past the pair of bodyguards, out onto the floor, until she was lost among the rush of technicians and security personnel swirling about in the final preparations for the news conference.

Doss appreciated Gary Dean's choice of venue. In this room it was nearly impossible to get a shot that didn't include a chandelier. Nice credibility enhancer. Spoke well of the wealth and power of the state. Gave people confidence.

He'd learned about setting from his predecessor Ramsey Haynes. "Remember," Haynes had told him on the day he'd been sworn in, "half an hour later, all they remember are the pictures."

When the chief and the sheriff veered left, toward the rear of the stage, where the assortment of dignitaries necessary to present a united front were in the process of assembling, Doss spoke to the nearest bodyguard. "Tommy," he said, "ask those two gentlemen if they would be so kind as to step up here and have a word with me."

Directly in front of the governor, three technicians gave a bank of microphones the finishing touches, while another pair scanned the stage area with light meters.

He watched, from the corner of his eye, as Tommy Shannon lumbered over to the pair, watched as they stopped walking and cast quick glances up his way. He had neither illusions nor complaints regarding either Dobson or Reinhart. As governor, he had his own State Police force and thus had no direct power over either of them. Dobson was appointed by the Seattle City Council and the mayor, and, although Reinhart was an elected official, the sheriff was sufficiently popular with both the public and the deputies union that he did not require the patronage of a lame duck governor.

He wondered if Gary Dean was smart enough to know how lucky Gary Dean had gotten. Dobson and Reinhart were both highly able administrators. Lifetime cops who'd risen through the ranks and were nearly universally respected by those whom they led. The kind of guys from whom you could expect a straight answer to a straight question.

"Governor," Harry Dobson said as they shook hands

at the top of the stairs. When his turn came, Dan Reinhart didn't say anything at all.

"Just wanted to be on hand," Doss said. "Let 'em know we're all on board and doing everything that can be done."

"Which is exactly what we're doing," the chief said quickly.

A momentary silence settled over the trio. "What do you think?" Doss finally asked. "What are the chances this threat is for real?"

"I've got over a hundred dead citizens who can attest to the reality of it," the chief said. "We have to treat tomorrow's threat like it's a done deal. We have no other choice."

Doss nodded and looked away. "Our esteemed mayor doesn't want me to declare a state of emergency and call out the National Guard. What do you two think?"

Dan Reinhart took the lead. "Between the city, the county and the feds, everything's being done that can possibly be done. Having soldiers standing around on street corners isn't going to make things better."

"Amen," the chief said.

"Speaking of the feds . . ." the governor said.

Neither man blinked. "What about them?" Harry Dobson inquired.

Doss offered a thin smile. "Because of you two, I've spent most of the morning with feds so far up my behind I could taste Brylcreem." The governor waited for a laugh but didn't get one. "Last I saw of them they were on the phone to the State Department." He sighed and looked away again. What all three men knew had been left unsaid was that James Doss had spent the first half of his final year in office lobbying for a cushy ambassadorship somewhere in Europe where they made wine, and this wasn't going to help his chances a bit.

Before the mantle of guilt could be firmly fitted to his shoulders, the chief spoke up. "If they were on the phone to D.C. it must mean you refused to order the State Police to do their dirty work for them," Harry observed.

"Murchison would do it if you told him to," Dan Reinhart said quickly. "Clint's strictly rank-and-file."

"Yeah, and about five seconds later, that son of a bitch would issue a press release telling the world how appalled he was to have to do this, and that I gave him a direct order to do so." Doss waved an impatient hand. "Besides . . . I'm not ordering anyone's arrest on the basis of his middle name being 'bin.' "

He gave the pair a nod of appreciation and began to make his way through the crowd, shaking hands, gripping elbows and patting shoulders as he went along. Before his cologne had completely cleared the area, the mayor came trotting up the stairs. His eyes were bright behind small metal frames. His cheeks were flushed red. He took off his glasses and massaged the bridge of his nose.

"You fellas aren't exactly making friends and influencing people," he said while wiping his glasses with a hankie.

"We start acting like the gestapo . . . the terrorists win," Dan Reinhart said.

The mayor nodded and held up an understanding hand. "You're preaching to the choir. I'm on board here." He puffed his cheeks and blew out a gust of air. "But don't think I didn't hear about it. Congressmen. Senators. Certain City Council members who shall remain nameless. Hell . . . I had Bernie Pauls on hold for ten minutes," he said, naming the new head of the Department of Homeland Security. "I had to make him wait because our senior senator wasn't through ripping me up one side and down the other about our refusal to cooperate with the D.C. crowd." He gazed out over the ballroom. "It's like the President said this morning . . . we can't let them drag us down to their level. We've got to stand firm in the face of the pressure."

"Five minutes," was shouted from the back of the room, ending the conversation, sending the three men back down the stairs and around the corner, out of view, where half a dozen tables offering coffee and cold drinks had been hastily set up for the dignitaries. Ben Gardener stood in the corner, half a head taller than everyone else in the room. Harlan Sykes was huddled up with Mike Morningway and a contingent from Emergency Management Services. The mayor was animated, emphatic with a clipboard. Out in the center of the staging area, Bernie Pauls was huddled with Doctors Belder, Abrahams and Stafford for a little photo op session. Watch the birdie.

A sense of dread began to spread through Harry Dobson as he took in the melee. He watched intently as if something about the scene couldn't be trusted. He sensed he was experiencing one of those rare moments when it becomes apparent that one's senses cannot always be relied upon to relay information in an accurate and timely manner. Like a frozen moment in traffic when a glance out the side window of your car tells your central nervous system that your car is rolling backward. You stand on the brake, but the slippage continues . . . your leg pumps like a dog in a dream and still the car eases backward . . . until you realize it's the bus in the next lane creeping forward, not your car rolling backward . . . and a nervous little chuckle escapes your chest. A chuckle that assures you this was just an aberration . . . the exception that proves the rule . . . because god forbid you should be that far off base on a regular basis.

Harry Dobson's foray into the Twilight Zone was brought to an abrupt end by the arrival of Colonel Hines at his shoulder. He'd broken out the full array of medals and military campaign ribbons for the news conference, but his expression said he'd rather be nearly anyplace else. "Not your cup of tea, Colonel?" the chief inquired.

"I'd like it better if we were going to tell the people the truth," Hines said while sizing up the crowd.

"Which is?"

"Which is . . . which is . . . this is a joke."

"How so?"

The colonel made a rude noise with his lips. "We play at readiness. We create new agencies. We throw money at every new technology that comes down the pike. We do everything except what needs to be done."

"Which is?" the chief inquired.

"Commitment," Hines said.

"To what?"

"To the reality of the situation. To the fact that we don't live in Mayberry anymore, Chief. To the fact that the rest of the world hates our guts and wouldn't lose a minute's sleep if we all turned up dead one fine morning."

Hans Belder called from across the room, "Colonel Hines." He gestured with a hairy hand for the colonel to come join in the photo session. Hines tried to demur, waved back and shook his head, until it became obvious that Belder wasn't going to take no for an answer and so Hines excused himself and began to pick his way through the crowd.

Dan Reinhart whistled under his breath. "Old boy's got quite a burr under his saddle this morning."

"I hear it's permanent," said the chief.

"Guy's only slightly left of Attila the Hun."

"As far as Hines is concerned, Attila was soft on terrorism," the chief whispered, sweeping his eyes across the crowd. Stopping his gaze here and there on one face or another, moving backward and then onward again until something clicked like a roulette ball falling into the slot.

There she was. Lingering at the back of the crowd with a smile on her face and a cup of coffee in her hand. She'd been with the doctors yesterday. Same thing. Standing in the back. Keeping out of the spotlight. And then it hit him. This was the woman Corso had described from the bus tunnel. Wearing a tailored suit of an unusually warm fawn color and sensible shoes to match. He watched her for a moment. She had an air of competence about her. A sense that she was somehow above the proceedings.

The chief stepped around Dan Reinhart and walked over to the entrance to the walled-off area. Over to the governor's security chief, Tommy Shannon.

He leaned in close. "Who's the woman in the brown suit?" he asked.

Tommy was an old hand. Without seeming to move his eyes from the crowd, he scanned the room, picked her out, took her in, then reached into his inside jacket pocket and came out with a laminated list. After a quick perusal, he said, "Irena Kahn. She's with the Israeli delegation."

"In what capacity?"

"They list her as a cultural attaché. Diplomatic passport."

"Which makes her what?"

Tommy Shannon rolled his watery eyes. "With the Israelis, you never know," he said. "They're only slightly less full of bull than the Russians. She could be anything from a personal nursemaid to a government spook."

He told Tommy thanks and was told not to mention it. Without looking her way, he sidled over to the edge of the enclosure. When he felt as if he was as alone as he was going to be, he pulled his hand radio from his belt, pushed the red button and spoke.

"This is Chief Dobson. Patch me through to the Downtown Precinct station." A yessir and a couple of clicks later, he had Lieutenant Carmen Pirillo on the radio. "Carmen," he said. "I need a pair of plainclothes detectives at the Olympic Four Seasons. Five minutes ago," he said.

"On the way," came the response. "Anything else, Chief?"

"Hurry."

Harry pocketed the phone and quickly crossed the room, not wanting her to spend too much time out of his sight. It was no more than sixty feet from where he stood to where he had seen her last, but when he arrived, she was gone. He checked the back of the throng and then moved among the crowd, smiling and fondling elbows when necessary, but she had simply disappeared.

That feeling of disassociation and uncertainty washed over him again, leaving him cold in his center and unsure of what to do next. He turned away from the crowd and swallowed several deep breaths. That's when he noticed the coffee cup. Sitting on the starched white tablecloth. White on white, nearly invisible to the naked eye.

He strolled over and looked down at the table. Frosted orange lipstick was smudged along the nearest edge. A brown eye of coffee stared up from the bottom of the cup. Instead of a saucer, the cup rested on a cardboard coaster, which had been flipped upside down and written on. He moved the cup and picked up the coaster.

"Hey," a familiar voice said.

Harry pocketed the coaster and turned back to the room. Dan Reinhart had wandered over his way.

"He got it from *The Sopranos*," said the sheriff.

"Got what?" Harry asked.

"The line about tasting Brylcreem. Doss robbed it off *The Sopranos*. Uncle Junior said it to Tony a couple seasons back."

Harry looked incredulous. "You watch that crap?"

"It puts me to sleep."

As if on cue, a great rush of noise filled the air, as the doors were opened and the press rushed into the room. The ambient noise, which, until that moment, had consisted of little more than a low buzz of conversation, suddenly sounded more like a herd of cattle on the prod.

Harry watched from the corner of his eye as the other room filled, hoping to catch another glimpse of her. He'd decided he didn't give a damn who she was. Or about her diplomatic passport either. Nobody but nobody was going to stick a needle into one of his officers and walk away with impunity. Nobody.

"One minute," was shouted above the noise of the arriving crowd.

The governor adjusted his tie and smiled. The agency people began shuffling toward the stairs at the side of the stage. Tommy Shannon left his post at the bottom of the stairs to make a final sweep along the front of the dais looking for nuts who didn't belong in the front row.

Harry's eyes rolled over the remaining crowd looking for the woman. No sign of her. He could feel the blood rising to his face.

Harry reached into his pocket and pulled out the coaster. He was in the process of turning it so he could read the writing, when someone called his name.

When Harry looked up, he found himself staring into the unblinking eye of a handheld television camera. Jim Sexton from Channel Five stood in front of the camera with a microphone grasped in his hand and a look of determination etched on his face.

For a moment, Harry was confused. Jim was a stand-up guy. He knew the rules. What was going on here?

"Press corps's over there, Jim," Harry said with a nod of the head. He could feel the hot lights on his forehead.

Jim ignored him. "Chief Dobson. Were you aware that a county pathologist and her assistant were killed earlier today by the same virus that killed the people in the bus tunnel?"

Harry felt the sheriff stiffen. He kept his face as still as stone, looked directly into the face of the camera and said, "Yes, Jim, as a matter of fact, I was aware of that."

31

Patricia Mitchell pointed to a spot on her front porch. "The boy throws it right here every morning," she said. "I'm usually still in bed, but I hear the noise."

Satisfied that Jeffrey now knew where the paper landed every morning, she marched down the front stairs and stood on her well-tended front lawn. She pointed at the house next door, a run-down Victorian whose gingerbread filigrees hung from the eaves in tatters, whose last paint job was either gray or some putrid shade of green, whose sidewalks were pierced here and there by clumps of dried grass and weeds growing up through the maze of cracks which time and inattention had etched into the concrete walks surrounding the dwelling.

"It's them," she said. "Those Indian boys in there. You do your job . . . you investigate, and you'll surely find out."

Jeffrey Unger had been a customer service rep for the *Seattle Times* for a little under three years, and in all that time, he had never ceased to be amazed at how seriously people took their morning newspapers . . . especially the old folks, who seemed to have their daily lives programmed and who took any variance in the plan as a personal affront. Miss Mitchell was that way. You'd think somebody'd shot her dog or kidnapped one of her kids or something the way she was carrying on. It was like she expected a forensics team to come out and work the crime scene or something. All for twenty-five cents a day and a buck and a half on Sundays.

"How do you know it's them?" he asked calmly.

As he'd feared, she immediately went postal. "How do I know? How do I know? How could I *not* know? The minute those people move in there is the minute my paper starts to disappear every morning. It doesn't take Philo Vance to figure it out, sonny."

Jeffrey Unger kept the smile plastered to his face. "I mean . . . have you actually seen any of these young men taking your paper in the morning?"

She looked at him with a mixture of scorn and anxiety. "You're not the brightest bulb in the box are you, junior?" she said, before moving her gaze half a dozen houses up the street, where a couple of guys seemed to be canvassing door-to-door.

"Those nutsy goddamn Jehovah's Witnesses again," she said. "We oughta give 'em the mail to deliver . . . long as they're out there anyway."

Unger, ignoring both the personal insult and the religious slur, instead held up an idea finger. "Tell you what we're going to do," he began. "I'm going to have your carrier deliver the paper just like he always does. And then, on his way home for the day, I'm going to have him deliver you another. Just to make sure. That way we can both be sure you're getting your paper in the morning." Her facial expression suggested she was not altogether pleased. "How's that?" he asked.

She thrust her lower jaw out. "Crappy," she said.

He took a deep breath and asked the question he'd hoped to avoid. "What would it take to make you feel better about this thing? The *Seattle Times* is determined—"

"I want you to march right over there and tell those people to leave my damn paper alone. That's what I want. I want you to tell them how lucky they are to be here at all . . . to be going to a school like the University of Washington. I want you to remind them that being here is a privilege . . . not . . . not . . . some . . ." She sputtered her way to silence.

Unger held up his hands in surrender. These were the moments he dreaded. When his job forced him to face what cops had known forever . . . that confronting people, regardless of how you went about it, was a risky business. You just never knew what kind of a reaction you were going to get. "Okay," he said. "But you've got to let me handle this." He looked at her for agreement but didn't find it. "Okay? You'll let me handle it?"

She gave a grudging nod and folded her arms across her pigeon chest. Kept them that way across the yard, around the hedge and up the front stairs. The porch needed to be swept; Jeffrey Unger could feel crunching beneath the soles of his shoes as he mounted the stairs and pushed on the doorbell. Miss Mitchell stood glowering, one step down.

Seemed as if the door opened instantly. No gap whatsoever between his finger pushing the button and the door springing open a crack.

The darkness of the man's complexion could not obscure the flush in his cheeks. Unger reckoned the man to be somewhere in his late forties or early fifties, thick as a brick, with a flat emotionless look in his deeply hooded eyes that reminded Unger of certain fish he had kept as a child. "Can I help you?" the man asked.

Jeffrey Unger offered one of his business cards. The man looked at it like Unger was trying to hand him a turd. "Can I help you?" he said again.

"Oh . . . yes. I certainly hope so," Jeffrey Unger said. "This is Miss Mitchell . . . she . . . ah . . . lives next door here and she's . . . we've been having a bit of a problem with her newspaper disappearing in the morning. I was hoping we could . . ."

"We could what?" the man demanded.

"Talk things over. I was hoping we could talk things over."

"Talk about what?"

"I was hoping . . ." he began, and then bit it off when he felt the rickety stairs move as Miss Mitchell stepped up onto the porch beside him.

"Talk about them stealing my newspaper every morning," she said. "That's what in heck we want to talk about."

"I'm sure we know nothing about any such thing," the man said. "We have nothing to hide here." With that, he opened the door allowing them to see into the front room where five young East Indian men sat sprawled all over the furniture. The one in the red jogging suit had a wicked scar running down the entire side of his face. Another had a bad eye . . . looked like it had been burned with acid. The pair wedged into the armchair together looked as if they might have been brothers, or, if the languid tangle of their legs were to be read another way, perhaps even lovers.

"These young men are graduate students," the man said indignantly. "Engineering students at the university. I assure you . . . they have no time for any such foolish—"

With a grace and speed belied by her advanced age and general obesity, Patricia Mitchell burst through the doorframe and into the room. She pointed at the couch. "There it is," she shouted. "There's my paper right there."

She got halfway across the room before the one with the bad eye rose to his feet and stepped into her path. "I think you better . . ." he began, but it was too late then, as she already had an arm through the opening between Scar and Bad Eye and wasn't about to be stopped by anything short of a Mack truck.

From the doorway, Jeffrey Unger heard himself call her name, but the sound of his voice was lost in space as the old woman snatched the folded newspaper from the couch and waved it around the room like a trophy. "Here's my damn paper," she announced triumphantly. "Just like I said."

Except that Jeffrey's eyes weren't on the purloined paper. They were still glued to the couch where the shiny automatic pistol lay on its side, with its barrel pointing directly his way.

For a moment, the room seemed to fall into a state of suspended animation. Nobody moved. Silence hung like icicles from the walls, in the seconds before the guy with the scar picked up the gun and backhanded Patricia Mitchell across the face with all his might, sending her shattered glasses flying off into space, as she twirled nearly a complete circle before pinwheeling to the floor in a pile of tangled limbs and bloody spittle.

Without willing it so, Jeffrey Unger found himself rushing forward, his arms extended to break her fall, his mouth agape to cry in protest. A powerful hand tore at his shoulder, trying to halt his advance. He shrugged it off and kept moving her way. All around him, the room was set in motion. The one with the bad eye was bringing his fist up from the floor. Somebody tackled him from behind, forcing him to his knees, speeding him closer to the rising fist and the flash of jagged silver he noticed for the first time on his way down and then the icy sense of deflation in his abdomen, as if somebody let the air out of his balloon, right before the weight on his back drove him facedown onto the carpet, where his instincts took over in some survival reaction to the pain in his gut, sending him bucking like a rodeo horse, sending whoever was on top of him flying, allowing him to roll once to the right and drag himself to his feet.

Against all odds, Patricia Mitchell had also regained her footing. Half blind, broken-toothed and bloody, one hideous purple jellyfish of an eye winking and blinking as she flailed blindly at the surrounding air, she emitted a low keening sound from somewhere deep in her chest as she sought to damage her attackers.

For a fleeting moment, Jeffery Unger thought he might have peed his pants in fear. His shame and consternation were replaced by genuine terror when he looked down at himself and realized the warm liquid rolling down the front of his legs was not urine but thick red arterial blood. That he'd been stabbed. And then a powerful hand grabbed the front of his hair and pulled his head back ... back until he dropped to his knees again, until he was staring straight up at the ceiling like a supplicant at mass and the prick of steel twitched his throat in the instant before the ripping sound began, and the dam broke all over him and he threw his eyes upward in time to see the one with the scar step behind Miss Mitchell, raise his arm and then drive something into her back.

Then again. And again, until the old woman's great will to live sent her staggering across the room, dragging a pair of them with her as she sought salvation in the light, only to collapse in the corner behind the front door with three of them piled on top of her. The knife rising and falling as she groaned and writhed on the dirty brown linoleum.

The doorbell rang. The knife paused in midair. Everyone froze . . . except Patricia Mitchell, whose movements had been reduced to a series of spasms and ticks that rocked her out-of-control body like seismic tremors.

Holmes held up a hand. A hand that held a serrated commando knife. A hand red with blood sticking out of a shirtsleeve covered with blood, inside a suit jacket covered with blood. The doorbell rang again. Three insistent rings. Then another three.

Using his clean hand, Holmes pulled open the front door. Just a crack. No more than six inches before he stopped it with his toe and then leaned his face into the opening.

Two men. A Hispanic and a tall white man. The Hispanic was waving a gold badge in his face. Detective. Seattle Police Department. Reuben Santiago Gutierrez.

Fortunately for Holmes he didn't have to speak. The cop did it for him.

"We were hoping you could help us," the cop said. A pair of gold front teeth glittered in the afternoon sun.

Holmes managed a smile and a nod. Over his left shoulder, Patricia Mitchell's death throes had become more violent. Only the combined weight of a trio of men kept her from flopping about like a fish on a riverbank. Worse yet and far more immediate, one or more of her stab wounds had severed an artery somewhere inside her, sending a river of red running across the linoleum floor toward the front door, toward Holmes's foot in the doorjamb and the policeman standing no more than a yard away.

Holmes held his breath as the cop slipped a pair of photographs from a manila envelope. The river of blood had reached his shoe. The only thing preventing the dark syrupy line from running under the door and into the cops' view was the black rubber heel of his cordovan wingtip. The cop held the first photograph in front of his face.

Martin. Years before. When he was Brian Bohannon. His hair was black and he was thinner. Holmes felt a wave of regret. Not for killing him, but for having chosen him at all. For not going along with his instincts. For valuing insider information above character. A gray van? He shook his head, inwardly thanking himself for ditching the gray van and stealing another. The cop asked about the picture. No, he'd never seen that face before. The blood had found the gap beneath his instep and was worming its way beneath his foot. He pressed down harder on the foot, trying to flatten his arch. The floor emitted a long low groan. Sounded a lot like a fart. The cop looked up at him disgustedly.

Holmes smiled. The second picture was more recent. They'd cropped out the knife wound across the throat but there wasn't any doubt about it. Martin was dead of unnatural causes. And recently too.

Holmes shook his head and shrugged his shoulders.

Wished he could have helped. Sorry. The cop thanked him and returned the photos to the envelope. Holmes watched the pair until they were back on the sidewalk, turned right and disappeared behind the overgrown shrubbery. Only then did he close the door and turn back to the room.

32

"Guy never even blinked," Corso said.

"Who's that?" Gutierrez asked.

"Coupla houses back. The East Indian guy. When you showed him the autopsy photo, he never even blinked. Looked at it like it was a laundry list. Most everybody else winced or turned away or something . . . you know."

"Strong stomach, I guess."

"Sure didn't sound that way," Corso commented.

Gutierrez burst out laughing. "Can you believe that guy? Rips one with me standing right there in front of him." Shaking his head.

They picked their way carefully up the sidewalk. The ancient roots of the maples and elms lining Fifteenth Avenue had turned the chunks of sidewalk into a jumble, tilted this way and that, cracked and broken, lifted upward as if some giant hand had cast the pieces of concrete like dominos.

They stayed at it. Four more houses. All the way to the end of the block. Across the street, Dougherty and Charly Hart had finished their side and were headed back to the car. The strands of afternoon sunlight had withered to gray, leaving only the smell of leaves and saltwater in the air.

"I'm starting to think this guy Bohannon was just driving around aimlessly," Gutierrez said. He waved an arm. "With all that's going on, I'd hate to think we were wasting our time on a wild-goose chase."

They angled across the street to Hart and Dougherty. "Anything?" Gutierrez asked.

Charly Hart shook his head. "Had a bunch of people say they noticed a gray van parked in the neighborhood for the past week or so. I called it in. They're gonna send a couple of squad cars to sweep the area. Maybe we'll pick it up that way. You?"

"Bunch of scared people take one look at my badge and want to know what's going on downtown and whether they ought to get out of the city."

Hart looked at Dougherty. "Where to?"

"From here he went to Broadway, but we already did that, so I guess it's the waterfront next."

"Let's go."

"I need to use the loo," Dougherty said.

"We'll stop at the pizza joint," Charly Hart said.

The sight of the tall woman told Holmes what he needed to know. They were retracing Martin's route of the previous night. Investigating the dead man on her floor. Had to be. The tall white guy was probably her attorney. He expelled a huge breath. Whatever they thought they might know . . . it was too late now. But how close . . . how close to everything coming apart . . . to everything he'd lived for . . . to everything . . . he felt the rage welling in his chest . . . could hear the pounding of blood in his temples and feel himself beginning to sweat.

He kept the dusty curtain pulled aside until he saw them ease into traffic and disappear from sight. When he turned back to the room, the look on his face was enough to freeze-frame the five men who lay scattered about the floor like discarded toys.

He marched straight across the room to Wesley. "Give me the gun," he said.

Again, everyone stiffened. In the weeks before they'd left for Canada, it was all Wesley talked about. How when he got to America he could get a gun of his own.

"It's mine," Wesley said.

Holmes held out his hand. "Give me the damn gun." In a quieter voice this time.

Wesley shook his head, began to speak, and, in the amount of time it took Wesley's lips to twitch, Holmes snatched the gun from his hand and straight-armed him in the chest, sending him staggering backward, tripping over Jeffrey Unger's lifeless form, down on the seat of his pants with his hands spread out behind him.

Holmes stepped over the body and shook the automatic in Wesley's face. "Where did you get this?"

Wesley's eyes rolled in his head. He scurried backward like a crab until he reached the wall.

"Martin got it for him," Paul said. "First day we got here."

"All he does is play with it," added Samuel.

Wesley was on his feet now. "It's mine," he said again. "Give it to me."

Holmes ignored him. "All of you. Get your things." They were moving now. "Your canisters are in the cars. We're going to the hotel now instead of later tonight. You each have your room keys. The rooms are paid for. Do not contact one another once you get there. Hurry."

Wesley did not move. His scar seemed almost to glow. When Holmes stepped his way, Wesley steeled himself but did not break and run.

"It's mine," he insisted.

"Listen to me, Madhu," Holmes said, using his old name. "This thing is bigger than either of us. It's about our mothers and fathers and wives and daughters. It's about what happened to all of us and how they saw us as dogs."

"Give . . ."

Holmes showed the palm of his hand. "You remember your mother, Madhu?"

He watched as Madhu Verma processed the question. "I do," Madhu said. He pointed at his own head. "I remember the white streak in her hair."

"These are the people," Holmes whispered. "Perhaps they were not the people in charge. Perhaps they only read about it in the newspaper, or saw it on the television, but they are the ones who pushed it from their memory. They said, 'Ho . . . there are millions and millions of them. They really don't care that much about these things.'"

Wesley made eye contact with Holmes for the first time. "My mother was very beautiful," he said, daring Holmes to dispute the fact. "She was . . . I remember the food she cooked. The . . ." He stopped himself. Only lately had he allowed himself the luxury of thinking about his family and, even then, only in the vaguest of terms. Nothing that could bring a taste to his mouth or a picture to his eye. Before that . . . before that, staying alive had taken every bit of his energy. The present had completely swallowed the past.

Holmes put a hand on his shoulder. Wesley looked down at the hand as if he were going to bite it.

"Clean yourself up. Get your things," Holmes said. "We must go now."

Wesley hesitated . . . the muscles along the sides of his jaw rippled like snakes. He ducked out from beneath the hand and headed for the stairs.

Holmes watched as Wesley shouldered his way past the others, who by now were on their way down the stairs, each carrying a small black suitcase.

Holmes pointed at Samuel and Paul. "You have everything?" They said they did. He tossed Samuel the car keys. "Go," he said.

Paul cast his eyes at the bleeding bodies on the floor.

"Leave them," Holmes said. "It is over for them now."

Wesley came down the stairs at a lope and stood next to Nathan. Holmes tossed Nathan the keys to the van. "Get going," he said. "The van is a deep red color. It's in the supermarket parking lot."

Holmes listened to the sounds of their retreating feet as he looked around the room. The old woman lay in a crumpled heap, her skirt halfway up her thick thighs, her life's blood spread out across the cheap linoleum like a fan. The man's white shirt was, by now, nearly red. His lower left leg had come to rest at a horribly unnatural angle. Holmes winced, turned his eyes away and headed for the door with Bobby Darling trailing along in his wake. They turned right at the sidewalk and strode the block and a half to the black Mercedes parked under the overhanging trees along the curb.

Albert Lehane stood with his hands on his hips, watching the mayor's press conference on the huge plasma TV in the newsroom. His face was still tingling from the news. A hundred sixteen dead. Genetically engineered Eboli virus that killed immediately and then died immediately. Dean had introduced the assemblage of dignitaries onstage, given out the basic information and then allowed the Stafford woman to handle the scientific end of the briefing. Twenty minutes later, having assured the multitude that everything possible was being done, that names could not be released pending notification of next of kin, he'd begun fielding questions from the media. Predictably, he'd started with the national media, Wolf Blitzer from CNN, Dan Rather in a brown tweed jacket, and then worked his way down to the local affiliates, where Kitty and the number one team had gotten her question in first. Good girl.

And then . . . while a question was being asked and the camera was trained on the audience, somebody began elbowing their way through the crowd. Brows furrowed and heads turned but the jostling continued until the pair had pushed their way to the front of the crowd. Gary Dean looked down at the commotion and recognized Jim Sexton.

Albert Lehane leaned forward and squinted at the screen. "What the hell is he doing there?" he demanded. He looked up at Robert Tilden. "Did you send . . ." he began.

Tilden shook his head vigorously. "No sir . . . you sent him over to Harborview."

"I'll be goddamned. What in hell does he think he's doing?"

And then Jim was shouting at the mayor, who leaned over to listen and then straightened up with a quizzical look on his face.

"I'll have his ass for this," Lehane announced.

Gary Dean got back behind the mic. "The question . . ."—he cocked a boyish eyebrow—"so strenuously tendered . . . was as to whether we have had any additional deaths other than those in the bus tunnel." He looked down at Jim with a mixture of annoyance and pity and then back out at the crowd.

"As of this time we have no—"

Something stopped his recitation. "Excuse me," he said into the mic and then turned and spoke to someone behind him. When the camera angle shifted, Seattle Police Chief Harry Dobson could be seen whispering in the mayor's ear. Gary Dean was doing his best to keep his face placid, but a slight tremor in his cheek suggested otherwise.

He'd lost some of his color by the time he got back to the mic. "I am given to understand . . . and this is completely new information to me . . . I am given to understand that we have indeed had at least two more deaths." The room broke into a roar. "A county pathologist and her assistant . . ." But by then the crowd had begun to drown him out. The camera panned to Jim Sexton, smiling . . . Channel Five microphone clutched in his hand.

Albert Lehane pointed at the image and looked up at Robert Tilden.

"That's my boy," he announced.

33

The mayor was livid. "How could you hang me out to dry like that?"

Harry Dobson kept his face bored and his voice neutral. "The information *was* and *is* part of an ongoing homicide investigation. It's not the kind of thing we release."

"The information could be germane to finding these damn people who are threatening to destroy—"

Harry interrupted. "The feds sure as hell don't think so. The only information I know of that could possibly be of use to a terrorist investigation is the route that Mr. Bohannon took while driving around the city last night. I've got a pair of competent men checking that angle right now." He threw a hand at the collection of agency heads huddled on the far side of the room. "You think these ham-handed feds here could do a better job than my men . . . you're just plain crazy."

"Makes us look like small-time operators out for ourselves."

Harry shook his head. "I respectfully disagree, Your Honor. What it makes us look like is a competent law enforcement agency, following standard investigative procedures to the letter."

Harry reached into his jacket pocket and pulled out the coaster. "I think we better get our panel of experts back together," he said.

The mayor hesitated and then took the coaster from Harry's fingers. He adjusted his glasses on his nose and began to read. Harry watched the words form on his lips. "The next batch of virus will become airborne in thirty hours and will live for thirty days."

The mayor swallowed hard and read the message again. "Where did you get this?" he demanded.

Harry told him everything . . . except the part about how he believed this was the same woman Corso had seen in the bus tunnel.

"You saw this Israeli woman leave this on the table?" the mayor asked.

"No. I found it in the area she had vacated."

"So we don't even know for sure—"

Harry cut him off. "No, we don't."

"Then we better be careful about what we say."

"My thoughts exactly."

The mayor slapped the coaster against his hip in disgust. "Can this be true?"

"I don't know, but we darn well better find out."

The pager on his right hip went off. His wife. Third time she'd paged him in the past two hours. "If you'll excuse me," he said to the mayor as he reached for his phone. Gary Dean turned quickly and walked away.

"I saw it on the news," Kathleen said as soon as she picked up.

"It's ugly," Harry said.

"A hundred sixteen dead?"

"Hundred eighteen," Harry corrected.

"Are you okay?"

"I'm fine," he assured her.

She had something to say but was holding back. Harry could sense it. "What's up?" he asked, trying to make it easy for her.

"I made some calls this morning."

"Oh yeah?"

"Caregivers."

"Ah."

"Somebody who could be with Dad full-time."

"And?"

"It's steep." She named a monthly figure.

"We'll figure something out," he said.

"One of them could start now," she said. "Tomorrow."

Harry held his breath. "Why don't you stay there for a while. Interview a bunch of these people. Get me some names and addresses. I could make a call or two and have somebody over there run a little background check on all of them."

She wasn't fooled. "You don't want me back there do you?" When Harry didn't answer, she pressed. "I thought you told me things were okay."

"Just stay where you are for a few more days," Harry said.

A silence settled over the phone line.

"Listen . . . I gotta go," Harry said.

"Be careful," she said.

"I always am."

"I love you."

"Me too."

Dougherty stared distractedly out the side window of the car as they pulled a hard hundred-and-fifty-degree left turn off Denny Way onto the last little spur of Third Avenue. The white arches of the Pacific Science Center loomed overhead like the discarded cocoon of some long-vanished insect. She fell against the door as they leaned right around the corner onto Broad Street. Feeling Corso's eyes on the side of her face, she looked his way. Corso started to speak, but she cut him off.

"Don't," she said. "Just leave me alone."

He held up a restraining hand. Kept his mouth shut.

The light changed. Gutierrez wheeled the Ford through the intersection, put the left-turn signal on and moved over a lane. Elliott Bay came into view now, from this angle jagged and black as an agate out beyond the foot of Broad Street. To the north, over the top of Myrtle Edwards Park, a trio of grain tankers stood by the Pier Eighty-Six grain terminal, empty holds waiting to be filled with eastern Washington wheat before heading out through the straits for the green Pacific and Asia beyond.

"How far, miss?" Gutierrez asked as he wheeled the car along the deserted street.

"All the way down to the bottom and turn left," she said.

The Ford crested the hill and started down to the waterfront. Toward the half-mile tourist promenade along the edge of the bay, where a gauntlet of tourist traps, waterborne adventures and curio shops stood ready to separate the traveler from his folding money.

Even with the windows rolled up and a stiff breeze hissing around the car, the roar of the train whistle reached their ears. "Oh shit," Gutierrez said.

He jogged to the left again, over into the turn lane, and gave the car some gas, but it was already too late.

A block and a half ahead, the safety barrier had eased down across the roadway. The train whistled again, this time closer and louder. The deep roar of the diesel engines vibrated the car windows. Gutierrez braked the car to a halt less than a foot from the red and white striped barrier, then flopped himself against the back of the driver's seat in frustration. He looked back over his shoulder at Corso and Dougherty. "Could be a while," he said disgustedly.

He was right. Burlington Northern trains were not only prodigiously long but were restricted as to how fast they could travel through the urban core, an unfortunate combination of circumstances which often led to interminable waits at downtown train crossings as a seemingly endless stream of graffitied car carriers and container cars inched through the city, bringing crosstown traffic to a complete standstill.

As Corso sat and waited for the train to appear, he noticed Gutierrez's reflection in the rearview mirror. He watched as the detective reached up with a thick knobby hand and adjusted the mirror slightly, frowned and then turned and looked over his shoulder out the rear window of the car. His brown brow looked like a freshly plowed field.

"Now . . . what in hell is this about?" Gutierrez asked himself out loud. He popped the door lock and began to step out of the car.

Harry Dobson pulled open the door to his private office area and stepped inside. The outer office was quiet, and he was grateful for the calm. The serenity was, however, short-lived. Margy looked up. "Lotta people looking for you, Chief," she said.

"I'm sure," Harry said.

"The mayor's called four times in the past ten minutes," she said as Harry crossed the room and stepped into his private office overlooking Sixth Avenue. To the south, the Port of Seattle's orange loading cranes rose above the stadiums. He closed the door. Ten minutes was how long it had taken Harry to duck out the service door of the hotel and walk the five blocks to the Public Safety Building. He heard the click and then Margy's voice was coming from his speaker phone. *"The mayor says the experts will be gathering at one in the Critical Incident Room."*

Harry walked over and pushed the red button. "Tell him I'll be there. What else?"

"Lieutenant Pirillo from Downtown says you asked him to send a detective team to the . . ."

Harry winced. He reached out and locked the button down and then shrugged himself clear of his jacket. "Get back to him. Give him my apologies. Tell him I'll get in touch when things slow down."

"I've got a bunch of stuff for Detective Hart, who for some reason doesn't seem to be answering his radio."

Harry hung the coat in the closet and closed the door.

"Such as?"

"The Canadian Immigration report he requested."

"Bring it in here, please."

Click. Ten seconds later, the door eased open. Harry thanked her.

He began pulling electronic devices from his belt, shaking his head at the amount of equipment he carried these days—two phones, two pagers—until he found the one he was looking for. He held the transmitter in front of his mouth, pushed the big white button and said, "Detective Hart."

Almost instantly, the reply came, "Yes, Chief."

"The Canadians came up with . . ."

Charly Hart must have forgotten to release the SEND button, because he certainly wasn't speaking to the chief when he began to shout, "Hey now . . . goddammit . . . hey . . ." Harry could hear other voices. A woman screamed. The deep roar of an engine filled the tiny speaker until it buzzed. "Detective Hart," Harry called.

The roar of the diesel engines had begun rising in his ears when Bobby Darling felt Holmes suddenly stiffen in the driver's seat. The man's usually implacable features were a mask of confusion. He'd never before seen Holmes appear this concerned about anything.

"What's the matter?" he asked.

Holmes bobbed his head slightly, indicating the gold Ford Taurus in front of them. The one nosed right up to the red and white barrier. "It's those same cops," Holmes said.

"From the house?"

"Yes."

A shiver ran down Bobby's spine like a frozen ball bearing.

"What are they doing *here?*"

"Yeah," Holmes said.

And then a big hand reached up and adjusted the Ford's rearview mirror. Bobby could see the top half of the cop's face in the glass. He watched a question form on the cop's forehead. Watched as the guy swiveled his head and looked back their way in astonishment. Watched his lips move as he said something. Whatever it was he said got everyone's attention, as the other three people then followed suit, craning their necks to the rear, staring back at Holmes and Bobby.

"You think they—" Bobby started.

And then the train rolled into view. A massive soot-covered Burlington Northern diesel, pushed along by another and yet another behind that, like a parade of dirty green elephants, joined trunk to tail for the journey south. The wet scream of its whistle shook the car on its springs.

And then . . . they were moving. Instinctively, Bobby reached up and grabbed the safety strap as the big Mercedes lurched forward, slamming into the back of the car in front of them, forcing the Ford forward, slowly at first, then faster and faster as Holmes brought the gas pedal all the way to the floor.

Ahead, the Ford's driver was standing on the brakes and frantically working the gearshift lever . . . all to no avail, as the out-of-control car snapped the red and white barrier and skidded out onto the tracks, just in time for the lead locomotive to plow into the side, sweeping the Ford from the roadway like a leaf in a hurricane, sending it tumbling onto its side as the scream of tearing metal rose static in the air. The last image Bobby collected was of the car rolling yet again on its way down the tracks, of the roof collapsing, of pieces of the car being torn off, of a steady stream of sparks, of the plaintive wail of the train whistle in his ears as Holmes pulled a U-turn and went tearing back up the deserted street.

The feeling in Jim Sexton's chest was so foreign and so nearly forgotten that he came within a whisker of not recognizing the sensation when it arrived. And then . . . sitting in the passenger seat rolling down Third Avenue, he started getting radio reception from another galaxy. Sense images really. The first one green with a little bit of white . . . it took him a minute to recognize. A football field. And then . . . he was there . . . smiling in his red and gold uniform. Old number twenty-seven. Reserve safety for the Inglemoor Vikings. It was at that moment when the oft-run movie of his single moment of glory in an otherwise ignominious high school football career flashed before his eyes. Nineteen eighty-eight. The Bothell game. He's on the field only because both the starter Kerry Nash and his backup Richard Oyler have already been carted off with injuries.

They've got Bothell backed up to their own five-yard line. Bothell's fullback takes the ball on a sweep, when, without being hit, he just up and drops the ball on the ground. The ball takes one low hop and then bounces straight up in the air, where it lands in Jim's arms and stays there long enough for him to lug it the five yards for the score.

For a day and a half he's a piece of the continent, a part of the main, not just the dweeb who does the morning news on the school station, but one of the inner circle.

In many ways, for Jim Sexton, that thirty-six hours was as good as it ever got.

His pager beeped once. The station. The sound pulled him from his reverie and damped the warm glow in his innards. Pete looked over dubiously and then went back to driving. The unasked question was whether their actions made them conquering heroes or plague carriers. Jim lifted the radio handset from its hook on the dashboard and brought it to his mouth. "Jim Sexton here," he said.

"Robert Tilden here," came the reply.

Jim winced, waiting for the hammer to fall.

"Jim . . . er . . . wait a second . . . Mr. Lehane wants to have a word with you."

Jim rolled his eyes and pushed the button. "Okay," he said.

Ten seconds passed and then Albert Lehane's rough voice came rasping out of the speaker. "Jim?"

"Here, sir."

"Hell of a job, son. Hell of a job."

Jim and Pete exchanged relief-filled glances.

"Thank you, sir."

"That's what TV news is all about. Getting what nobody else can get."

"Thank you, sir."

"What I want . . ." Lehane began and then stopped.

Lehane was still holding the SEND button. Jim could hear another voice coming over the line and then the news director's voice again, half an octave higher.

"Where are you two now?" he demanded.

"Third and Bell," Jim told him.

"Get down to Elliott and Broad . . . we've got a report of a car-train accident."

"On the way," Jim said.

34

The car took one final tumble and then lurched to a stop, amid the groan of torn metal and the tinkle of broken glass. The steel carcass came to rest upside down, with Corso's face so close to a greasy railroad tie he could smell the creosote. The roof had been torn off, along with a piece of his right ear. He could feel pain in his shins but couldn't get his legs to move. He was able to turn his head just far enough to see Meg Dougherty, unconscious, bleeding from the nose and mouth, hanging from her seat belt on the far side of the backseat. He couldn't see the front seat at all.

"Hey," he called to Meg. "Hey." No answer.

And then his words were swept away by the sound of the locomotive backing up, and then the final jarring screech as the train became disentangled from the car's twisted remains and was eased backward up the track. The sound of fluids hissing on the car's hot engine block. The smells of smoke and antifreeze and motor oil brought back an image of watching his father work on his battered Buick under an elm tree.

And then the voices from outside. Calling for someone . . . anyone inside the car to speak. "Here," Corso rasped. "I'm here."

"Got somebody alive in there," he heard someone shout.

"No way," a voice scoffed.

"I'm telling you. I heard him."

And then a face was pressed right up to his . . . upside down. Lots of gray stubble on his jowly face. "You hang in there now, buddy. We got help on the way."

Wasn't often you beat the cops to an accident scene. They set up the shot so that both the throbbing locomotive and the twisted husk of the car were in the frame. The red light on the front of the camera told him they were rolling. *"This is Jim Sexton reporting for King Five News from the corner of Broad Street and Elliott Avenue where a midday collision between a passenger vehicle and a freight train has left the car little more than a steaming chunk of scrap metal."* Pete used the telephoto to pan slowly in on the smoking car. The sound of sirens could be heard in the background as Jim began to trudge up the tracks toward the wreckage. *"Bystanders believe there may be as many as four people trapped inside the car at this time. The condition of the occupants is not known."*

When Pete aimed the camera back his way, Jim bent at the waist and picked up a twisted piece of sheet metal. *"The power of the locomotive has literally torn the car to pieces,"* he intoned. *"One can only pray for the safety of anyone trapped inside."*

He kept walking toward the wreck, talking as he went along, Pete trailing him with the camera. *"The sound of sirens is in the air now as emergency crews*

rush to the scene." He kicked a piece of debris out of
the way and kept moving down the tracks, even as the
first aid car arrived, siren whooping, light bank blazing. "*As yet there is no word on how this accident may
have occurred, but one thing is for certain . . .*" The
rest of his narration was drowned in a sea of sirens as
a fire truck and half a dozen police cars arrived on the
scene simultaneously. Jim picked up his pace, trying to
cover the last thirty yards between himself and the accident before anyone told him to back off. Police cars
skidded to a stop at both adjoining intersections,
blocking Broad Street from both directions.

A pair of EMTs were at the car now, lying on the
ground, peering into the car's interior. Pete brought the
camera to bear just in time to catch one of them getting
to his feet and waving frantically at the fire truck,
which immediately roared to life. Shouts filled the air,
until one of the police cruisers blocking the bottom of
the street was backed up, allowing the fire truck sufficient room to make a wide turn at the foot of Broad
Street and nose into the narrow alley between the train
tracks and Elliott Avenue. Jim looked around. Everyone was too busy to take any notice of him. He
couldn't believe his luck. "*Keep shooting,*" he chanted
at Pete Carrol.

They had a plan now. While four firemen stood by
with a variety of firefighting equipment, a cable was
pulled from the side of the fire truck to the far edge of
the car. Took a minute to find the right place to attach
the hook and then the whine of a winch could be heard
above the idling sounds of the train and the fire truck.

At first the car refused to budge, then with a loud
pop began to skid sideways until something caught,
providing enough resistance for the car to begin to flop

itself over onto its one remaining tire. With shouts and caution, gloved hands inched the car inexorably over. At the point where it was resting on the passenger door, a fireman crawled under the wreckage, leaving only his booted feet sticking out from the pile of twisted metal while he surveyed the inside of the car. He lay still for a full minute before wiggling out from under and motioning the crew to continue winching the car upright.

Jim moved closer. *"As you can see, rescue teams are on the scene. In just a minute here we ought to be able to see . . ."* He continued to drone on, until something caught his eye. He bent at the waist and picked it up. A license plate, folded nearly in half. He put the mic under his arm and pried the bent metal open. Washington. He looked around and allowed himself a smile.

They had the car right side up now and were carefully tending to the occupants. Pete was changing cassettes. Jim watched as the firemen sawed through the hinges on both passenger doors and then used the Jaws of Life to pry the doors completely off the frame, giving them far better access to the people inside the car.

When Pete looked his way for guidance, Jim simply twirled his finger as if to say: "Keep it rolling. No sense in doing voice-over here. We'll let the pictures tell the story." Jim Sexton watched in silence as one by one the car's occupants were eased out of the wreck, placed on rolling gurneys and then lifted into aid cars.

He turned to Pete. "First the station. Then Harborview."

"Get Transportation on the line. Get me the make, model and plate number of whatever Gutierrez and Hart signed out and then put out an all-call on the vehicle."

Margy headed for the outer office at a lope. His voice stopped her halfway.

"Route everything that comes into every precinct for the next hour through this office. I want to see everything."

She turned to leave but had to bring herself up short to avoid running head-on into her assistant Jamie Celestine, who was on her way in. As her presence in the inner office was somewhat out of the ordinary, she shrugged a silent apology.

"Your wife, Chief," she said. "Line four."

Harry nodded his thanks and then waited for the click of the door, before picking up the phone. "Hey," he said in as light a voice as he could manage.

"I know you're busy," she said.

The degree of the understatement nearly caused Harry to laugh. He took a deep breath and swallowed his cynicism. "Whatcha need?" he asked affably.

"Have you got time to talk?"

He used his fingertips to massage his left temple. Seemed like there was a bulging vein there he'd never noticed before. "As a matter of fact . . . I'm . . . no, I don't."

Her disappointment was palpable. "I just wanted to—"

The office door opened. Margy stuck her head inside.

Harry cut his wife off. "I gotta go."

"Oh . . . I . . . I didn't—"

"Bye," he said and hung up.

"Gold Ford Taurus. 879PLN."

"Get dispatch to—"

"Already did." She waggled the papers in her hand. "Got . . ."—she counted—"four domestic violence . . . a missing person . . . an assault . . ." She looked up. "Nothing you'd notice," she said.

And then Jamie Celestine was in the doorway again. Harry was sure it was Kathleen, calling back to say she was worried about him, or to finish whatever it was she'd called about, or both and so, for the briefest of moments, he felt a sense of relief when she began to speak. "Dispatch says the last contact with Detectives Hart and Gutierrez was from Capitol Hill."

Harry rolled his eyes and thrust one arm into his coat. "I'll be at City Hall. Page me when you've got something solid."

Holmes nosed the front of the Mercedes hard against the garage wall and turned off the engine. Anybody wanted to look at the front, they'd have to tow it. He took a deep breath and again told himself how he'd done the right thing. How he and the cop had made eye contact. How there was no doubt whatsoever that the cop had recognized him. How he'd had no choice but to deviate from the plan and put the operation at risk. No choice at all.

Took him a moment to pry his fingers from the steering wheel and look around. Three floors down and across the street, the hotel parking lot was three quarters full. The red Subaru was angled into one of the slots in the middle of the lot. The van was parked out near the sidewalk. He turned off the engine and sat back in the seat. The others had made it safely. He took what felt like his first breath in five minutes and looked over at Bobby Darling, who sat flushed and sweating in the passenger seat, his knuckles bone white as they gripped the overhead handle.

"The others are here," Holmes said. "Let's go."

Only then did Bobby Darling drop his hand to his lap and look around. The Edgewater Hotel was just that . . . right at the edge of the water. An old-fashioned L-shaped structure that flowed along the jagged shore-line for half a block.

"Let's go," Holmes said.

Bobby looked at him as if he'd never seen him before.

"Whatever they knew . . ."—Holmes snapped his fingers—"is gone now."

"That wasn't . . . I mean . . . we weren't supposed to—"

Holmes jumped in. "Once the battle begins, all plans are out the window," he said. "He knew me from the house. He knew it, and I knew it." He pointed to the south.

"It's right there. Did you see it when we drove in?"

Bobby looked away and nodded. "It's much bigger than I thought possible," he said. "It's bigger than a mountain."

"Your moment will be bigger too."

Bobby mulled it over and then reached for the door handle.

35

Hans Belder flipped the plastic evidence bag containing the coaster onto the table. "Of course it's possible," he said. "The same technology used to accelerate the life cycle of a virus could . . . theoretically at least . . . be used to slow the process down."

Isaac Klugeman held up a moderating hand. "Much more difficult, however," he said. "An abbreviated life cycle would be far more easily attained than . . ."—he gestured at the coaster with the back of his hand—"something like this."

Belder nodded gravely. "I concur. Life is always easier to shorten than to prolong. It is unfortunate but true."

"And, of course, there's the matter of the host," Helen Stafford said.

"It cannot live without a host," Belder added. "That fact is the very nature of the beast. A virus is neither dead nor alive. It's somewhere in between, which is to say, a virus is alive only so long as it can move from host to host."

"Unless . . ." Klugeman began and then changed his mind.

"Yes?" Belder threw the word out as a challenge.

"Unless . . ." Klugeman pointed down at the coaster. "The thirty hours part is easy," he said. "It could be done in the same manner as the material in the bus tunnel. Instead of a spore like ragweed or whatever they used . . . a spore that releases its load immediately upon contact with air . . . they would need one whose viability they could control."

"Something organic?"

Klugeman shrugged. "Organic or engineered . . . it wouldn't matter."

"But the viral life span?"

"Once it was delivered into the air, the virus would have to be able to feed on some part of the host in order to survive for any length of time on its own."

"Like?"

Klugeman thought it over. "Perhaps something as simple as a pinecone," he said. "When the individual seed breaks off the cone, it takes a small piece of the cone with it. That small piece acts as a . . ."—he waved a hand—"as a placenta for the seed. It keeps the seed alive until the proper combination of moisture and soil makes it possible for the seed to take root on its own."

"Think about it," said Colonel Hines. "They somehow introduce the virus into the hotel where we're all staying. We inhale it. Suddenly we're all carriers. We're on our way home. We've got spores on our clothing that we pass on to our fellow passengers. We go home and interact with the other people in our lives . . . infecting them . . . they interact with others . . ." He cut the air with the flat of his hand. "You get the picture. For the next week or so . . ."

"Longer," Belder said. "If the Walsdorf Conjecture is correct . . . and it appears to be . . . then it's likely that the incubation period of the virus has been similarly extended. Which of course exponentially increases the number of contacts by individuals, which increases the number of . . ."—he rolled his hand in a circle as if to say "and so on and so on." He seemed unwilling to go on.

"You realize what we are talking about here of course," Klugeman said.

"The doomsday virus," Hines said immediately. "You're talking about the beginning of the goddamn end is what you're talking about."

Belder turned away. Rubbed the corners of his mouth with his thumb and forefinger. "At this point in history, I would like to think there could be no such thing as a doomsday virus. I would like to think our knowledge of both chemistry and genetics is sufficiently far along to prevent anything so dreadful." He braced both arms on the table and looked out at those on the other side from beneath his thick bushy eyebrows. "I will say, however . . . the scenario which Dr. Klugeman has described . . . might push our systems as close to catastrophe as I am willing to imagine."

"It's the apocalypse," Hines said. "The end of the world as we know it."

"It would take the caregivers first," Klugeman said. "They'd be treating people for headache . . . for nosebleeds . . . for fatigue . . . for any number of common ailments for days . . . weeks before they realized what they were dealing with." He looked around the room. "The doctors, the nurses . . . the support staff . . . their colleagues, their families and friends . . . they would be among the second wave of dead."

"Without the professionals . . ."—Belder made a helpless gesture with his hands—"we would be at the mercy of the virus."

"Have you informed the federal authorities of this?" Klugeman asked Harry Dobson.

"They laughed at me," Harry said. "Told me somebody was having me on. Said they had a hot lead on a Hamas cell operating out of Portland."

As a buzz of conversation began to spread around the room, the pager on Harry's right hip began to vibrate. He pulled it from his belt and checked the number. He excused himself, walked around the table and stepped out into the hall where he dialed for his messages. Margy's voice. A half octave too high.

"We've got an emergency report on a car being hit by a train down on the waterfront." She paused. "The make on the plate comes up as one of ours." He heard her breath catch. "879PLN."

36

Corso and Charly Hart came up the hall together. Other than the stark white bandage they'd used to reassemble his right ear, Corso appeared little the worse for wear. In truth, however, he'd seldom felt as bad as he did at that moment. Every joint in his body ached. He had a pair of half-inch divots in his shins where the twisted sheet metal had pinned him to the backseat. It was all he could do not to groan every time his left foot hit the hard tile floor.

Charly Hart had not been quite so fortunate. The process of being dragged by a locomotive had shattered one lens in his glasses, broken his right wrist, which now rested in a bright blue sling, ripped a four-inch gash above his right eye which had required thirty-seven stitches to close, and tweaked his back to such a degree that he now shuffled across the floor like a man who had quite recently been administered a spinal tap. Maybe two.

More troubling to Charly Hart than his own injuries was the plastic tray he carried in his good hand. A tray containing his partner's notebook, wallet and badge, his watch, his gun, his cell phone, his car keys and eighty-seven cents in change. Unless the docs were way off base, Reuben wasn't going to be needing this stuff anytime in the foreseeable future. Some of it . . . maybe never again. Charly was also worried about Reuben's wife Inez. She was a big-time drama queen. High-strung. Made a big deal out of everything. No doubt about it . . . she'd take the news real hard.

The shuffling counterpoint of Charly's feet was the only noise in the hall as they shouldered the swinging doors and entered the last fifty feet of corridor. Beyond the next set of doors lay the chaos of the Emergency Room. Chief Dobson and a guy in a tweed sport coat stood just inside the final set of doors, engaged in animated conversation.

Some primal call pulled Corso's eyes to the right, toward the storage area behind the admitting desk. The woman from the bus tunnel. She'd found herself a green lab coat and a stethoscope. Looking very nonchalant and official. Standing there like she owned the joint. Corso motioned to Charly Hart, but Charly was so beat up and fixated on getting to the end of the corridor he didn't notice Corso turn right and belly his way through the swinging doors.

She stood her ground. Didn't move a muscle as Corso walked over and stood directly in front of her. She was better-looking than he'd imagined and a bit more exotic. Her eyes sloped down at the corners tending her a slightly Asian quality.

"You seem to pop up in the strangest places," he said, taking her in.

She smiled. "So I've been told." She reached up and touched the bandage on his ear. "For a man in a train wreck, you don't seem very much the worse for wear."

"I come from hardy stock."

Her eyes narrowed. "Good breeding material, eh?"

"Train-resistant anyway."

Her laugh was girlish, but something in her eyes belied any notion of flirtatiousness.

"Speaking of trains . . ."

"Yeah?"

"You're on the right track."

"Oh really?"

"This is not about Arabs."

"Maybe you ought to inform the feds of that."

"I'm afraid that's not possible."

She stepped behind the deserted nurses' station and leaned back into the shadows. A movement in Corso's peripheral vision pulled his eyes toward the light in the hall, where Charly Hart's facial expression and hand gesture signaled his confusion as to how he'd managed to lose track of Corso; he beckoned "come on" with his good hand. Corso smiled and indicated he'd be along in a minute.

When he turned to say something to the woman, he found himself alone. He hurried around the counter and tried the knob on the door next to the desk. Locked. He smiled for the first time in days.

Charly Hart stuck his head through the swinging doors. "Where the hell did you get to?"

"Did you see—" Corso began.

"See what?" Detective Hart wanted to know.

Corso hesitated. "Never mind. I was just checking things out," Corso said, walking toward Hart and the door.

Together, they approached the chief and the guy in the sport coat, whose conversation had become, if anything, more animated.

"Get them the hell out of here," the chief was saying.

"I can't do that," the other guy said.

"It's your hospital, isn't it?"

"We've been to court with them before about this . . . more than once . . . and lost. You know that, Chief. They have a right to be here. As long as they're not interfering with hospital operations, they have every right to be on the premises."

"Make 'em wait outside."

"No can do."

Dobson pointed a finger Charly Hart's way. "I've got officers here. Injured in the line of duty. They've got a right to some respect . . . to some privacy, for god's sake."

The guy threw up his hands. "I agree with you, Chief. Unfortunately, the Sixth Circuit Court of Appeals doesn't. As far as they're concerned, the press has as much right to be here as we do."

The chief waved a disgusted hand and turned his back on the guy, who, seizing the opportunity to get out from under, ducked out the door.

The chief waited for Corso and Hart to negotiate the last ten yards. He looked down at the tray Charly Hart carried and blanched.

"How's Gutierrez doing?"

"Not so good," Charly Hart said. "He was trying to get out of the car when the engine hit us. They think he had one foot out the door when the car rolled over on it and damn near severed his foot."

Harry Dobson looked away in pain. "What about Miss Dougherty?"

"She's got a level two concussion and a knot on her head the size of a cantaloupe. They're keeping her for a couple of days for observation," Corso said.

The chief was scowling now. "How does an accident like this happen? What . . . nobody saw the . . ."

Corso and Charly Hart passed a quick look. For the first time since the wreck, they had a minute to think and realized they were the only ones who actually knew what had happened. Everybody else thought it had been an accident. Charly Hart motioned with his head for the chief to get back from the door. Dobson got the message, stepped in close.

"Wasn't an accident, Chief," Charly whispered. "The car behind us pushed us out onto the tracks."

The chief looked from Hart to Corso and back. He was silent for a full minute. "I don't believe in coincidences," he said finally.

"Me neither," said Corso. "We must have touched a nerve somewhere in our travels today."

"But you've got no idea where?"

Both men said they didn't.

"What kind of car?"

Corso shook his head. Charly Hart shrugged. "Something big, square and dark. By the time I looked back, it was already locked on our back bumper, so I couldn't see the grille."

"Gutierrez saw something," Corso said. "He saw something that really got his attention . . . something in the rearview mirror."

"What?"

"Had to be something in the car behind us. We were the only two cars waiting for the train."

"Did he say anything?"

"He said, 'You're not going to believe this.' "

"That's it?"

"That's it."

"And then?"

"And then the car was on us."

"Can Detective Gutierrez—"

Charly Hart jumped in. "He's out of it, Chief. Everything goes well . . . the docs are saying he might be able to talk to us something like tomorrow night."

"By tomorrow night it might not matter."

Jim Sexton could feel the eyes of envy. In these days of press releases and tightly managed news, it wasn't often anybody gained a serious advantage on the competition. Once was rare. Twice in the same day . . . unheard of. The footage of the train wreck had aired before the victims ever arrived at the hospital and had since been picked up by the national media. Beth had called to say her sister Judy had seen Jim's report on CNN. It was all he could do to keep an idiotic grin from hijacking his face.

No point in asking Dobson anything. He was pretty sure he'd worn out his welcome with the chief. Pete had the camera rolling while the chief held forth on how he didn't have anything to say. No . . . he wasn't giving out the officers' names . . . no . . . he wouldn't identify what were rumored to be two civilians in the car, one of which had to be the tall guy in the back, standing there looking blandly out over everybody's head. Jim was sure he'd seen the guy before, more than once, but just couldn't put a name to the face. The chief was winding up. No . . . he had no further statements at this time. Good-bye.

And then Jim began to wonder what the chief was doing here anyway. Yeah . . . the accident had been spectacular and all, and Harry Dobson had never been particularly averse to a little free face time, but with all the other stuff going on . . . spending an hour with a couple of injured officers . . . what was that about? Nobody was dead.

Jim watched as the chief turned his back on the retreating media horde, reached into his inside pocket and set several folded pieces of paper on the tray the skinny cop was clutching to his chest. After exchanging a couple of words, the chief gave the cop a pat on the shoulder and disappeared down a hall to the right.

Holmes hung the DO NOT DISTURB sign on the handle and closed the door. Bobby Darling sat on the edge of the bed staring at the ceiling.

"Soon," Holmes said. "Soon."

Bobby nodded and threw himself back onto the bed, arms and legs spread like he was making snow angels. "You think we'll all get home?" he asked.

Holmes considered his answer. "No . . . probably not," he said.

"Me neither," Bobby said.

"And even if we did . . ."—Holmes emitted a bitter laugh—"even if we all got back . . . we could very well fall victim to our own actions."

"I don't let myself think about that," Bobby Darling said. He glanced over at Holmes, who now stood placidly looking out the window. "What do you not allow yourself to think about?" he asked.

"Me?" At first, Holmes seemed offended by the question. He stood by the sliding door to the balcony scowling out into space. "I don't allow myself to think about the years in between . . . when my family and I . . ." He had to stop and collect himself. "I try not to think of the many times when I would be out . . . at night . . . walking among the fields and the smell would rise from the ground . . . the smell of nothing natural on this earth would rise from the wet soil . . . and how I would go to my prefect in the morning and tell him how I felt certain such a smell could not be good for people . . . how I was concerned for my wife and children . . . and how he would wave me away like a bug . . . just tell me it was a 'residual' effect. That was his favorite word, *residual*. Told me I worried like a woman." Holmes shook his head in disgust. "Of course, he and his family lived many miles away in Nora Dehi. He came in by train every morning. I should have known. I should have followed my instincts."

"He lied to you."

"But I should have known."

Bobby sat up. "But how could you have . . ."

Holmes threw back the drapes revealing a four-mile stretch of wind-whipped waves, wild and whitecapped, shattering against one another in a frenzy of movement. In the distance, Bainbridge Island seemed to float on the surface of the water.

"Look at this," he said to Bobby. He checked his watch. "In four hours it begins." He pointed north. "Right out there somewhere . . . our moment begins."

Bobby bounced himself onto the floor and ambled over to the sliding glass door. He took the last few steps tentatively, as if he were approaching the rim of an open pit. Holmes took notice of his reticence. "Does the water scare you?" he asked.

"I don't swim," Bobby answered, his eyes as wide as saucers.

Holmes snapped the lock and slid the door open. Bobby took a step back as a rush of air fanned the curtains, waving them halfway to the ceiling. Holmes stepped out onto the balcony and peered down into the inky recesses of Puget Sound. After a minute, the color of the water found its way into his eyes. His face was grim when he looked up at Bobby.

"I should have known," he said.

* * *

Charly Hart set the tray on the ledge running all the way around the room and picked the papers from the top with his working hand. He shook the pages open and peered at them through his shattered glasses, turning his head this way and that in a vain attempt to find a clear field of view.

Corso walked to his side. "Didn't I hear your boss say you ought to go home and take it easy?" Corso said.

Even through the starburst lenses Corso could see the hardness in the detective's eyes. "I've got a partner getting his foot sewn back on," Hart said. "Way I see it, there's no going home." He gestured with the papers . . . toward the door. "You got somewhere to be . . . feel free. I gotta figure out what happened today that gave some asshole the urge to crush us all under a train."

Corso held out his hand. "Lemme see," he said.

The detective hesitated for a moment and then dropped the pages into Corso's hand. Corso looked them over. Four pages. CITIZENSHIP AND IMMIGRATION CANADA printed across the top. A list of maybe fifty names, sorted in a variety of ways. Some kind of legend or glossary on the last page.

"What name did you say Bohannon was using?" he asked Charly Hart.

"Magnusen, Martin Magnusen."

Corso flipped over to the second page. There it was. Crossed the border at Blaine last Tuesday afternoon at one fifty-three. Carrying an Indian passport of such-and-such a number. Listed his occupation as student. Corso read the data out loud.

"That squares with what the tattoo guy told us," Charly Hart said.

"There's a number after his name. What's that about?"

"Starts with a nine?"

"Uh-huh."

"Nine means he's a male."

"Nine-dash-one."

"One's Caucasian."

"Dash-five-six."

"Not a Canadian citizen."

"Dash-seven-zero-dash-three."

Charly shook his head and winced, wishing he hadn't. "Look on the back page."

Corso followed the list with his finger. "Means he's a student."

"Dash-three."

"No idea."

"Country of origin: India."

"How many other nine-dash-one-dash-five-six-dash-seven-zero-dash-threes we got?"

Took Corso a minute. "None."

"Anything close?"

Again Corso scanned the data. "Got several nine-dash-four-dash-five-six-dash-seven-zero-dash-threes."

"What's the four?"

Corso rolled his eyes down the page. "Race: East Indian."

Charly Hart started to shrug but thought better of it. "We didn't run into any—"

"We did," Corso said. "The guy with the shark eyes."

"What?"

Corso told him the story. Hart wasn't impressed. "It's not much," he said. "Just some guy who farted and a feeling you've got."

"I'm telling you . . . he never even blinked at the autopsy photo."

"I can't be . . ." He threw his good hand into the air. "We've got nothing going on with the Indians. They've got no reason to hate us. Why would anybody from India want to do Americans harm?"

"Everybody hates us."

Charly Hart sighed and looked away.

"Call your boss. We're gonna need some help," Corso pushed.

Charly Hart peeked over his shoulder at Jim Sexton, who had surreptitiously slid over in their direction, trying to hear what was being said. Mr. Nonchalant, standing there now trying to look all cool and disinterested.

"You want to give us a little privacy or what?" Charly Hart asked.

Jim shot him a half smile and a two-fingered salute as he bumped himself off the wall and started across the room. Charlie watched him go, making sure he was out of sight before he walked back into the corner of the room. He checked again, then pushed the button and said, "Chief Dobson," into the speaker.

"Yes, Detective," was the immediate reply.

Charly checked his back again. "I think we got something here," he said.

"Something like what?"

Charly told him. The reply was a little slower in coming this time.

"Just a hunch of Mr. Corso's? That's what you've got?"

Charly swallowed hard. "Yes sir."

"What do you need?"

"A Tac Unit to the U District. Fifteenth Street. Last block before Ravenna."

"Ten minutes."

"We need another car," Charly Hart said into his palm.

"I'll send a unit for you."

Pete Carrol had stopped loading the gear into the back of the mobile unit and was gazing over at Jim Sexton in amazement. His jaw dropped as he listened to the chief say, "I'll send a unit for you."

Jim snapped the walkie-talkie phone closed and threw a crooked grin his way. "You heard the man, Petie. U District. Fifteenth right before Ravenna."

Pete grinned back. "You on a roll now, baby. A serious roll."

37

The black-visored quartet bent low as they made their way around the sides of the house, staying close to the building and beneath the windows. Two to the left. Two to the right. The pair on the right deployed themselves on either side of the old-fashioned cellar doors, while the other two duck-walked all the way around the corner of the house and disappeared from view.

Protected from head to toe by black Kevlar body armor, the seven members of Special Weapons and Tactics Squad Number Three looked considerably more like androids than they did like human beings.

The guy whose name tag proclaimed him to be Sergeant Nance was running the show from a hundred feet up the street, which had been blocked at both ends by police cruisers to prevent civilians from blundering into the middle of the operation.

Nance turned to Charly Hart. "Good to go," he said.

Charly nodded. Nance whispered into his shoulder-mounted microphone and the show began, as another trio of storm troopers burst out of the overgrown shrubbery and sprinted for the front door. Two flattened themselves against either side of the door while the third swung a massive metal battering ram against the knob, sending the door crashing inward with a bang.

Nance, Charly Hart and Corso were a third of the way across the street when the pair of SWAT cops suddenly reappeared on the front porch. The one on the right made sure the splintered door stayed closed while the other one used one hand to pull the guy with the battering ram down from the porch and the other hand to indicate that everyone concerned should stay back. Insistently back. Way back.

Nance's earpiece squawked. "How many?" he asked his microphone.

Charly Hart's mouth had already formed a question when Sergeant Nance pushed another button on his radio. "Need a haz-mat team to . . ." He ran through the address and zip code. "Level Four. I've got officers who are going to need decontamination." He listened. "Now," was his answer to an unheard question.

He turned to Charly Hart. "Got at least two corpses in the house. Blood all over the place. Looks like what I hear the victims in the tunnel looked like." Corso held his breath. Nance went on. "I don't want my crew in there until we know what's going on."

Charly Hart said he understood. He used his good hand to find his phone.

Jim Sexton had the volume turned all the way down and the speaker pressed tightly against his ear. He lay in the damp beauty bark between a pair of azalea bushes whose gnarled limbs curved and twisted about one another like praying fingers. Two shrubs down, Pete Carrol lay on his belly, the camera trained on the front door of the house across the street, where everything had come to a sudden halt.

"Chief," the skinny cop said into the speaker.

"Detective Hart."

"We've got bodies. Lots of blood. Looks a lot like what they found down in the tunnel. We've called for a haz-mat team. They're saying twenty minutes."

"I'm on my way to City Hall. Keep me informed."

Jim Sexton crawled along the edge of the front porch and whispered in Pete's ear. Told him what was going on and how he ought to save his tape until the haz-mat team arrived. The soft whirring of the camera stopped. Pete slipped his Mariners cap over the lens and lay the camera on its side in the bark.

"We wait," Jim mouthed.

Pete understood. He rested his head on his forearm and closed his eyes.

Holmes checked his watch and then snuck a quick look at Bobby Darling, who lay stretched out on the other bed watching some cartoon peopled with yellow-faced characters. He seemed to be calming down a bit. The incident with the train and the size of the target had gotten Bobby a bit more excited than Holmes would have preferred. His experience with Bobby suggested that the kid was reliable only so long as the plan was well structured and remained more or less on track. Forced to improvise, the kid tended to panic, which was why he'd paired him with Brian and planned on sending them out last. By the time they left the hotel, the others would already have completed their assignments.

Five-thirty. Two hours until Wesley and Nathan reported for duty. Two and a half before Samuel and Paul left. Fifteen minutes later it would be Bobby and he. An hour after that, it would all be over. In more ways than one.

He'd hoped to survive. That's the way the plan had been presented. That they could do what they had to do and then get away, but the minute they got specific about the plan and how it might actually work, he'd realized that chances of any of them walking away were fairly remote. Wasn't rocket science. Hell . . . even Bobby had figured out they were on a suicide mission. When you're taking directions from a man who doesn't care whether he lives or dies, it's pretty safe to assume he doesn't hold your safety any more dearly than he holds his own. So when Brian became a liability and it became obvious to Holmes that he was going to be forced to get more involved than the plan originally called for, he was ready. Not necessarily eager, but ready.

Funny how, even among those with nothing to live for, dying was more palatable in the abstract than in reality. How the closer the hour came, the deeper the blackness of the pit became and the colder the air rising up from the depths below. How the mind begins to fill with unanswerable questions when the final hour slinks round at last. The questions nobody's ever come back from the grave to answer. The questions bridging the gap between being and nothingness. The place where faith begins.

The haz-mat team leader was pulling off his gloves as he came down the front stairs. His mask was perched on top of his hood. And then another pair of orange-clad firemen backed out the front door, similarly unmasked and unconcerned, leaving the front door ajar as they came down onto the lawn. The tiny ovals of face visible inside the tightly drawn strings looked bemused. Fearless leader gestured with his bare hand.

"Come here," it said to Charly Hart and Corso and Sergeant Nance.

Charly Hart's injuries were beginning to catch up with him. He moved with all the grace and agility of a Hollywood mummy as he and Corso made their way down the jumbled sidewalk. At one point it took Corso's steadying hand on his elbow to keep him upright. By the time they arrived, haz-mat had already spilled his story to Sergeant Nance.

"What do we got?" Charly Hart asked.

The guy started to turn his back. "Like I told him . . ." he said over his shoulder.

"Tell me," Hart said in a tone that stopped the guy in his tracks.

The guy turned slowly. Gonna tell the cop what he could do with his attitude problem. The sight of the battered Charly Hart froze the reproach in his throat, however, and, in a spasm of lucidity, he discerned that he was probably dealing with a desperate and deranged man here and it might be better to hold the grief.

"Oh . . . you . . . the train," was all he said.

Charly Hart gave him a nod small enough to pass for a tremor.

"Got two bodies. One male. One female. Not a bio. Multiple stab wounds. Hell of a struggle. It's a mess. You're gonna need a forensics team in there."

Corso watched the air drain out of Charly Hart. Watched him wobble and then reach for his pocket.

"Better safe than sorry," Sergeant Nance said with a dishwater grin.

38

When a soft tap sounded on the hotel room door, Wesley held a finger to his lips and tiptoed across the room. He checked to make sure the door was double locked, fondled the Buck knife in his front pocket for a moment and then pressed his eye to the little optical peephole.

The image was distorted and disjointed, like looking at the world through a piece of broken glass, but it was Holmes all right. Standing in the hall swiveling his head back and forth as he checked the corridor. Wesley snapped the locks and pulled open the door.

Before stepping inside, Holmes checked the hall one more time. Satisfied that he hadn't been observed, he hurried into the room and relocked the door.

"You're ready?" he phrased it as a question, although that's not what he meant. Wesley waggled a hand as if to say "more or less."

"Remember . . ." Holmes began his litany. "Take your time. Your best opportunity to leave will be among all the others. If they let you work together . . . that's fine. If not . . . you just go about your business on your own. You know where to meet afterward." He paused long enough for Wesley and Nathan to indicate they'd been listening. "This is our moment," he said.

Both young men looked frightened and tentative. Wesley was playing with something in his pocket. Nathan's hands trembled slightly.

"It's all right to be afraid," Holmes said in a low voice. "We've been afraid for years. Afraid to go outside. Afraid to breathe the air. Afraid that someday we might wake up and it would happen all over again." He made a rude noise with his lips. "We know all about afraid. Fear has become our friend."

They nodded without conviction.

"Come on. Time to get going," Holmes said.

Jim Sexton was stiff and cold. The forensics team had been in and out of the house for an hour and a half. Darkness had begun to settle on the street like a mantle. Last week's rain had leached up through the beauty bark, dampening him to the bone. He smiled to himself and shivered slightly in the breeze. They had some great exclusive footage. The SWAT team busting into the place. The haz-mat team arriving. The EMTs and the bodies coming out on gurneys. The crowd of uniforms milling around in front of the place. The arrival of the feds and the heated argument that followed. All of it was great. Pete was right. He was definitely on a roll. All he needed now was to get this stuff on the air.

Jim was weighing the merits of returning to the station with the footage, when the phone in his pocket squawked. He grabbed it quickly and jammed the speaker hard against his ear.

"According to Canadian Immigration, they're all from something called Madhya Pradesh," the woman's voice said.

"From what?"

"It's an Indian state." When Charly Hart didn't respond, she added, "Somewhere out in the middle of the country is what they told me."

"Thanks. Anything else?"

"The card found on Mr. Bohannon's body is a key card. The lab says it could be used to open a dock gate or a garage door or the doors in any one of a dozen local hotels. The only prints on it are his own."

He thanked her again and must have neglected to remove his finger from the SEND and RECEIVE button because a third voice could suddenly be heard coming from the speaker.

"Where did she say they were from?"

Charly Hart mimicked the sounds he'd heard.

"Madhya Pradesh," voice three corrected.

"Something like that. What about it?"

"Bhopal is the capital of the state of Madhya Pradesh."

"So what?"

"So Bhopal is the one place in India where you just might find a bunch of people who have a score to settle with the United States."

"How's that?"

"Union Carbide."

Jim Sexton rolled over onto his dry side. "Holy shit," he whispered to the wind.

"December second, 1984. I remember the date because it's my sister's birthday and the year because it was the first time I ever saw my work on the front page of a newspaper," Corso said. "I was fresh out of college and green as cabbage. Working for the *Atlanta Constitution.* They gave me the assignment of collecting all the

Bhopal information off the AP and Reuters wires and compressing it into two columns a day. I didn't get a byline or anything. It was strictly wire service attribution, but for me it was a big deal. Up until then I'd never done a story more urgent than a charity flower show."

Two houses up, a trio of yellow-jacketed forensic technicians appeared on the front porch carrying an assortment of evidence bags and boxes. "Looks like they're finishing up in there," Charly Hart said. He began to move slowly up the street as Corso continued to talk. "So anyway . . ." Corso went on, "Union Carbide has this big pesticide factory out in the middle of India. It's in India because there's no way the EPA or any other government agency lets them put anything like that here. Way too dangerous to put near white folks."

"I remember now. There was a leak or something."

"Or something. Forty tons of methyl isocyanate leaked from the Bhopal factory. Five hours later an area of forty square kilometers with a resident population of almost half a million people was covered with a cloud of lethal MCI gas. People woke up with their eyes burning out of their heads. With their lungs full of fluid. Within three days, eight thousand people died . . . mainly of cardiac and respiratory arrest. Another twenty thousand suffered permanent chronic injuries."

Charly Hart looked over at Corso. The strain of the day had etched deep lines at the corners of his mouth. "That many?"

"That was just the beginning," Corso said. "When the smoke clears, the Indian government sends in teams of police and bureaucrats and scientists to get things cleaned up. Within two years, *they're* dying at a rate fourteen times the national average. Cancer is everywhere. Women are giving birth to stillborn children who don't even look like human beings. Different skull shapes. Extra fingers, extra eyes. You name it and they're giving birth to it."

Charly Hart stepped on an uneven piece of concrete and stumbled. Corso put a restraining hand on his elbow. "Next thing you know the Indian government finds itself every bit as liable as Union Carbide, so they agree to some shitty settlement with the company . . . works out to less than five hundred dollars a victim . . . doesn't even begin to cover medical expenses let alone damages. Then, before you know it, Dow buys Union Carbide and the whole company just disappears down the corporate gullet . . . leaving absolutely nothing that anybody can sue. Dow says it's not responsible for Union Carbide. The government blames Dow. Just as neat as can be."

In the gathering twilight, the neon yellow coat stood out like a beacon. She was maybe forty, with a handful of stiff brown hair pulled back into a ponytail and a look on her face said she didn't want to dance. "Two dead. One of each. Multiple stab wounds. The woman . . . name's Patricia Mitchell . . . lives next door." She caught the question on Corso's face. "She was wearing a medic-alert tag. The male works for the *Seattle Times*. Name's Jeffrey Unger. He's a route manager."

"Anything else?" Charly Hart asked.

"Looks like anywhere from six to eight people've been living in there for three or four days," she said. "We lifted a truckload of prints. Anything that looked new enough . . . we took a picture of."

"So."

"E-mailed the prints to the FBI. Got a special priority. Over a hundred prints we got only one hit." She shook her head. "These people must have been living in a cave or something."

"Whatdya get?"

"Came from the FBI print link with Interpol. Name's Rodney Holmes. Used to be an Indian cop." She stopped for a moment and read to herself from the card before going on. "He's the chief suspect in the murder of a police captain he used to work for. You read between the lines it says they know he did it but just can't make a case." She read some more. "Says here he blames the death of his family on some kind of chemical spill or something." Hart and Corso exchanged looks. "He's been arrested half a dozen times for assaulting government officers. Arrested again in 2001 by the French police in the town of Toulouse. Demonstrating against a chemical spill that killed thirty people there." She made eye contact with Corso. "Dipped under the radar early last year and hasn't been seen since."

A car alarm began to honk in the distance. Nobody paid any attention.

"That's it? All those prints?"

She shrugged and made a face. "What can I say? It's statistically aberrant. You'd think they'd be in somebody's computer somewhere."

"Yeah . . . you would," Charly Hart agreed.

She turned to leave. "We come up with anything else, I'll let you know."

Charly thanked her, watched her amble off and then turned away. He pulled off his shattered glasses and massaged the bridge of his nose. "None of this—" he started to say and stopped. "None of this amounts to a damn thing," he said finally. "We can't even tie Bohannon to the house, let alone to a terrorist plot."

"We've got the Indian connection."

"Yeah and there's an Indian restaurant up the street, but that don't help us either," Charly Hart said disgustedly.

"What if . . ." Corso said.

The detective waved his glasses in frustration. Engines were starting all around them. Shouts flew through the air. The techies and the haz-mats were gonna have to move before the SWAT team could get out, but nobody was going anywhere until the cruisers angled across both ends of the street were moved.

Corso went on. "If I'm planning this thing, there's a Plan B." He jerked a thumb at the house across the street. "Someplace to go if the house gets too hot. Someplace close to the target. Someplace where I can go through the final preparations for whatever it is I'm planning to do."

"Gotta be the germ doctors down at the Weston," Charly Hart said. "Nothing else makes any sense." He looked to Corso for agreement but didn't get it.

"Did I hear Bohannon was carrying a key?" Corso asked instead.

"Electronic. Could open anything."

"A room at the Weston?"

Charly Hart set the glasses back on his nose. He hesitated and then pulled the phone from his pocket. "Hey . . . ah . . . hello . . ." he said.

"Can I help you?" Same woman's voice.

"Who'm I talking to?"

"Jamie Celestine," she said. "I work in the chief's office."

"I need the chief."

"Can't be done. He sent all nonessential personnel home. The chief and the rest of the bigwigs are down at City Hall putting together an evacuation plan."

"Was that you earlier . . . about the Indian information."

"The chief wanted you kept informed."

"They tell you which hotels that key could be from?"

"Just a sec." Papers rattled. "It's a Texas Instruments key code system. Used locally by . . . the Airport Hilton, the Airport Marriott, the Airport Holiday Inn, the—"

"Downtown," Charly Hart interrupted.

"The Camlin, the Vintage Park and the Pioneer Square Hotel."

"Not the Weston?"

"Nope."

"Damn," slipped out. "Oh . . . sorry," he said.

"And the Edgewater, but that's not downtown."

"Say again?"

"I said the Texas Instruments system is also used at the Edgewater."

Charly Hart looked out over the tops of his glasses at Corso.

"All of a block and a half from where we kissed the train," Corso said.

"But nowhere near the Weston."

"I'm like our boss," Corso said. "I don't believe in coincidences either."

"Sergeant Nance," Charly Hart hollered.

The SWAT cop had one boot in the street and the other in the black armored van. He stopped his upward motion, put both feet on the pavement and stepped around the open door. He removed his baseball cap and raised his eyebrows.

"Don't run off quite yet," the detective said.

39

S amuel made a noise like a bird.

"Me too," Paul answered.

Nearly twenty years ago, on a cloudless night in the week before his sixth birthday, the MCI gas had seared Samuel's larynx, burning the vocal cords from his throat, leaving his voice little more than an odd collection of clicks and whistles. Since that day, only Paul had been able to make out what he was saying. Samuel leaned his arms on the roof of the car and squawked again.

"We'll do it just like we practiced," Paul said.

Samuel swallowed in that noisy way of his and slid into the driver's seat. His movements were slow and deliberate. Before today, his only experience driving a car had consisted of a couple of hours tooling around a deserted British Columbia parking lot early one Sunday morning, with Holmes talking him through it from the passenger seat.

His hands shook slightly as he turned the key and started the engine.

"Seat belts," Paul reminded.

They buckled up. Samuel took a deep breath,

dropped the car into reverse and backed slowly out of the parking space. He shifted gears and, with a lurch, they rolled across the parking lot toward the street.

Traffic was light. Tourist season was over. The waterfront had taken on the forlorn look of an abandoned amusement park. As they bounced into the street and started south, the squeal of tires suddenly filled the air. Paul turned his head in time to see a huge black police van slide around the corner, light bar blazing, the roar of its engine getting louder and louder as it swallowed the distance between the two cars.

"Watch where you're going," Paul admonished his cousin, whose eyes now bounced frantically between the rearview mirror and the street in front of the car. He made a noise in his throat that others would have taken to mean he was going to spit.

"The others will take care of themselves," Paul said. "Go."

"I don't know, Officer . . . I mean the privacy of our guests . . . I'm going to have to call my supervisor."

"We don't have time for that." Charly Hart clapped his hand on the desk hard enough to bounce the brochures and then slid the sheet of paper closer to the kid. "Are any of these people registered here?" he growled.

"I can't . . ." the kid stammered. "My boss would . . ." When he lifted his hands from the computer terminal in a show of helplessness, Corso slapped the computer around in a circle and used his forearm to drag the keyboard and mouse across the desk.

"Hey now," the young man pleaded. "You can't be—"

The sight of the SWAT team entering the lobby froze the words in his throat. Using only his hands Sergeant Nance directed three of his men to cover the rear stairs and another trio to stand by. The six or eight guests in the lobby backed themselves up against the walls, palms flat, eyes wide. The front door opened. A middle-aged couple dragging a pair of flowered suitcases stepped inside, took one look at the unfolding scene and, without a word, beat a stiff-legged retreat back outside.

"All of them," Corso said. "Singh and Kimberly in two forty-one. Holmes and Darling in three fifteen and Rishi and Singleton in two hundred."

"Unless you've got some sort of official paperwork . . . I'm afraid I'm not going to be able to—" That's when the kid noticed the huge guy with the battering ram and again his words caught in his throat. "Oh no . . . you . . ."

Rather than drive all the way down to the waterfront, where they would surely be spotted by subsequent waves of police cars and given the boot, Jim Sexton had opted for a left turn onto a narrow section of railroad right-of-way running parallel with the street. The venue looked good when they started down, but the narrow lane got thinner and thinner as they moved along. Now the KING-TV remote truck was stuck. Wedged between the slumping railroad grade and the white wall of the parking garage. The van had slid downhill and now had its side pressed directly against the cinder blocks at an angle which prevented the passenger door from being opened. "Get us out of here," Jim shouted from across the front seat.

"Gonna tear it up," Pete countered. "We better call a

tow truck. You know how the brass are about damaging the equipment."

"Get us out of here," Jim shouted again.

Pete shook his head. Lifted his hands from the wheel in refusal. "Not me, man . . . No way I'm gonna . . ."

Jim stuck out his left leg. Put his foot on top of Pete's and forced the accelerator to the floor. The van first began to vibrate and then to move haltingly forward with a metallic scream, the tires throwing up great hunks of gravel as they dragged the side of the vehicle along the uneven bricks for twenty yards before popping back out into the light, where they teetered on two wheels for a second as the van decided whether or not it was going to fall all the way over onto its side, wavering in the wind before coming to rest at such a precarious angle they were both afraid to move.

Holmes fed his final pair of quarters into the machine and pushed the button. Two dollars for water. He shook his head. In his mind, he began to recite his oft-repeated litany about how these depraved and degenerate people deserved whatever happened to them. How they were users and spoilers. How their own uncaring arrogance would be the instrument of their doom. How he was merely the arrow loosed from the bow of atonement. How . . . how . . . He stopped and cocked his head. His ears took in a sound he hadn't heard in years but would never forget. Deep and rhythmic. The sound of good leather. The squeak of gear, of rivets and straps and the tink of metal against metal. He recognized the sound at once. The sound of soldiers moving fast. His head began to throb.

He stepped over to the edge of the mezzanine and

looked down into the second-floor hallway just in time to catch a glance of a black-visored trooper jogging down the hall with an automatic weapon slung around his neck. Without willing it so, the two bottles of water slipped from his hands and landed soundlessly on the carpet.

He turned and ran. Sprinted up the three stairs, around the corner and down the hall. He jabbed the plastic card into the door lock but got only a red light for his trouble. He tried again. Another red light. He heard shouts and the splintering of wood. Then a moment of silence before the sounds of boots could be heard on the stairs. He forced his hands to work . . . to slowly swipe the card . . . to wait for the green light, before bursting into the room and slamming the door behind himself . . . before grabbing the wing chair from the desk and jamming its padded back beneath the doorknob in the second before the door bent inward from the force of a blow. And another and another as he dragged Bobby Darling across the room to the sliding door and the balcony beyond.

The cold night air washed over his skin as he grabbed Bobby around the waist and lifted the struggling bundle above the rail.

"Oh . . . no . . ." Bobby cried. "I cannot . . ."

Holmes watched the door begin to disintegrate . . . watched the wing chair fall to the carpet, watched a black visage fill the gap and then, with Bobby Darling pressed hard to his chest, he threw himself off the balcony into the rushing darkness below.

40

Overhead, the banks of mercury vapor lights rained an eerie glow onto the five acres of tarmac below, bathing the scene in an ungodly purple radiance which was neither light nor dark but merely a respite from the night.

Nathan eased the van to a halt just outside the gate and rolled down the window. It was of no importance that he kept his face deep in the shadows, because the closest guy didn't bother to look up from his fingernails. "Names," was all he said, as if, regardless of the circumstances, everything else was unquestionably somebody else's problem.

"Singh and Kimberly," Nathan announced.

The other man—the one standing just inside the gate—ran his finger down a list he had on a clipboard. "Got 'em here," he said. "They're new." He jammed the clipboard into his armpit and rummaged through a battered cardboard box resting against the fence.

When his hands reappeared, they held a pair of ID cards dangling from bright red lanyards. He came forward several strides and handed them through the window to Nathan, who thanked him and put them gently on the seat next to his hip.

Only then, as he stood close to the van, was the man able to catch a glimpse of Nathan. He winced and pointed. "Park over there with the rest of them."

Nathan felt the man's horror. He could sense discomfort with the same degree of certainty with which others could feel a spring breeze. He allowed his eyes to follow the finger toward a dimly lit area to the north, where half a dozen men with flashlights directed the parking of the cars. The way they moved their arms reminded Nathan of the men who'd guided the airplane into the gate at Montreal on the night they'd arrived, their long orange arms enfolding, beckoning them forward and forward and forward . . . as if toward the promise of a warm embrace. He looked over at Wesley, who sat transfixed, staring out the side window at the reason why they'd come.

"Keep your IDs in sight at all times," the guy said and then waved hard with his arm, as if to hurry them along. "Let's go now," he said.

He pulled the clipboard out from under his arm and watched the taillights recede into the gloom before he turned to his partner and spoke.

"You see the face on the driver?" he asked.

"What about it?"

"Guy looked like he had a fire on his face and somebody put it out with a track shoe." He picked at his own face with pincerlike fingers. "Looked like he had pieces of gravel or glass or something sewn all up under his skin.

"Lotta ugly people," his partner commented.

"Not like that, man. Not like that."

*   *   *

"Don't move, man. Just stay still."

Pete didn't need to be told. He'd unbuckled his seat belt and had one hand out the window, hanging on to the roof, and the other locked so tightly around the steering wheel his knuckles were bone white in the gathering darkness.

"It's going over," he said through his teeth.

Jim waved him off. "I'm gonna move your way."

When Pete began to shake his head, the van began to teeter. He stopped and waited for the balance to stabilize, then watched helplessly as Jim Sexton grabbed the steering wheel and pulled himself upward until his hip rested on the side of the passenger seat.

"Go on. Climb out," Jim said.

Pete was more than willing. He used the roof for leverage, easing his hip out the window frame, until only his feet dangled inside the vehicle; then, one by one, he brought his legs out onto the door before stepping upward and disappearing from view altogether.

Jim moved carefully into the driver's seat and surveyed the scene. The van had come to rest at a thirty-degree angle. The driver's side wheels were a good four feet higher than those on the passenger side. All the equipment in the back of the truck had shifted downhill, making the balance even more precarious.

The squeal of tires pulled his eyes downhill, but the roof was in the way.

"What's going on?" he shouted out the window.

"More cops." Pete answered. "Lots more cops."

"Shit," Jim muttered to himself.

"What?"

"Stand clear."

"Oh no, man . . . don't . . ."

Jim found the accelerator and raced the engine. The

roar sent Pete clawing his way up the railroad grade until he stood huffing and puffing on the tracks, his heart hammering, his shoes full of gravel. "Gonna go over, man . . . gonna go over," he chanted as Jim dropped the transmission into first gear and fed it a little gas. The van inched forward, sending a cascade of loose dirt rolling down the hill.

Pete covered his eyes with his fingers as Jim began to point the front wheels downhill in a desperate search for equilibrium. He closed his eyes and began to picture the scenario where he explained to the bosses that . . . no, he personally wasn't driving when everything went to shit. Had to word it just right. Not ratting old Jimbo out, but rather just calling a spade a spade. Just the way it was, man.

He peeked out from between his fingers just in time to see the upper part of the grade collapse and begin to slide down the hill. The whole slab was sliding toward a four-foot drop into the parking lot below when Jim Sexton gave the engine full throttle, sending the van crawling across the moving expanse of earth like a bug on a floating leaf.

The tires spewed up rooster-tails of dirt as the van picked up speed, gaining sufficient momentum to bounce the front wheels up onto the grassy berm separating the sidewalk from the railroad right-of-way. Pointing the nose toward the sky . . . lurching forward and up . . . and then, as if by magic, the landslide picked up speed and disappeared over the edge of the retaining wall, leaving the van sitting benignly on the sidewalk.

"Holy shit," was all Pete could think to say.

He recalled when he used to swim in the river as a boy. When they traveled to Fessil Park to visit his mother's sister. He remembered the way his innards seemed to cool in the muddy water, leaving him feeling nearly hollow, like a tube of skin through which the cool water flowed. In those moments, he came to understand why the people scattered the ashes of the dead upon the sacred river. How a soul could never rest until it was returned to the river from which it had sprung and so given its eternal relief from the sun in the cool currents of the underworld.

But the cold was never like this. The ache never this deep. The urge to die never this strong. Holmes took in a great gulp of air and began to scissor his legs again, mindless of direction, moving with the tide, holding Bobby Darling across the chest, pumping for all he was worth . . . left, right, north south, it didn't matter . . . anywhere but down into the icy depths below his feet.

Bobby began to squirm in his arms. Holmes held him closer, whispered in his ear. "Parag," he whispered. "It's all right, Parag. We will make it."

And then . . . a powerful wave pushed them sideways and down, dragging them beneath the bubbling surface for what seemed like an eternity before thrusting them up once again into the cold night air where they shook the water from their eyes and gasped for breath and then suddenly . . . Holmes blinked in disbelief . . . it seemed as if they were in a forest of great looming trees, angled this way and that, each trunk reaching for the night sky with bare black arms.

Holmes reached out, half expecting to find it all an apparition, but instead found it hard and slimy and real. He threw his free arm around the nearest tree and held tight as he swung Bobby toward the trunk.

"Hold on, Parag," he said. "Hold on to it."

Instinctively, Bobby complied, wrapping his arms around the slippery surface and squeezing for all he was worth. His black hair had washed completely down over his face. The chattering of his teeth made a sound like a small, badly tuned motor.

Relieved of Bobby's weight, Holmes looked around. It took his eyes a moment to adjust to the dim light. The trees of this forest were the underpinnings of a pier. Ancient poles driven deep into the bottom of the bay. Out over Parag's shoulder, he could see the south facade of the hotel. The current had pulled them two hundred yards south. Two full piers down from where they had gone into the water just minutes before.

And then . . . as he fought to control a shudder, he lost his grip on the piling and slid down under the water again, the water cresting his chin and then his nose and mouth . . . until his foot hit something. Something solid. He pushed off and bobbed to the surface. He looked around, loosened his grip on the pole and did it again. Just to be sure.

"Parag," he whispered. "Parag."

Bobby disengaged one hand from the piling for long enough to wipe his hair from his face. His lower jaw quivered violently. His lips were blue. He opened his eyes.

"The bottom," Holmes said. "It's right beneath us."

Holmes watched as Bobby Darling groped downward with his foot and discovered he could stand with his chin just above the waterline.

Holmes pointed toward shore. Toward the floating dock and the sailboat and the concrete stairs rising to the street. "Just a little farther," he said.

41

Charly Hart slammed the phone on the bed. "Son of a bitch," he snarled. He checked his watch and looked up at Corso who stood with one foot on the balcony and the other on the carpet.

"Problem?" Corso asked.

Hart threw his good hand into the air. "What kind of crazy son of a bitch throws himself off the balcony on a night like this?"

"Son of a bitch who really don't want to get caught."

Hart nodded grudgingly, struggled to his feet and shuffled out through the sliding doors onto the balcony. Three stories below, Puget Sound gleamed like a cabochon. A full moon, veiled and pale, rode high over Bainbridge Island, sending a silver stake of light shimmering across the expanse of water, narrowing its beam . . . thinner and thinner, until it seemed to point directly at the room in which they stood.

Corso stepped all the way outside and leaned over the rail, where a pair of Coast Guard runabouts skirted the pilings, the narrow beams of their halogen searchlights spearing the darkness beneath his feet.

"Reuben's still in the operating room," Charly Hart

said, as he snuck another peek at his watch. "What in hell can they be doing all this time? It's been four fucking hours, for christ sakes."

Corso rejected several responses, opting to keep his mouth shut. Thus encouraged, Hart went on. "I guess Inez came all the way unglued down at the hospital. Hadda be sedated. They got her in the room next to where Reuben's gonna be." He stared off into space. "Woman's a soap opera waiting to happen. One of the great fucking drama queens of our time." Catching the bitterness in his own voice, Charly Hart clamped his jaw closed.

Corso put a hand on his shoulder. "Let's see what's going on downstairs," Corso said. Charly didn't answer. Just turned and started pushing his feet toward the door.

Samuel checked the zipper on his coveralls and then did the same for Paul.

"Who are you two." The voice came out of nowhere in the seconds before the face emerged from behind the battered aluminum trailer where they'd just been issued their haz-mat suits. He was older than Holmes. Maybe fifty. Needing a shave. Wearing the same two-tone brown coveralls they were sporting. NORTHWEST SANITATION sewn across the back. One size fits all.

"Rishi and Singleton," Paul told him.

"You new?"

They nodded in unison. He pointed across the lot . . . to a larger, newer portable building where a line of men walked in one end dressed like they were now and emerged from the other end with tandem breathing devices resting on top of their heads and silver canisters strapped across their backs. "Hurry up," the man said.

"Hustle over there and get yourselves into your gear. The party's about to start."

Samuel and Paul passed a quick look. The plan was to sidle back over to the car . . . to get their facsimile canisters, then to join the rest of the crew over by the west gate.

When they failed to move, the guy stepped in closer, eliminating any question as to what he'd been doing behind the trailer. His breath smelled of old cigarettes and new whiskey. His etched fingers were yellowed at the ends.

"Let's go, fellas," he bellowed. "Ain't no fashion show here."

He took Samuel by the elbow and began to move him across the yard. Paul trailed along in their wake, casting furtive glances at the Subaru as he moved along.

"Hope to God you two ain't gonna be this pokey all morning."

"Oh man . . . it's fucked. Took the whole damn antennae mast off and everything." Pete slapped his hands against his sides. "They're gonna go ratshit over this. Absolutely ratshit."

"Don't worry about it," Jim Sexton soothed. "We're on such a roll, they'll never even mind."

He said it, but knew it wasn't true. These days you could find Jimmy Hoffa's body and there'd still be some bean counter demanding you justify the pick and shovel. The bottom line was king at KING-TV. And, although it was not a word he generally used . . . because Beth went absolutely ballistic . . . "fucked" was precisely what the van was. A deep crease ran the entire length of the vehicle; in places the paint had been ground all the way down to the bare sheet metal. The passenger window was sprung and would no longer roll up. Worse yet, as Pete had so aptly pointed out, the microwave antennae had been torn completely loose and at some point had been run over by the tires, leaving twenty grand worth of high-tech equipment little more than a twisted assemblage of wire and metal, ready for immediate recycling.

"Let's get real clear here, man," Pete was saying. "*I* wasn't the one driving when all this . . ." He waved a hand at the carnage. Before he could drum up the proper phrase, however, it became apparent to him that Jim wasn't listening, but instead was staring intently at a pair of men crossing Elliott Avenue arm in arm. Considering the neighborhood, it would have been easy to write the sight off as a pair of drunks helping one another across the street after yet another afternoon of drunken debauchery. Problem was . . . they were soaking wet. Not the kind of wet you get from the rain. The kind of wet you only get from swimming in your clothes. The kind where you leave big wet tracks on the sidewalk as you move along.

"What do we have here?" Jim asked himself.

A block and a half to the west, the night was aflame with pulsing emergency lights . . . red and white and blue and red and white and blue . . . ricocheting off the bricks, dancing on the clouds, as what seemed like half the police cars in town had converged on the Edgewater Hotel.

They watched in silence as the pair crossed the sidewalk and disappeared inside the Belltown Parking Garage. Monthly Rates Available.

"You don't suppose . . ." Jim started.

"Don't even start, man," Pete jumped in. "Next thing I'm going for a ride in is a tow truck."

For the second time in as many minutes, Jim wasn't listening. He'd pulled the walkie-talkie from his pocket and had it pressed tightly to his ear.

". . . went off the balcony. Got two Coast Guard and two of our own boats scouring the water side," the skinny cop was saying.

"What about the others?" Sounded like the chief.

"Rooms were empty. We're doing a door-to-door."

"Keep me in the loop," Click. Silence.

And then, half a block down the hill, a black Mercedes nosed out of the parking garage. Stopping for a moment in the middle of the sidewalk while the driver surveyed the scene. The gentle rocking movement sent one of the chrome headlight rims rolling out into the street. A rhythmic ticking sound said the fan was hitting something as it went around.

The driver turned left . . . heading south. Without willing it so, Jim Sexton found himself trotting toward the van. He could hear Pete carping in the background . . . something about giving it a rest . . . as he slid into the driver's seat and turned the key.

He was down the hill and around the corner before he realized the van was dragging something. He shrugged and turned up the radio. Warren Zevon. "Werewolves of London."

42

Wesley shifted his weight from foot to foot. Nathan gave him a little bump with his hip as if to tell him to relax, but it didn't do any good. If anything, Wesley seemed to get more energized by the contact, so Nathan bumped him again and threw a scowl his way. From the corner of his eye, he watched Wesley's right hand clenching and unclenching around something he was holding. He looked away.

The foreman of their cadre—they called the work groups "cadres"—was finally winding down. Other groups had been inside for at least ten minutes, while they were still standing outside receiving instructions. Nathan was ready. Everything had gone according to plan. They'd switched backpack sprayers, queued up and nobody had been the wiser. Their hour was finally at hand. Nathan looked up, forcing his eyes to take in the sheer scale of the world they were about to enter. He stifled a shudder.

"Harris," the foreman called.

"Yeah," somebody yelled back.

"Got a new partner for you."

"Another one?"

"Some folks just can't stand prosperity."

Harris strolled up from the far end of the line. Like everyone else, he was clad from head to toe in blue. SANITATION MANAGEMENT SERVICES INC.

"Singh," he called out now.

Nathan held his breath as Wesley stepped forward. The one called Harris beckoned Wesley to come closer, then took him aside. "We're working C deck, you and me." He looked Wesley up and down. "You ever done this kind of work before?" Wesley shook his head. Harris reckoned how it didn't matter much either way as it wasn't what he called "rocket science" anyway. Nathan watched as Harris and Wesley walked toward the far end of the queue and eventually disappeared from sight.

"McGruder," the foreman called.

"Let me guess," the man on Nathan's right said.

"Another training opportunity."

McGruder stuck out a hand. "Must be you," he said to Nathan. "I know most of the rest of these monkeys."

Nathan shook hands. The guy patted him on the shoulder. "Gonna be workin' right across the hall from Harris and your buddy." He smiled. "Like old Harris there said, this ain't exactly rocket science."

"Come up with a hotel maid on her way home from her shift, says she saw a couple of East Indians get into some red Japanese car and drive south," the cop said. The cop spread his hands as if to say, "Sorry but that's it."

"Thanks," said Charly Hart. He looked around at the awesome array of police equipment. "Police garage is empty tonight," he commented.

The cop nodded. "Whatever's not down at the Weston is right here."

Another uniformed officer was chugging up the sidewalk in their direction. Guy needed to get out of the squad car more often. His sizable stomach bobbed like a melon as he jogged along. By the time he slid to a stop in front of Charly Hart, he was so out of breath he had to take some time to compose himself before he was able to deliver his message. Even then, the words came out in a series of gasps.

"Down there . . ."—he pointed north and panted a couple of times—"they got a place . . ."—couple more deep breaths—"looks like somebody came out of the water."

"Show me," Hart said.

Luckily for the out-of-shape cop, Charly Hart wasn't up to rapid movement. They trudged along in silence for the better part of two hundred yards. The wind had stilled and the tide was at slack, leaving the surface of the water as flat as glass.

Two piers down they came to an unexpected break in the tourist traps, a little dock where a sailboat stood ready to take folks out for a little cruise of the bay for a mere twenty bucks each. Plus tax.

A Harbor Patrol cop stood at the bottom of a set of concrete stairs. He wore a dark blue SPD baseball cap, a black wetsuit and a bright orange life vest. He pointed at a collection of blotches and footprints covering the central portion of the stairs. At least one of them had been barefoot. The outlines of his toes were visible in the dim light.

"Looks like something went up here," the HP cop said. "Not too long ago either."

Corso looked down at the sidewalk. The same wet trail crossed the concrete sidewalk and then disappeared on the black asphalt of the street.

"Hell of a long way from where they went out the window," Charly Hart mused. "Guy musta been an Olympic swimmer."

The cop shook his head. "Half an hour ago the tide was ebbing hard. The way it swirls around in this part of the bay, it could have dragged 'em down here like they had a motor. All they hadda do was keep their heads above water." He made an arc with his arm. "Big eddy just spit 'em out here under the building. By the time they were out of the current, with the tide all the way out, they could probably stand. Just walked on out."

Charly Hart thanked him and turned back toward the street.

"Maybe a dog," Corso said.

"Just what I was thinking," Hart said.

He got on the radio and called for a K9 unit. "Foot of Broad Street."

A blue SPD cruiser slid to a stop at the curb. One cop driving, another riding shotgun. Passenger leaning forward in the backseat in that awkward way of people wearing handcuffs. Driver popped the door and stepped out onto the sidewalk. Stocky Asian guy whose name tag says T. Masakawa.

Hands Charly Hart a wallet and a laminated ID card. Jerks a thumb at the man in the backseat. "Picked up this guy walking down the railroad right-of-way. Peter Carrol. Works for KING-TV. Mr. Carrol here just couldn't manage to be forthcoming about what he was doing there, so we brought him along."

"Let's get him out here."

Although a glance at the ID hadn't rung a bell, Charly Hart recognized him immediately. "It's Parka Boy's cameraman," he said to no one in particular. "Where's your buddy?" he asked.

Pete Carrol shook the handcuffs. "What's this about?" he demanded. "Since when is it illegal to be walking around the city?"

"Since we've got terrorists threatening to kill everybody and you don't seem to be coming up with the right answers."

Charly waved his good hand at Officer Masakawa. "Let him go."

Pete stood on the sidewalk rubbing his wrists. Charly stepped in close, took Pete by the shoulder and led him across the sidewalk to the top of the stairs. He bent at the waist and put his nose right up to Pete's. "I'm only going to say this once, Mr. Carrol. What's going on here is serious business. It's got nothing to do with that 'who gets the story first' bullshit you spend your life chasing. This is for real." He pointed at the wet spots on the concrete. "We think we've got a couple of terrorists who came out of the water right here. I'm sure you want to do everything possible to help our investigation. I'm also sure that's the way your federally licensed employers back at the station would want it to be." He moved even closer. Insisting on eye contact. "Don't you think so?"

Pete Carrol nodded.

"Yes what?" Charly Hart wanted to know.

"We seen 'em."

Charly Hart took a deep breath. "Seen who?"

"The wet guys."

The story came out of him like it was under pressure. Wrecking the truck. How he wasn't the one driving. How much trouble they were gonna be in. The two wet guys limping into the parking garage. "Couple minutes later they come driving out in a big black Mercedes. Front end all messed up, dropping parts all over

the street." He waved a tired hand. "Nice rig, but the
thing was a mess."

Corso and Charly Hart passed a look.

"Went south on Western," Pete Carrol said.

"And Parka Boy?"

"Right on their tail."

Jim knew right away what was going on. He'd covered the original story. Back when all the hoopla
about the cruise ship industry coming to Seattle
turned into a story of how the boats kept coming back
from the inside passage with boatloads of sick people
and didn't know what to do about it. Back when the
promise of seven days floating around Alaskan ice-
bergs regularly morphed into seven hundred seriously
unhappy people with the trots, many of whom were
also spending their free time projectile-vomiting the
buffet lunch into marine heads. Some kind of virus
the ship lines said. Naturally, bookings went the way
of the buffet lunches, and for a while, it looked like
the whole cruise ship thing was going to be over before it began.

After it happened three or four times, the cruise
lines started hiring teams to disinfect the entire ship
between cruises. Hundreds of people spraying god
knows what carcinogens all over the place to keep the
passengers from losing their lunches. Must have
worked, though, because he couldn't remember a similar story this whole cruise season.

And there they were, the wet brothers, half a block
up the street, changing into dry clothes before reporting for work and shouldering themselves into pairs of
green coveralls. Jim Sexton clung to the chain-link
fence and watched as the duo dressed. Must have been

a hundred people milling around in the same coveralls. Most of them wearing black backpack sprayers.

Weird though. Coupla guys driving a Mercedes, on the run from the cops, working for ten bucks an hour on their way out of town. Spraying disinfectant all over the *Arctic Flower.* THE FUN SHIP, as the sign proclaimed. That's when the first tingle of fear ran down Jim's spine.

43

"**F**ifteen minutes," the foreman bawled. "Right back here in fifteen minutes. Don't be late." He waited a minute and then yelled again. "Back here at nine-twenty. Fifteen minutes."

Paul followed the others down the long corridor and out onto the deck. Once outside, everyone pulled off their breathing devices and feasted on the cold night air. Some even unlaced their hoods, pulling them from their heads, the men wiping sweat, the women shaking out their hair. Samuel stood leaning against the far end of the rail. Paul moved that way, careful to seem nonchalant and unhurried as he passed among the others.

"We've got to do something," he whispered to Samuel. "We can't be the only ones to fail."

When he looked for agreement, he saw only doubt. Even fear perhaps.

"We have to try," he insisted.

Samuel gave a tentative nod and a squawk.

"I don't know how. We've got to get back to the car."

He grabbed Samuel by the arm and led him down the deck, toward the midpoint of the ship where the elevators stood. The area was nearly deserted as Paul pushed the down button and waited. The door slid open with a muted whir. He shepherded Samuel into the car and breathed a silent sigh of relief as the door slid shut.

Less than a minute later, they stepped out onto Pier Forty-Seven. The air was colder and wetter than it was up on deck three. He tightened his grip on Samuel's arm and led him across the tarmac toward where they'd parked the car. The pier was a blaze of activity. People moving in all directions at once. Vegetable trucks and forklifts and centipede baggage carriers skittered everywhere. Shouts from the longshoremen filled the air, as they hustled to cram last-minute deliveries into the yawning freight elevators. North, toward the bow, two dozen immaculately uniformed crew members engaged in knots of animated conversation at the foot of a gangway marked in bright white letters: SHIP'S CREW ONLY. A pair of beefy security officers stood ready to enforce the ban.

Paul skirted the tail end of a segmented baggage carrier as it came clattering by, only to find the little red car now buried three rows deep in the parking lot. The sight sent a shiver through Paul. He hesitated for a moment and then stopped altogether as he noticed the driver's door standing wide open. Samuel squawked a question. Paul pointed.

"Did we leave the door open like that?" he asked.

Samuel reckoned he didn't have any idea.

"Hey," a voice called.

Paul followed the sound of the voice. The front steps of the trailer. The same man as before. "Come on over here, you two," the man said, beckoning with his arm. Instead of complying, Paul walked quickly over to the car, bent at the waist and slipped the upper half of his body inside. When he reappeared, his face was blank.

He looked at Samuel, who stood stiff and silent, and then back to the man on the steps.

"I took care of it for ya," the guy said, coming unsteadily down the stairs. Once on solid ground, he steeled himself and started their way at a measured gait. "What you doin' down here anyway? You on a break?"

Samuel nodded.

Up close, the man reeked of whiskey. His eyes were filigreed with red as he swept his gaze across the two young men. "I seen you forgot your equipment, so I run it back to supply for ya." He squinted his eyes and waved a grimy finger in their direction. "Y'all come back next year y'all gonna have to be more careful how you handle the gear." He grinned, showing a yellowed set of teeth, broken and irregular as fence posts. "You don't want to be havin' no company equipment in y'all's backseat neither. Folks get to thinkin' you was stealin' or somethin'." He chuckled. "'Course ain't no reason at all anybody gonna be stealin' a damn sprayer. Lest you got one hell of a case of roaches at home or somethin'." He laughed at his own joke and then checked his watch. "Y'all best be getting back upstairs. Six more minutes and you got to be there. They'll dock you for sure."

Samuel made a noise even Paul couldn't translate.

"I . . . I . . ." Paul stammered, "I left something."

"In the car?"

"On the sprayer. My watch," Paul said touching his wrist with his forefinger. "I fastened my watch around the . . . the . . ." He stopped, at a loss for words.

"Around the wand?"

"Yes, around the wand."

The guy slapped his side disgustedly. "Well that was

a dumb-ass thing to be doin', now wasn't it?" He beckoned to his right, out in front of the equipment trailer. "Come on with me. We'll see if we cain't find the damn thing and get you fellas back on the job before it costs you boys hard-earned money."

Paul gestured with his head, telling Samuel to follow along as he started around the front of the trailer. When he looked back over his shoulder Samuel hadn't moved an inch. From long experience, Paul knew the look. Samuel was close to panic. He wanted to remind Samuel what Holmes had said so many times. "You have to be prepared to improvise. Once the first battle starts all plans are out the window." Instead, Paul turned and said to Samuel, "Just stay right there, I'll be back in a minute." Again, no response.

He ran a couple of steps and caught up with the man, following along silently as they wove their way among a maze of containers and equipment, finally coming to a stop beside an oversized wooden crate. RECHARGE was stenciled on the side in black.

The man stopped at the box, looked down and then ran a hand through his greasy hair. "I'll be damned," he said to himself. A smile eased itself across his face. "Coupla hours ago," he said, "the damn thing was empty."

Paul hustled forward. The bin was filled with an army of backpack sprayers. Seventy or eighty, something like that. Identical. A great big giant pile of them, all thrown together in a great jumbled mess waiting to be carted off.

Paul must have made a noise. "Take it easy now," the guy said. "It's just a watch." His eyes nearly closed when he smiled. "Weren't no diamond-crusted Rolodex or nothing was it?"

Out in the reaches of his vision, Paul caught a movement. Samuel was walking away. North toward the entry gate. "I . . . I've got to . . ." Paul stuttered, moving that way.

"Hey now," the guy said. "Y'all can . . ."

The sound of his feet hissing on the tarmac prevented Paul from hearing whatever the guy said next. He skipped twice, broke into a jog for a few feet and then began to run headlong after the rapidly retreating Samuel.

"So what if . . ." Corso began. "What if you wanted to pull off a terrorist act in a major city." He waved a hand. "You gotta know that when it comes to terrorism, as far as Americans are concerned anyway, what we're talkin' about is Arabs and nothing but Arabs. You can pretty much figure for sure they're not even gonna go looking for anybody else until they run out of Arabs." Charly Hart sat on the front seat of a patrol car with his feet hanging out the door.

Corso looked down for agreement, but got nothing more than a grimace. "So the first thing you do is get yourself a crew together. Something other than Arabs. People with an ax to grind against the United States. People with nothing to lose. People who've already lost everything they had because an American corporation was more interested in profits than it was in human misery."

The look on Charly Hart's face said he thought Corso's assessment was a bit harsh. "What?" Corso said. "That seems out of line to you?" He didn't wait for an answer. "Remember the heads of the major tobacco companies? Remember those guys? Standing up there in front of God and Congress, raising their hands, swearing they had no idea that cigarette smoke was habit-forming. Remember those turkeys?" Corso's tone was bitter. "A real high point in American history," he said.

Charly fiddled with his watch. Corso went on. "Problem is, though, you gotta come up with people who are all the way under the radar screen. People who have no connection whatsoever with any kind of terrorist organization." A small twisted smile appeared on his lips. "Which pretty much limits you to amateurs."

Charly Hart glared up. "This whole thing stinks of amateurs," he snapped. "It's what keeps me wondering if we don't have our heads up our collective asses, if maybe we're not making something out of nothing."

"Coupla carved-up bodies isn't nothing."

"Isn't international terrorism neither," the detective countered.

The radio began to squawk. Charly Hart leaned farther inside the car and listened. From where he stood in the street, Corso couldn't make out the words. He waited until the noise stopped and Charly Hart sat up in the seat. "Units have completed a sweep of lower downtown," Hart said. "Nada. No East Indians. No beat-up Mercedes. No nothing."

Jim Sexton leaned back against the hood of the van. A sticky valve ticked rhythmically in the night air as he surveyed the scene inside the enclosure. He watched the small army of green-clad bodies lining up by the side of the cruise liner, primed and ready for work, and thought how it looked like one of those old science fiction movies where uniformity was the order of the day and everybody dressed the same.

He'd lost track of the wet guys when they'd stepped

into the equipment shed. Everyone who exited the shed was masked and dressed and ready to go, so there was no telling one from another.

They were going on board now. Crowding into the freight elevators, waiting to be lifted to their respective decks. Jim's scalp tingled at the sight. He knew what he had to do. He reached into his pants pocket, pulled out the phone and flipped it open. Silence. He pushed the SEND and RECEIVE button.

"Hello," he said tentatively.

Two responses came at once. "Dobson here." And "Hart."

Jim opened his mouth but nothing came out.

"You rang?" said the chief.

"Not me, sir," said Charly Hart.

"Had to be one of us," the chief said. "Only people on this channel are you, me and Gutierrez."

"I . . ." Charly Hart began. He looked over at Corso and scowled. "Hang on a second, Chief," he said.

When the detective tried to rock himself upright and failed, Corso stuck out a hand and gently pulled him to his feet. Hart walked to the rear door of the cruiser and pulled it open. The black plastic tray rested in the middle of the backseat. He bent at the waist and used his good hand to rifle through the contents. Notebook, wallet and badge, watch, gun, the car keys and eighty-seven cents in change. He patted around the area for a moment, then straightened up and held the phone to his mouth. "Reuben's radio is gone, sir," he said.

"Gone?"

"Last time I looked, it was with the rest of his stuff," Charly Hart said.

A strained silence ensued. "You out there," the chief

said after a moment. "You with the stolen radio. Do you hear me?"

Jim Sexton's fingers trembled as he turned the volume knob all the way down and put the phone back in his pocket.

44

Harris pulled the spraying wand from the clips on the side of his backpack. He pushed the brass lever and sent a thin spray of disinfectant arcing out into the air. Satisfied, he directed his attention to Wesley and Nathan.

"We gonna do the rails all the way down this side," he said. "Then we gonna come back and we gonna do the staterooms along this side all the way to the middle of the ship. Damn near two hundred rooms. Gonna take us all night long." Nathan answered with a grunt. Wesley was staring out over the water, toward Bainbridge Island and the Olympic Mountains beyond. "You hear me?" Harris asked.

Wesley brought his eyes around and nodded. Nathan pulled his mask into place.

Harris ran the sprayer along the top of the rail, sending a narrow mist down onto the metal. "Just like this," he said. "Not too much, not too little." He released the lever. "You'll get the hang of it. You ready?"

Wesley nodded again but didn't move.

"Let's go, man," Harris prodded. "Put your mask on."

Wesley used his left hand to slide the mask down over his face, then reached for his wand. He fumbled and failed to remove it from the trio of metal clips holding it fast to the side of the canister. A disgusted noise escaped from beneath Harris's mask.

McGruder, who'd been using the bathroom, strode around the corner and crossed the rear deck to join them. He retrieved his backback from the deck and shouldered it on.

Harris watched as Wesley made another feeble attempt and then pushed the mask back up on his forehead. "Come on, man," he mumbled. "Come on, man, what's the matter wid you, man? What you got in your hand there?"

Wesley pulled the hand behind his back. Harris looked at McGruder, who likewise removed his mask for a better view. "You see what he's got there?" Harris asked again.

"Lemme see," McGruder said.

Wesley pushed the hand even further behind his back. He had begun to shake his head when McGruder reached out and grabbed him by the arm.

Behind his mask, Nathan's breath caught in his throat. Wesley's eyes were taking on that steely sheen they always got before he went crazy. Nathan shouted an admonition into his mask, but no one heard.

Wesley growled and jerked his arm free. The violent movement sent McGruder's arm reeling into space, where it banged against the bulkhead before flopping back to his side. Harris pointed. "Fucker's got him a knife there," he said.

McGruder stepped forward. "What the hell's the matter with you, man? You got no call to be walking around here with a shank." He stuck out his hand.

"Gimme that damn thing," he demanded. When Wesley failed to move, he reached for his arm again.

The movement was swift and nearly gentle. Looked like Wesley tapped him on the chest as a way of telling him to stand back. Like he had magic powers or something, because the tap stopped McGruder in his tracks, left him standing there feeling around on his chest with a look of astonishment etched on his face. And then the flower came in season.

A red gardenia bloomed on the front of McGruder's coveralls, small and wet in the center, before the circle widened and color began to spread across his narrow chest. He reached for Wesley again; his eyes were wide and his hands were red, as he pawed the air. Wesley stepped to the side and tapped him twice more. And then a third time as McGruder began to sink to his knees.

Harris was quicker than he looked. Before McGruder hit the deck, he lifted his wand and sprayed Wesley full in the face keeping his fingers clutched around the brass lever . . . keeping the flow coming . . . filling Wesley's eyes . . . soaking his hair with pine-scented disinfectant. Wesley staggered backward, rubbing his eyes, slashing at the air with the knife. Harris began to scream. "Help," he cried. "Somebody help me."

"So you bring this crew of anything but Arabs across the Canadian border," Corso was saying. "Lord knows they got their share of East Indians in B.C. so nobody ought to bat an eye. You make 'em out to be grad students at the U. You put 'em up in one of those perpetual rentals in the U District. Someplace where the residents change with the semesters. Someplace where unless they've got two heads, nobody's gonna notice their comings and goings. You bring Bohannon along because he knows the area and because he's got his own ax to grind." Charly Hart gave a grudging nod.

"Problem is . . . no matter how slick you set it up, you're still working with amateurs." The detective started to say something, but Corso waved him off. "Let's face it, Hart, the world is not chock-full of people who're willing to strap their asses to five hundred pounds of dynamite and then push the button. You gotta find some nut who thinks he's going directly to heaven after the explosion." Corso waved a disgusted hand. "You know, up there in the clouds with the seventy virgins and all that crap."

"Didn't know you could still find that many virgins," Charly Hart groused.

"So you get your people in place," Corso continued. "You pick a weekend when all the germ doctors in the world are in town for their annual symposium . . . exactly the kind of people you could reasonably blame for the kind of thing that happened in Bhopal, except they're not the target. You've got something else in mind 'cause you know they're gonna have the germ doctors guarded like the mint and you figure that while they're expending their resources in one area you can wreak havoc with a bunch of amateurs in another."

"Under the radar."

"Exactly."

"Except."

"Except Bohannon gets antsy and wants to create a little havoc of his own." The radio began to squawk again. Charly Hart leaned into the car and listened. Corso watched his expression change from boredom to confusion to concern.

"Got some kind of disturbance down on Pier Thirty. Some maniac with a knife," Hart said.

"What's on Pier Thirty?"

"Cruise ships."

Charly Hart propelled himself off the seat. Banged his head hard on the doorframe. He rubbed his head as he scanned the street, looking for a driver. Corso read his mind. "I'll drive," he said.

Hart shook his head. "Against regulations."

"You got a better idea?"

Charly Hart was still massaging the top of his head when he threw himself back into the passenger seat. "For god's sake don't hit anything."

"Hey, hey," the guy yelled. "Where in hell do you think you're going?" Samuel stopped and looked around. He pointed out to the deserted street.

Guy shook his head. "That suit's company property," he said. "Ain't no way you're leaving with the damn thing."

Samuel began pulling wildly at the Velcro, trying to extricate himself from the coveralls. Before he was sufficiently unfastened to free his shoulders, Paul jogged up to his side and put his lips close to Samuel's ear. "We'll leave quietly," he said. "We'll get back to the border." The words seemed to have a calming effect. Samuel's motions became more deliberate, his fingers less frenzied as he pulled the suit from his body, lifting his feet one at a time to pull the coveralls over his shoes. The guy sauntered out of his kiosk. "We don't pay no partials," he said. "You don't finish your shift, you don't see a dime."

"That's all right," said Paul, holding his coveralls out at arm's length.

The guy shook his head. "What?" he sneered. "You think I'm gonna return those to supply for ya?" He emitted a dirty laugh. "You wanna take them back . . . you get your own asses over there, and I'm not gonna . . ."

Paul opened his hand and dropped the coveralls on the ground. Samuel followed suit. Together they turned and walked out through the gate.

"Hey," the guy was yelling, "you get your asses back here and . . ." The rest of his words were lost in the sounds of their own breathing and the scuff of their heavy shoes on the street as they picked up the pace, trying to put as much distance between themselves and the voice as they could. Alaskan Way was a half-erased pencil drawing, the buildings ghostly apparitions, as an offshore flow had carried a light fog in over the city, leaving the rose-colored streetlights to shed lonely cones of light along the darkened street. They walked half a block before another set of lights bounced down onto the street. At the sight of a Seattle police cruiser, Samuel emitted a harsh croak. Paul reached out and touched his arm. "Just keep walking," he said. "They have no business with us." As if to argue, the cruiser's engine roared as the driver cut directly across both lanes and jerked to a halt ten yards in front of them. In little more than a second, the cop was out of the car with his gun drawn, resting his arm along the roof of the car as he took aim.

"Down," he screamed. "Get down in the street."

Before Paul's mind could process the situation, Samuel took off running. "Stop," rolled through the silvery air, and then again, "Stop." Paul stood open-mouthed as the cop stepped out from behind the car, dropped to one knee and again took aim. Paul opened his mouth to shout, but any sound he might have made was lost in the *boom* of the pistol. He turned. Samuel was still running in that awkward gait of his. The gun boomed again and Paul watched in horror as Samuel was thrown forward onto his face, finally sliding to a stop in the street with his limbs still twitching. Without willing it so, Paul began to run toward the cop, shaking his arms and shouting Samuel's name. His real name. "Suprava." He heard a shout. "Stop." And then the pistol roared again, sending a bright white flame out into the night. The bullet entered just beneath Paul's right eye, deflected off his sinus cavity and exited the skull slightly behind his left ear. He was dead before he hit the asphalt.

45

Corso pushed the accelerator to the floor. The SPD cruiser fishtailed slightly before gaining traction and rocketing down Alaskan Way. Charly Hart hung on to the overhead handle with his good hand and braced himself with his feet.

Half a block down, the radio began to scratch out another message. Mostly streams of numbers. The only words Corso caught were "officer involved." Then "Pier Fifty-Six."

"I thought it was Pier Thirty," Corso said, horsing the wheel to the left.

"This is something else," Charly Hart said through clenched teeth. "Shots fired by an officer. Suspect down. Right up ahead here someplace."

Before they could exchange further words, they rounded a slight bend in the road and there it was, an SPD cruiser parked diagonally across the street, driver's door open, radio spewing static into the quiet, light bar ablaze, red and blue bolts of light bouncing off the foggy air.

Corso slid the car to a stop, half on, half off the sidewalk. Out where the two sets of headlights intersected, a uniformed officer knelt in the street, using his finger to check the pulse of somebody lying in the street. Ten yards closer another body lay facedown on the concrete, a crimson halo beginning to form around his dark head.

Wasn't until they were right on top of him that they recognized the cop. Same guy who brought them that Pete Carrol character. T. Masakawa.

His mouth hung open. His eyes looked like he might start to cry. He looked up at Corso and Hart. "This one's alive," he said. As if on cue, an approaching siren could be heard. And then another . . . closer. "Roll him over," Charly Hart said. "Keep the airway clear."

T. Masakawa did as he was told. Carefully, as if he were handling a child, he rolled the victim over on his back. The slug had plowed a trough through his shoulder. Contact with the street had broken off both front teeth and painted a seeping stripe down the center of his face. East Indian. Maybe twenty-five or so. His eyes were closed and his breathing was shallow but regular.

T. Masakawa began to babble. "I . . . I mean they were . . ." He looked over his shoulder at the other man, still and silent in the street. "That one came at me," he said. He looked down at the man cradled in his arms. "I told him to stop. Twice, I think."

Charly Hart reached down and put a hand on his shoulder. "You did the right thing, Officer," he said. "The want was for double homicide. The description said armed and dangerous."

The cop blinked and shook his head. "I never wanted to . . ." he began. "I never . . ." He looked down at his side. "My gun . . . I never . . ." He began to cry.

"It's all right," Charly Hart intoned. "You did what you had to do."

The *whoop whoop* of the siren was right on top of them now. Orange pulsing lights joined the red and the blue in a macabre dance. A guy in a white shirt had left the fenced-in parking lot two blocks up and was trotting their way. A red and white aid unit rolled around the corner behind them. Another police cruiser slid to a halt a block down.

Charly Hart squeezed the officer's shoulder and looked over at Corso. "I'm staying with the officer here," he said.

"I gotta see what's going on at the boat," Corso said.

Hart kneaded the kid's shoulder and nodded his understanding to Corso. "I'll have to say you stole the car."

"Okay," was all Corso said before sprinting back to the car and throwing himself into the driver's seat. He jammed the lever into Drive and bounced down off the sidewalk with a squeal.

Two blocks down, the silhouette of an enormous ocean liner etched itself on the sky. A floating hotel bigger than an office building. Corso ignored the red light at the corner.

What had begun as fifty pounds strapped between his shoulder blades was feeling hollow and light now. As he sprayed a toilet in the first-class section, Bobby Darling mulled over what he was supposed to do when he ran out of virus. Find the foreman. Say he was out of disinfectant. Ask for another backpack. They'd said he'd probably need three or four before the night was over. Put the used ones in the orange bins marked RE-CYCLE. Get a new one from the white bins marked FULL. Simple as that. Keep working until the job was done. Then he and Holmes would walk off with the rest of them, collect their pay and disappear into the city. Bobby felt a glow of satisfaction as he dusted his gloves together and started toward the front of the ship. Considering how things had started, the plan had gone well. Only thing he was sorry about was that he didn't have another load of virus to spread about the ship. Kill twice as many of the sons of bitches.

"What have we got here?" Harry Dobson demanded.

The officers looked among themselves for a volunteer. When none was forthcoming, a balding sergeant stepped forward, hat in hand.

"Got a guy up on deck there with a knife," he said. "Him and his buddy are part of the cleaning crew they bring on board between cruises. We've got one dead, one cut up pretty bad." He pointed at the ship. "They ought to be bringing the vics down pretty soon here."

"Where are the perps now?" Dobson asked.

"They got him and another guy locked in a walk-in freezer."

The chief's face darkened. "What about this situation required my presence?"

The sergeant ran a hand over his face. "There's this window where you can look into the freezer."

"And?"

"Well, every time somebody makes like they're gonna open the door and take these guys into custody, one of these guys threatens us."

"With his knife? You called me over a—"

"No sir, he keeps threatening to spray whoever opens the door. He's got this canister strapped to his back. He keeps brandishing the sprayer thing." The cop demonstrated by waving his hand around in a spraying motion. "Like he's got something real dangerous in there or something."

"They're East Indian," another of the cops said.

Harry stiffened like a metal rod had suddenly been driven through his core. The muscles along his jawline were in knots. Before he could muster a response, a metallic clatter pulled his attention toward the ship, where a pair of medical technicians were pushing an aluminum gurney across the uneven boards of the pier.

"Guy that got cut up," one of the cops said.

Harry called for them to stop and walked in that direction. Halfway there, he stopped and looked back over his shoulder. He thought about asking for a gas mask. One of the units they all carried in the cars. Then changed his mind.

"Can he talk?" Harry asked the nearest EMT.

Guy nodded. "Says his name's Harris."

The chief walked close enough to make eye contact. "Mr. Harris," he began.

The other EMT slipped both hands beneath the man's shoulders and lifted him into a sitting position. He was a dissolute fifty-five or so. African American, his hair grown out like Don King's; a nasty-looking cut ran the length of his right cheek. Looked like it might have gone all the way through into his oral cavity. The pink flaps of skin had been sprayed with a yellow antiseptic and were being held together by a trio of metal clips. Both of his hands were bandaged the size of boxing gloves. He fixed his eyes on Harry Dobson. "Fucker's crazy," he said. "Crazy as a goddamn loon."

Harry let him rant for a moment and then thanked him for the information. "What I need to know, Mr.

Harris, is whether either of those men sprayed anything onto the ship."

"Didn't get that damn far."

"This is very important, sir," Harry said in his most serious voice. "If you're not sure, just say so."

Harris's voice rose an octave. "I'm tellin' you, man, I was the crazy bastard's partner. Neither of them India boys was out of my sight the whole time we was on the damn boat." He started to wave a hand but thought better of it. "Next thing you know, that fucker shanks McGruder."

Harry spoke first to the EMTs. "Take Mr. Harris and put him inside your unit." He pointed to the far end of the dock. "Park down there and do everything for him that you can. I'll get you out of here as soon as I'm able."

The closest took a step forward. "Is there a situation here, sir?" he wanted to know. "Should we be . . ."

"I suggest you take whatever precautions are available to you at this time."

The guy started to ask another question, but Harry cut him off. "I'll let you know if there's any change in status," he said in a tone designed to stifle further query.

Harry walked back to the collection of cops. "Get a perimeter on any and all exits from the ship," he said. "Nobody goes on. Nobody gets off." He cut the air with the side of his hand. "Nobody," he said again. "Go."

Everyone moved at once. The sounds of barked orders and scuffed shoes were muffled by the thick night air as Harry pulled his cell phone from his pocket.

"Emergency Services," he said.

Soon as he got somebody on the line, he told them what he needed.

Before he could pocket the phone, another police cruiser came sliding into the lot. He was about to go ballistic on the officer for driving so recklessly when the door bounced open and out stepped Corso.

"It appears you may have been right," Harry said.

46

Charly Hart pushed the walkie-talkie button. "Chief?" he said.

The response was sharp and immediate. "I thought I told you to go home."

Charly ignored him. "I've got two of our suspects here, Chief. One dead. One wounded. A patrol officer named—"

"Mr. Corso has apprised me of the situation," the chief said. Charly Hart could be heard to swallow. "These are the guys we've been looking for, sir," he said after a pause.

"Are you certain?"

"ID says Paul Rishi and Samuel Singleton. Same names we got from Canadian Immigration."

"Seal off the area. Nobody in. Nobody—"

"Don't think we need to, sir."

When the chief failed to respond, Charly Hart went on. "Don't think these two ever got their virus canisters on board." Charly told him the story. "So we went through the bin the guy says he set their equipment in and lo and behold, down at the bottom are a pair of backpacks. Full. Seals still intact. Right where the guy says he put 'em. Everything else in the bin is empty."

"I'm going to send a CDC team your way," the chief said. "In the meantime, nobody goes aboard the ship and nobody gets off."

"Yessir."

"How's the officer?"

"Pretty broke up about it, sir. Never had his piece out before."

"Get him some help."

"Already did, sir. Except this time of night the only thing I could come up with was a grief counselor."

"Keep me posted," the chief said.

"Yessir."

Harry pocketed his phone just as the elevator door slid open. He stepped to the side, allowing Hans Belder and Isaac Klugeman to precede him from the elevator car.

"CDC team came up negative," Harry said. "No trace of the virus."

"Sounds like you may have gotten lucky," Belder said as he passed.

"I pray to God," Harry said.

"Sometimes luck is better," Klugeman added with a grim smile. A muted *ding* announced the arrival of the second elevator, crammed with people from the FBI, the CIA, the Centers for Disease Control, Homeland Security and every other agency that could be squeezed into an elevator. Corso and the guy from Scandinavian Cruise Lines stayed in between the two groups as they walked all the way to the stern of the ship, where a knot of police officers milled about the rails, engaged in low-key conversation. The sight of the chief coming their way brought about an instant improvement in posture.

The dozen or so cops backed away, making room for the official delegation to enter the metal corridor marked EMPLOYEES ONLY. At the far end of the space, a huge stainless steel food locker covered nearly the entire width of the area. Fifteen by fifteen with a four-foot-square window to the right of the door. Somebody had slipped a thick, greasy bolt through the eye beneath the handle. Put the nut on too. Nobody inside was going anywhere.

The chief and the scientists bellied up to the window. The feds hung back at the end of the hall. Corso straightened up and looked over the top of the trio. Two guys in blue coveralls walking back and forth inside, trying to keep warm. A pair of black breathing devices lay on the floor. Nearest guy had an unruly mop of black hair and a wicked-looking scar zigzagging down his face like a slalom course.

The other guy looked fairly normal until he reached the far side of the space and turned back the other way, revealing a withered ear, shriveled and brown as a dried apricot. He was pleading his case, whatever it was, to the guy with the scar, who, quite obviously, wasn't buying it. From their positions outside, Corso and the others were unable to hear so much as a whisper.

Harry looked over at Corso. "One of these the guy you and Gutierrez saw?"

"Nope. One we saw was older than these two."

"You get a look at the guys we got up the street?"

"Neither of them either."

"So where's the guy you're describing? There were six of them in addition to this Holmes guy. I got Bohannon in the morgue, got two here and two up the street. Where's this Holmes character?"

Corso shrugged. Harry turned to the guy from the cruise line. "How long before they run out of air?"

"Two days," the guy said. "Give or take."

"How cold is it in there now?"

He stepped around the corner and consulted a gauge. "Thirty-four."

"How cold can you make it?"

"Forty below."

Belder let go a low whistle. "Forty below is the end of the virus."

"Minus twenty-five would be sufficient," Klugeman added.

"It would kill it?"

"Absolutely," Klugeman said.

"Unless, of course, it had been engineered to withstand that kind of cold," Belder cautioned.

"What would be the point?" Klugeman snapped. "That sort of engineering is far too costly and time-consuming to be used frivolously." His scowl did not encourage disagreement. "I mean . . . what would be gained? There is no strategic value to a cold-tolerant virus."

At that point, the one with the scar noticed he had an audience. His thick lips folded back into a sneer. He crossed the room in three quick steps and slashed at the window with his knife, causing Harry and the doctors to flinch a step backward.

He began to shout but could not be heard by those outside. Scattered bits of spittle appeared on the inside of the window as he yelled himself red in the face. The second man crossed to his side, spoke to him and then took him by the shoulder. Scar shrugged off the hand and took another swipe at the window with his knife. The violence of the movement sent the other guy skittering back against the rear wall, where he watched in horror as Scar separated a brass spraying rod from his backpack, aimed it at the window and let loose a thick stream of what could have been a thin broth. He kept at it until the window was completely covered and he was no more than a shadow behind the glass.

Klugeman stepped forward; he put his finger on one of the many brown specks at large within the solution. He beckoned Belder to his side. "See," he said, "some kind of airborne pollen." He tapped the glass with his fingernail. "The virus is inside the little pod. Exposure to air opens the pod. The pollen containing the virus becomes airborne."

Belder slipped his glasses over his nose and peered intently at the area. After a moment, he looked back at the chief. His face was the color of oatmeal. "The doctor is correct. And once Marburg is airborne . . . once it discovers lungs . . ." He waved an uncomprehending hand. The words congealed in his throat.

"You have no choice," said Klugeman. "You must kill the virus."

Belder nodded gravely. "Freeze it," he said. "By the grace of God, you have the opportunity. You must seize it."

A buzz of conversation ran through the crowd in the passageway. Harry turned to face them. "Any of you gentlemen care to do the honors?" he asked.

The crowd went suddenly silent. Which made the voice from Harry's pocket all the more audible. "Hey," it said, "Chief Dobson."

Harry turned his back on the feds, pulled out his

phone. "You listen to me, whoever you are," he whispered.

"You gotta get down to Pier Eighteen while everybody's still on board."

Harry appeared dumbfounded. "Eighteen?"

"*Caravelle*," said the guy from Scandinavian Cruise Lines.

"What about *Caravelle?*"

"Dey got a ship down at Eighteen."

"What ship?"

"Anodder cruise ship."

"There's only two," Harry insisted. "I watch them come and go every weekend. In Saturday morning. Back out on Sunday."

"Dey do it every October. Last cruise of da year," the guy said. "Dey got a lot of comps from when they had the sickness, so they put on anoder ship. Keep da refunds down."

"Something's not right here," came the electronic voice. "I don't know what these guys are doing, but—"

Harry held the phone to his mouth. "You listen to me, whoever you are. We're on the way, and when we get there you damn well better be there waiting for us. Do you hear me?" No answer. "I will find you," Harry said. "Know that. I will find you." Silence. Harry pointed to the jittery crowd. "Everything we have to Pier Eighteen."

They didn't have to be told twice. Harry then pointed to his own men. "Seal off this entire deck. I don't want anybody up here at all." When they were slow to disperse, he hollered, "Go," and things got moving. He beckoned for a sergeant. Sent Belder and Klugeman with him. A minute later, only Harry Dobson and Frank Corso remained. They passed a long look.

"You better go," Harry said.

"Might be best if we were both here."

"It's not your job."

"It's all of our job."

Jim Sexton stood with his elbows resting on the round metal rail, the chief's voice still ringing in his ears. Hard as he'd tried, he'd been unable to convince himself to wipe the phone clean of prints and throw it into the Sound. He'd have preferred to think that this inability to take definitive action was a matter of good character. A sense of the heroic which allowed himself to put the good of others before his own well-being. He'd massaged that notion for a full fifteen minutes before reluctantly rejecting it.

Who was he kidding anyway? The reason was baser and far more pragmatic than that. Problem was that plan wasn't going to work. Sooner or later, when all the excitement died down, somebody was going to notice that the timing of today's piece showed that he seemed to be getting to the story before the cops, and sooner or later they were going to demand an explanation, which sooner rather than later would lead to Pete, and, quite simply, no sane plan could hinge on Pete. Simple as that. So much for rising above self-interest. He closed his eyes and hoped for an inner voice to lead him from the darkness.

47

"Eight hundred fifty-seven feet at the waterline," the captain said. "A little over seventy-seven thousand tons." He looked around, making sure everyone was duly impressed. "We cruise at twenty-five knots with a range of nearly four thousand miles." Sitting there, partially obscured by the fog, the ship looked more like an office building tipped over onto its side. Black down below, all white and shiny up top, it seemed unreasonably large and most certainly incapable of sustained movement.

"Accommodations for just over two thousand guests and eight hundred crew members," he was saying. "Two pools, five separate dining rooms, a casino, six hot tubs. It's got a running track all the way around."

The sight of five space suits stepping out of the elevator brought his spiel to an abrupt halt. Corso stood among the assembled multitude of government functionaries, seventy yards upwind from where the CDC crew members made their appearance.

They watched in silence as the space suits waddled over and handed their test kits to a similarly clad figure who disappeared inside a mobile laboratory, while they lined up at the rear of a small tanker truck, where they took turns rinsing one another off with a pressure washer. Ten minutes later, when the last man was presumably decontaminated, they shed their biohazard suits and disappeared behind a cordoned-off area at the extreme edge of the pier. By that time, the air was permeated with the smell of chlorine bleach.

"How many crew members are on board this time of night?" one of the FBI agents asked the captain.

"About two hundred," he answered.

"Passengers?"

The captain shook his white mane. "No passengers till six A.M."

"What about the cleanup crew?"

A bald-headed guy in a pair of forest green overalls stepped forward. "I got a hundred forty-one people on board. Fifteen women, a hundred and twenty-five men." He checked his watch. "They're due to get off for lunch in eleven minutes."

Corso watched as the CDC lead pressed his earpiece deep into his ear and stepped away from the rest of the group. If his facial expression was any indication, the news wasn't good. He watched as the guy took a deep breath before opening his mouth. "Ladies and gentlemen," he began. All eyes were on him. "Preliminary tests on the wipe kits show the presence of the virus." A buzz ran through the crowd. "In some cases trace amounts, in others truly alarming levels of toxicity." He waved off the barrage of questions. "They're working on more specific test protocols as we speak. Sometime in the next hour or so, we should have a much better idea of what we're dealing with here." The buzz started again, "But," he began again. Silence. "It doesn't look good. Anyone who's been on board is going to have to be isolated indefinitely. Anyone who's on board now, which is somewhere in the vicinity of three hundred fifty people, well, I would say their chances of having been exposed to the virus to one degree or another are quite high."

This time the buzz broke out in earnest, as groups broke off from the main body and huddled on their own. Corso watched as the mayor used his index finger to pound in a point with the governor. Watched as the FBI and CIA broke into separate knots of whispered conversation that seemed to repel one another like the opposing poles of a magnet.

"This is insane," Harry Dobson muttered.

"Actually, in its own little way, it was a hell of a plan," Corso said. "While everybody's looking the other way, you hop on three cruise ships and contaminate six thousand people from something like twenty-three countries. You stretch out the incubation period of the virus a little bit and everybody gets all the way back home before they start feeling sick. And even when they do, first thing they assume is that they got the standard ship sickness. They go to their doctors." Corso twirled a hand in the air. "Worldwide epidemic, doomsday, god only knows how many dead before it's over."

"Damn near everybody," Harry Dobson said. "That's what's so crazy about it. Whoever these people are, they have no regard whatsoever for human life. It's like they're willing to kill everybody, willing to unmake the entire planet, just to prove some point they want to make."

"Ever been to India?" Corso asked.

Harry shook his head.

"Falling through the cracks in India isn't like it is

here," Corso said. "You fall through the cracks in India, you end up all the way on the bottom, 'cause there ain't no other place to fall." He snapped his fingers. "You wake up one morning and you're a garbage eater. Living on the streets of some city with all the others just like you. In the blink of an eye, you go from your mama's knee to living with people who purposely maim themselves in colorful ways . . . who gouge out an eye or cut off their fingers to make begging easier. People who'll cut your throat with a piece of glass over something you found in the trash."

The chief was paying rapt attention now, but Corso was just about through.

"There's no message here, Chief," Corso said. "If they wanted to send a message they'd have gone after the germ doctors. This isn't about politics. This is about suffering and the human need for revenge."

They milled around in silence for a moment. Up close to the overhead lights, the fog moved inland as a translucent sheet of white, folding itself around the *Arctic Flower* like tissue paper and then rising off the water in stages, to envelop the Alaskan Way Viaduct and then move upward toward the stadiums beyond.

Corso watched as Harry Dobson looked his way and scowled. Wasn't until Harry took a step to the left that Corso thought to look behind himself, where a pair of cops approached warily, as if they weren't at all certain they wanted to be this close to whatever in hell was going on. Between the officers, propelled along by the elbows, a hooded apparition in a burgundy ski jacket stiff-legged it their way.

"Guy says you want to see him, Chief," said the shorter of the two officers.

"Wouldn't take no for an answer," added his partner.

Before the chief could speak, the hood pulled a hand out of his pocket and thrust it forward. A black cell phone rested in the palm. Harry stared at it for a minute and then left it there; instead, he took a step forward and pulled the hood from the man's head. Jim Sexton came into view.

"I should have known," the chief said, snatching the phone and putting his nose right up on Sexton's. His hands were twisted into knots. "You make me sick, you know that? You put people's lives at risk over some stupid story, you—" He unknotted one hand and grabbed hold of Sexton's jacket, jerking him even closer.

Corso put a restraining hand on the chief's shoulder. "We've got company," Corso said. The ship's captain, Belder, Klugeman, Mayor Dean, the governor, the guy from the sanitation company, and a pair of FBI field agents all walked a respectful half step behind the guy in the brown cashmere topcoat as they made their way across the tarmac toward Corso and the chief. As they approached, the chief let go of Jim's jacket and smoothed his own clothes with his hands.

The mayor took the lead with the introductions. "I don't know whether you two have met," he began. He indicated the guy in the topcoat. "Harry, this is Bernard Pauls, chief of Homeland Security." Pauls nodded but failed to offer a hand. "Mr. Pauls, this is Harry Dobson, chief of police for the city of Seattle." Harry returned the nod.

"Governor Doss has wisely called out the National Guard. They'll be sealing off this section of the city in just a minute here," Pauls said. "We're going to need some volunteers from among your ranks, Chief."

"Volunteers for what?"

"We'll need to get the terrorists off the ship before we make any decisions regarding the disposition of the people on board."

Harry waved a hand at the FBI contingent. "What about these guys? Half the Bureau's in town. Send them on board."

"The Bureau doesn't have the necessary equipment on hand," Pauls said in an even voice. "The time lines for getting bioequipment from Quantico aren't workable at this point. I'm sure you understand. It's a law enforcement issue."

"You've got some fucking nerve," Harry said.

A collective gasp. "Chief," chided the mayor.

"First you tell me you don't need my help. You turn my whole damn department into traffic cops while you run around chasing every Arab in town. Then, after a couple of my men break the case, and we're suddenly faced with the possibility of a plague, you want my men to go on board a death ship for you. You want them to risk their lives to clean up your mess so's nobody will notice how you botched the investigation."

"I'd hoped our mutual professionalism could rise above—" Pauls began.

"Professionalism my ass," the chief spat. "We're talking about people's lives here, Mr. Pauls." He pointed across the deck at a pair of CDC staff in space suits. "There's people inside those suits, Mr. Pauls. People with wives and kids and gutters to clean and car payments to make, and every one of them is taking his life in his hands as we speak. As far as I'm concerned, the basic FBI 'cover your ass' drill doesn't work around here."

"I've consulted with Deputy Chief Gardener," Pauls said.

"You can't send firemen after these guys, for pity's sake."

"Harry," the mayor interjected.

"You gonna volunteer?" Harry snapped. He waited a beat and then said, "If not, maybe you ought to keep out of this."

Gary Dean's fleshy neck visibly reddened but he kept quiet. A shout broke the silence. Then another and another until it started to sound like a ball game was about to break out. Corso looked in the direction of the commotion. Two of the upper decks of the *Arctic Flower* were lined with green uniforms, waving their hands and shouting at the people down below. "Lunchtime," Corso said. "They want to get off for lunch."

"We've sealed the staircases and are holding the elevators at ground level," Pauls said. "The ship's crew has locked themselves into the employee areas. The cleaning crews are stuck on their respective decks. Lunch is going to have to wait."

Harry turned his back in disgust. He opened his coat and pulled a cell phone from his belt as he walked away. The group watched in silence as he spoke into the mouthpiece for several minutes, pocketed the phone and walked back their way.

"I'll have six men ready to go in fifteen minutes," Harry said.

"Do we have a confirmed ID on the suspects?"

"Just a pair of names. Roderick Holmes and . . ."

"Robert Darling," Corso filled.

"Pictures?"

"No, the Canadians claim they can't come up with those until Monday, but these guys are East Indian. How many East Indians can there be on board?"

"Seven," said the guy from the cleaning company.

"You're kidding."

The guy shrugged. "Immigration makes us keep track. We got a big turnover. We get a lot of transients, lotta Mexican workers . . . they come, they go." He lifted his hands in resignation. "Ain't exactly workin' for Microsoft, if you know what I mean."

"We have a number of East Indian crew members as well," said the captain. "I'm not sure exactly how many, but certainly not more than five or so, at this time of night."

Harry was disgusted. "There are over three hundred people on board that ship. How are we supposed to . . ."

"I've seen one of them," Corso said.

"I've seen both of them," came another voice. Jim Sexton freed his elbows from the pair of cops and stepped forward. "As close as I am to you now," he added. "I'd for sure know if I saw them again."

Pauls wasted no time. "Perhaps if these gentlemen were willing . . ."

Harry shook him off. "They're civilians. There's no possible way we can allow them on board."

Pauls looked at his watch again. "The terrorists have been on board for nearly four hours now. Presuming that message about the shelf life of the virus was any-where near correct, we've only got another three hours to get this resolved before it becomes airborne, which, if our scientific friends here are to be believed, will re-sult in a catastrophe."

Harry looked over at Corso. "You understand what he's asking you to do?"

"I understand," said Corso.

"Me too," said Jim Sexton.

Harry thought it over. Looked up at the governor. "Let's have the Guard bring them lunch on board. We'll say we've got a toxic spill down at dock level. That way everybody will have his mask off and we'll have support people on board in case we get any resistance. Once they're eating, we'll send my men on board."

48

At first, Bobby Darling, like all the others, wondered why they were not being allowed to get off the ship for lunch. Then came the announcement that there'd been a toxic spill of some sort down below. Unlike all the others, however, Bobby knew better. The sight of the Bradley armored vehicles parked nose to nose across the gate, of the horde of soldiers and policemen swarming like maggots, wiped any trace of hunger from his innards, replacing the urge to eat with a shaft of cold remorse that somehow they had been found out and had thus failed in their mission. He cursed and got to his feet.

His knees were unsteady as he abandoned his position on the rail and went looking for Holmes. People were sitting everywhere, pulling open the box lunches the soldiers had brought. He smiled his way to the center of the ship, where the same soldiers who delivered lunch now guarded the elevators. He kept moving, all the way around the front of the ship and back down the far side.

He hadn't seen Holmes since they'd started working. A finger of panic traced his spine as it occurred to him that he and Holmes might not be on the same deck. Took him ten minutes to get all the way around, back to where he'd left his unopened lunch. No Holmes. The realization that he was alone made him nauseous and slightly dizzy. Bobby took a moment to compose himself and then leaned far out over the rail. A trace of talk and laughter rose to his ears. The deck below was likewise filled with people sitting and eating their lunches. He walked to the stern and tried the door marked STAIRS. Locked. Then around the deserted side of the ship, trying all the doors, every locked entry pushing the sense of panic deeper into the pit of his stomach until finally he yanked on a handle and found himself looking at the inside of a safety locker.

The oxygen had a sweet taste, as if the air had been dusted with powdered sugar. Corso and the cops were working their way down the landward side of deck three. Thus far, they'd encountered two East Indian men. Neither was the guy with the snake eyes. Mostly it was college kids, deadbeats and green card refugees. The free food, combined with the announcement that lunch today was going to be an hour seemed to have assuaged any prior hostilities and suspicions. Mostly they wanted to know what got spilled and how it was going to interfere with getting off shift later. Corso was within two hundred feet of the stern and a big open area he thought maybe they called the fantail. Maybe a dozen diners sat with their backs to the rail, chatting and sipping at Cokes.

"Hey, *cabrón*," a dark little fellow called. "What kinda chit dey speel down dere?"

Corso smiled at him through the plastic faceplate. *"No sé,"* he said into the microphone.

The guy waved a disgusted hand Corso's way. *"Pinche Bebosa,"* he said.

Corso was fumbling for a reply when the last guy in line got to his feet and headed for the stern. Something about the thickness of his neck and the blocky, almost square head caught Corso's attention. He moved that way. "Hey," he called. The guy kept walking.

At that moment, a barrage of shouts and laughter went off behind him. He threw a quick glance over his shoulder. A piece of white rope, with an orange and white life preserver on the end, was hanging down from above. From the way the rope was shaking, it was safe to assume somebody was trying to climb down from the deck above. The three cops swam people out of their path on their way to the rail. Corso turned his attention back the other way just in time to see the heavyset guy disappear around the corner, to the right. Corso stretched his long legs to the max, moving as fast as he could without running.

Holmes took the apple out of his mouth as soon as he saw the rope . . . had to be Bobby. "Parag, Parag," he chided silently. "Oh no, Parag." And then he watched the three guys in the white suits fan out and move that way with a practiced assurance that could only mean cops and the fourth one . . . the tall one . . . was nearly on him now. He got to his feet, and moved quickly in the other direction. An amplified voice called, "Hey." He kept walking. Didn't break into a run until he was sure he was out of sight and then gave it all he had across the width of the vessel.

He had, for the past half hour, been ruminating on their present situation. Where things had gone wrong. Whether or not the whole team had been compromised . . . a great likelihood as far as he was concerned. And what he might do to both maximize the damage and effect his escape, neither of which, at this point, seemed in the least bit likely.

Once he saw the rope and then the cops, all bets were off. He was only sorry that he'd run out of virus. He'd have loved to have gone down spraying. As it was, they'd made their statement. Before it was over the name Bhopal would be on the world's lips once again and they would remember. At least he hoped they would. The only thing he was sure of at the moment was that he had no intention of being taken alive. Instead of sprinting down the deserted side of the ship in an attempt to elude his pursuer, he stopped just around the corner, pulled down the zipper on his coveralls and fished his knife from his pants pocket. He took his time zipping up and opening the blade. American policemen were quick with their weapons. Everyone knew that. He didn't imagine he would have any difficulty getting them to help him finish the game.

He counted three and stepped back around the corner. Only the tall one was in view. The others must have stopped to deal with poor Parag. The tall cop stood fifteen feet in front of him, feet spread, his long arms hanging loosely from his sides. And then the cop spoke. "It's over, man," came from a tiny speaker at the top of the helmet.

And then he saw the face behind the plastic and knew he had seen it before, at the house with the cop who had asked him about Brian Bohannon.

"It will never be over," he said. "Not so long as I'm alive."

"So . . . don't be alive."

"You're not a policeman." It was a statement. "Policemen don't say things like that."

"No. They don't."

49

Having climbed over the rail without being noticed, Bobby Darling swallowed hard and swung out into space. The rope was thinner and less easy to grasp than he'd imagined. He tried to get another loop around his ankle and failed, leaving his entire weight suspended from his hands and arms. Ten seconds in and his muscles were already screaming for relief.

As he mustered the courage to loosen his grip and slide down the line, the breeze blew him around in a slow circle and then another, before slackening and allowing the rope to twist him back the other way. He tightened his grip and mouthed a silent prayer that when he stopped twisting in the wind, he would end up facing the ship. Unlike so many other nights, the gods were listening. He took heart. Once stabilized, he began to loosen his fingers, one by one, until he started to slide downward. The friction burned his hands right through the gloves. He squeezed with all his might and came to a halt about halfway down.

He took a deep breath and for the first time looked past his feet, causing a muffled shout to jump from his throat and the blood to run backward in his veins. The dock was barely visible through the fog. The people looked like insects. He pressed his eyes closed and rested his forehead against the quivering rope. "Just a little farther, Parag," he said to himself. "Just a little farther."

They were nearly at the back of the ship. Jim first. The three cops trailing along behind, just like they'd worked it out. Didn't want to look too threatening as they moseyed along. He'd encountered a lot of good-natured ribbing about the moon suit and passed three East Indians, two men and a toothless woman, but neither of the pair he'd seen at the parking garage.

The suit was air-conditioned, but Jim was sweating bullets. He moved slowly, forcing himself to concentrate on the faces, hoping for all he was worth that this foolish act of bravado would somehow make up for whatever reprisals would be in store over the wrecked van and the purloined radio. He'd risked his life, hadn't he? For the common good and all. Howya gonna come down hard on a guy like that? Yeah, that was it. No way they could forget what he was doing here today.

The last group of diners rose in stages as he approached, picking up their garbage as they went forward, moving over against the bulkhead so he could pass.

His mind was so full, he nearly walked right on by. If the white rope hadn't squeaked from the dangling weight, he probably would never have noticed it looped around the white railing.

Jim wandered over and looked down. At first glance, his brain failed to process exactly what it was he was looking at. "Hair," he thought. "Something with hair." About the time he figured out it was the top of some-body's head, the guy looked up and Jim needed wonder no more. He was sure. This was the smaller of the pair from the garage. A high-pitched keening noise rose from the kid's chest to Jim's ears as he turned and motioned for the cops to hurry.

They covered the distance with practiced ease. Jim pushed the speaker button on his throat. "That's one of them," he said pointing down the rope. All three officers leaned out over the rail and looked down.

"You sure?" the nearest cop wanted to know.

"Positive," Jim said.

The cop pushed his radio button and began to talk.

Jim watched as the cop talked back and forth with whoever he had on the other end.

The cop pushed the speaker button. "They won't send anybody else on board," he announced. "They say we should pull him up, get him secured and wait for instructions."

At that moment, the other three officers appeared on the rail one deck down, like reflections of one another. "We got him surrounded," Jim thought. A mad chuckle escaped his throat, forcing him to turn away.

Holmes held the knife down along his side. On his left, an ornate modern bar ran half the width of the ship. In the cold gray light, the jungle of neon tubes looked like untended vines. Four leather-topped stools at each end, twelve running the long way. Down to the dance floor and the individual tables at the far end. On his right, the deck arched out from under the roof, flowed under the painted white rails until your eyes took off for the horizon like a plane on a carrier.

"What now?" Corso asked.

Holmes shrugged. "I don't know," he said.

"You're the last one. The others didn't make it."

Holmes nodded. Shouts could be heard in the distance. "I'm going to kill you," Holmes said.

"Why?" Corso asked.

Holmes could feel the fear in himself. The natural revulsion for the unknown that each man carries in his heart. Fear of the pain. Fear of how he might react in that final moment. How one might taint a lifetime with an instant. But there was no panic in this one. No tears. No remorse. Not this one.

"Because it's what men do in moments like this," Holmes said.

Four powerful strides and Holmes was on him. Corso was ready, legs braced, hands ready to defend himself, but the sheer force of Holmes's impact threw them both to the deck before either man could gain an advantage. The moment Holmes wrapped an arm around him, Corso knew he was in trouble. His moon suit was far too cumbersome for self-defense. It left him pawing at his attacker like a schoolgirl as they rolled about the floor, swinging wildly, seeking leverage on one another.

Not only that, but this Holmes, whoever he might be, was ungodly strong. He had one arm clamped diagonally across Corso's ribs, squeezing Corso's bulk like he was a doll. Corso slammed an elbow back at his attacker, but the padding from the suit robbed the blow of any significant force. He rolled once, twice, but the man had his legs around him now and was beginning to squeeze the breath out of him. Corso used both hands to wrench the man's ankles apart. He filled his lungs with a bolt of fresh air and rolled over, teetering with his knees in the middle of Holmes's chest, for the first time feeling he might have gained a slight advantage.

And then, in an instant, Corso felt the air rush from

his suit and a burning pain in his chest that refused to allow him to breathe. He heard the hiss of oxygen and the sound of something cracking as he struggled. He clutched at his side, when another blow bowled him over backward, banging his head hard on the deck, swimming his vision.

As he sought to regain his senses, Corso could feel hands around his helmet. He opened his mouth to speak just as Holmes tore the helmet from his head and pressed his face to Corso's. For an awful moment, Corso thought the other man might be going to bite him in the face. He turned away just as the shouts began in earnest. Next thing he knew, he was being jerked to his feet and dragged backward like a puppet. Corso gasped for breath, trying to breathe around the arm pressing his throat, trying to ignore the excruciating pain in his side. And suddenly there they were, in the mirror behind the bar. Corso red-faced, flailing with one arm, Holmes with a burly arm around Corso's neck, holding him upright, dragging him around at will, and in the other hand a black Commando knife pressed hard to Corso's throat. "Get back . . . get back . . . I'll kill him . . . I'll kill him," Holmes shouted at the pair of cops who had suddenly appeared, guns in hand.

"Easy," said the nearest cop. Dropping his gun hand to his side. "Easy."

50

"**O**n three ... you ready?"

Jim watched the officers jockey for position along the rail. Each man trying to find a space where he could get a purchase on the rope and use his strength to haul the guy up the side of the ship. They hunched together in a quivering mass of muscle waiting to explode into action like a bull bucking out of the chute.

Jim kept his distance. When they made the first pull, he leaned over to see what the guy's reaction would be. Naturally, he looked upward in horror. Eyes wide, teeth bared. And then he loosened his fingers and slid down the rope in what, at the moment, seemed to Jim one of the most pathetic acts of futility he'd ever witnessed. Fifteen feet below the guy's locked ankles, an orange and white life preserver swung to and fro in the night air. Where did the guy think he was going? Only thing under the life ring was a couple hundred feet of foggy air. "Pull," ricocheted through the air and another four feet of rope curled onto the deck. "Pull." And still more line came on board.

When Jim looked down a second time, the kid's face

was transformed. Devoid of the horror he'd exhibited just a minute before, he was looking up, but not at them, with an air of expectation. He was focused on something above them. Something high in the sky. Jim craned his neck and looked up the side of the ship. Nothing but steel, and patches of glittery fog sliding across the dark sky.

The kid shouted something, but Jim could not make out the words. "Pull," sounded in the night and then the kid let go of the rope. Not to slide, but to fly, as the sleeves of his coveralls began to flutter in the breeze, as the weight of his torso began to pull him backward, arms and legs stretched out at his sides like he was making a snow angel in the clouds.

The sudden lack of resistance sent the officers staggering back against the bulkhead, dumping them in a heaving irregular pile on the deck, leaving Jim Sexton the only one to witness the kid as he floated past the life ring, turned a full somersault in the extended position of a skydiver, and then hit the dock facedown, with a sickening crack such as Jim had never heard before. Jim brought a hand to his mouth and turned away.

Corso waved at the kneeling officer with his free hand. "Don't," he screamed as the cop sighted along his arm, looking for any opening that would allow him a head shot at Holmes, who jerked him higher, trying to keep Corso's head in front of his own as he sidestepped along the deck. The second cop had fanned out to the right in a flanking movement, leaving Holmes vulnerable from both sides. The blade dug harder into Corso's throat.

"You will tell them?" a voice in his ear.

Corso didn't answer. Couldn't answer.

"If I let you live . . . you will tell them what I say?"

Corso managed the smallest of nods. As Holmes began to whisper in his ear, the second cop had made his way to a position nearly parallel to theirs. He held the black automatic in two hands and braced himself to shoot. Corso closed his eyes and waited to die.

And then the pressure of the blade relented, and just in the instant when he was more concerned with being shot than with having his throat cut . . . he heard the noise . . . just as he'd imagined it would be . . . the crackle of cartilage and the sudden rush of arterial air as his throat came open to welcome the night, the warm gush of blood running down over him like a flash flood, cooling as it traveled down inside his suit and across his chest . . . and then the deck coming up fast beneath him as he dropped to the seat of his pants.

He looked down to find himself covered with blood. Was amazed to find he could look up again and see the cops creeping his way. He touched his throat with dis-believing fingers and found it whole. His mouth fell open. For some unfathomable reason, he stuffed his fingers into his mouth and then looked up to the cop.

Electronic words tumbled from the helmet speaker. "Son of a bitch cut his own throat," the nearest cop said, in wonder. "How in hell do you muster up the *huevos* to do that?"

The other cop was on the radio. "Second suspect se-cured," was all he said.

Charly Hart limped along behind the scattered knots of dignitaries until he found the chief, standing off to the south side of the yard, with Ben Gardener and a cou-ple of people from Emergency Services. Everything on Pier Eighteen had been moved as far away from the ship as possible, while the CDC team worked at securing the area around where the body had landed. Word so far indicated that the body was hot. Hot as anything they'd ever tested, which undoubtedly explained the intense deliberation with which they now worked the scene. In order to slip Bobby Darling's lifeless corpse into a hazard bag, they'd been forced to slide a piece of plywood under the remains, as the fall and subsequent impact had jellified the flesh into something more akin to cranberry sauce than human tissue.

The chief noted Charly's approach, excused himself from the group and walked Charly's way. "You seem to be having trouble with the concept of a direct order, Detective," Harry said without a trace of humor.

"Yessir."

"I hear we got lucky."

"Yessir. The other two sites test out negative. Not a trace of the virus anywhere except those two sprayers we retrieved."

"Wish I could say the same."

"Bad?"

"Not as bad as it could have been . . . but bad."

"What about the perps?"

"They're both down." The chief nodded at the CDC crew as they sprayed decontaminant over the half acre nearest where the body had landed. "One of them either jumped or fell off the side of the ship, depending on who you ask. The other one cut his own throat up on deck three." Harry winced and shook his head in disbelief.

"Did they . . ."

"Sprayed everywhere. Infested everything except the crew areas, which, thank god, they couldn't get into."

"What now?"

"We don't know," Harry said. "We're not set up to deal with this many potential carriers." He jerked a thumb toward the federal contingent. "The brain trust is working on that right now."

A deep rumble filled the air, and then another, almost in harmony with the first, a throbbing two-part bass, coming from everywhere at once.

"They say Reuben's gonna be okay," Charly Hart said.

"That's what I heard."

"Probably isn't gonna be joggin' anymore, but at least he'll be able to get around." Charly waved a hand. "Play with the grandkids, that kind of thing."

A wet whistle wailed in the stillness. Once, twice and then a third time.

A tugboat. Red and white, *Crowley* painted across the side, had wedged itself between the *Arctic Flower* and Pier Eighteen and was slowly but steadily pushing the massive ship's prow away from the pier. As the bulk of the ship displaced the surrounding air, the fog scattered and it became obvious from the black smoke percolating out of the stacks that the ship's diesels were running.

As Harry began to move forward at a lope, the *Arctic Flower*'s running lights suddenly blinked on, all bright and twinkly and cheerful. The Fun Ship grinning in a gruesome parody of the moment at hand.

"What's this?" Harry wanted to know.

The governor put on his command face. "We've decided to deal with it in situ," he said. "It's the only thing that makes sense."

"In situ?"

"We're keeping everybody on board."

"For how long?"

"Until it's over," the governor said.

51

"**S**TAND CLEAR," the voice boomed over the loudspeakers. "STAND CLEAR OF ALL SECURITY GATES AND WATERTIGHT DOORS." And then the horn, like the dive horn on a submarine, bouncing its rough squawk off the steel walls, coming from everywhere at once and nowhere in particular. "STAND CLEAR." It started over again. "STAND CLEAR OF ALL . . ."

The cop grabbed Corso by the hand and pulled him to his feet. The maneuver caused Corso to wince, as the sharp pain in his ribs returned with a vengeance, turning his vision white, leaving him short of breath and reeling.

And then the shots began. One, two and then a burst of four or five, automatic weapons fire, somewhere up by the center of the ship. "Stay here," the cop ordered. "I'll come back for you."

Another burst of fire rapped around the walls. Corso nodded and massaged his side, trying to pant some air back into his lungs as the cop took off running toward the front of the ship.

To his right, the collapsed form of Roderick Holmes

lay sprawled on his back, his big hands loose and comfortable, his dark face serene. Wasn't till then Corso remembered what he'd promised. He closed his eyes and listened again. Heard the words being whispered in his ear. Second time through, his lips began to form the sounds as if the thoughts were his and not those of the dead man at his feet.

"STAND CLEAR," scattered his thoughts like leaves. "STAND CLEAR OF ALL SECURITY GATES AND WATERTIGHT DOORS."

And then the clash of metal on metal began to rumble through the ship like a drumroll. That maximum security lockdown beat. That hydraulic bolt-snapping, greased-door-sliding moment when the steel eyelids come down and all movement ceases.

He could hear shouts from the deck above. A glance over at Safeco Field told him they were moving even before his ears picked up the throb of the engines. Before he could collect his thoughts, he heard his name being called. "Hey, Mr. Corso. Hey."

Massaging his ribs and moving slowly, Corso made his way over to the starboard rail. The cop who'd promised to come back for him stood sixty feet up the deck, his fingers entwined in the thick mesh of a security gate. A similar gate barred the way, not ten feet in front of Corso's face.

Corso looked up. What had earlier appeared to be nothing more than stanchions for supporting lifeboats had cleverly morphed into a series of white security gates, some of which now segmented the deck into sections of varying length.

"This is as close to you as I can get," the cop said. "They got it locked off both ways. Whole center of the ship is crew quarters, so you can't get through that way either. Everybody's stuck where they are. Probably trying to keep the cross-contamination down. Keep everybody separate from everybody else."

"Where we going?" Corso asked.

"No idea."

"How many people in your area?" Corso asked.

"Sixteen," said the cop. He managed a weak smile. "Looks like you got the bar all to yourself," he commented.

"I've heard worse ideas," said Corso, turning away.

The caption read: "Governor of the State of Washington, James F. Doss." CSPAN, CNN, FOX, MSNBC, ABC, NBC and CBS occupied the alpha camera positions with the rest of the affiliates bringing up the rear in descending order of rank. From where Doss stood, the sea of whirring red lights looked like rats in the darkness. Doss pulled his little half glasses from his inside coat pocket and slipped them onto his nose. He squinted through the lights and made eye contact with the technician at the PE mixer board for long enough to get the okay sign.

"Ladies and gentlemen," he began. "The purpose of this briefing is to fill you in on the situation as it presently stands and perhaps to give you some idea of what you may be able to expect in the coming days. At the conclusion of the briefing, we will take a limited number of questions." He paused for effect and then went on. "Let me begin by stressing how much more dire this situation could have become had it not been for the stellar efforts of the Department of Homeland Security, the Federal Bureau of Investigation, the Centers for Disease Control in Atlanta, Georgia, and any number of other agencies without whose efforts we could be looking at disaster today."

They were all lined up behind the governor, doing their official dais routine. Belder, Klugeman, Pauls, Payton, Helen Stafford, Marty Morningway and a bevy of others.

"Beginning at approximately eight-thirty last evening, three teams of terrorists made their way aboard cruise ships bound for Alaskan waters. Masquerading as maintenance workers, their intention was to infect the crew and passengers of these ships, nearly eight thousand people in all, with a deadly virus and thus instigate a plague of worldwide proportions." He made a gesture at the crowd behind him. "Without these ladies and gentlemen you see standing before you tonight, they most certainly would have been successful in their mission."

A smattering of applause ran through the crowd. "I am relieved to report that two of these teams were apprehended before they managed to do any harm whatsoever."

He paused to let the numbers speak for themselves. "The third group, however, was at least partially successful."

He took a deep breath. "At this time there are approximately three hundred sixty people on board the *Arctic Flower*. We believe it is possible that every one of them could potentially be a carrier of this deadly disease." The numbers rushed through the crowd like a gust of wind. "Faced with such staggering numbers of potential cases . . . consulting with some of the world's foremost scientists and health care professionals, we have determined that our best option is treating the victims on board." He pushed his glasses up and read from a paper in front of him. How many isolation units would be required to treat the victims in a traditional hospital setting . . . how many more would be required for the people who treated the first wave of victims and the people who then treated them . . . The numbers brought the crowd to a stunned silence.

"At this moment, we are launching an unprecedented medical treatment and cleanup program aboard the *Arctic Flower.* If our information is correct, and we believe it is, the incubation period for this virus is between ten and twenty days and the life span of the virus will under no circumstances exceed thirty days."

The MSNBC section just couldn't hold it together for another second. "So what you're saying then, Governor," someone shouted, "is that you're going to keep these people on board until you can be sure which of them have the virus and which do not."

"That's correct," the governor said.

This time the roar began to rise from the back of the crowd, where friends and relatives of those on board had found their way to the edges of the gathering.

"You just can't keep people like that," someone shouted. "What if somebody wants to be treated by his own doctor?"

Payton from the FBI stepped forward. "Under the provisions of the Patriot Act . . ."

The crowd buried him in boos.

Soon as they heard over the loudspeaker they were going to get fed, they'd ordered thirteen meals. There were only eleven of them, but they wanted to be sure they had enough food for the long haul. Seemed silly. Like somebody pointed out . . . nobody ever starved to death on a cruise ship. But what the hell. They were all stuck here together. Majority rules. Thirteen meals. Early on, Jim Sexton had wandered up to the next gate and shot the breeze with a couple of the cleanup guys who were trapped in the next forward section. They had nineteen people, including two women. While the people in Jim's section had taken the news of their isolation with a certain stoic grace, the group immediately forward had apparently erupted into something a bit more exciting, eliciting a couple of fights and a good deal of general hysteria of the "we're all gonna die, we're all gonna die" variety. If the noises heard bouncing around the boat immediately following the announcement were any indication, a great many other people had objected to their enforced quarantine. It had been long after midnight before the shouts had subsided and Jim had been able to get a few hours of fitful sleep.

An awsome array of toiletry articles, new coveralls and new respirators had arrived with breakfast. Along with a nicely written, not too pushy list of do's and don'ts for "making your stay with us a happy one: Stay in your suit and mask as much as possible. If not, stay in your cabin as much as you can. Stay away from public areas. Shower often." Things like that.

Most of the people in Jim's section had taken the suggestions to heart and hadn't been seen or heard from since, apparently preferring to ride out their quarantine in solitary confinement. Things could, after all, have been worse. They had twice as many staterooms as they had people. Each of which was lavishly equipped. Each wired for cable television and phone service. What with three sumptuous meals a day . . . hell, if you subtracted the specter of agonizing death, most of these people had it better than they'd ever had it before. Sort of an American dream come true . . . strings attached of course.

Jim had taken more or less the middle ground. The notion of these little spores drifting around bespoiling his lungs with every step kept him in his room the majority of the time. The frank realization that most likely they'd all been in contact with the virus already allowed him a couple of strolls a day through the section of the ship on which they were confined, which explained what he was doing all the way over on the starboard side, poking his nose into every open door, when he discovered the Caravelle Internet Café.

A dozen Compaq computers were spread around a tony little room. "Keep in touch with friends and loved ones," the sign admonished.

"Yeah, sure," Jim thought.

One of the first things he'd done, after they'd been apprised of the situation and after they'd picked out staterooms for themselves, was to call Beth. Second thing he'd done was to wish he hadn't. She'd already been notified by the station and had seen the story of his heroism on TV. Predictably, the heroic part of his present predicament had been lost on Beth, whose sole concern was the precarious nature in which Jim's actions had left the family. Would the station continue to pay his salary? Would his health benefits still be available? How could he have done something so thoughtless and stupid in the first place? What was he thinking?

Forty-five minutes of remonstrations had reduced Jim to claiming his cell phone battery was getting low and he'd better get off. He'd promised to keep in touch.

The station he hadn't called at all. After an hour of watching the news, all he knew for sure was that the media was playing up how he and this Frank Corso guy had been assisting the authorities with the investigation when they got caught in the lockdown. Short bios and small pictures of Jim and the six cops who were trapped on board what was now being called the Death Ship. Long bio and scads of pictures on this Corso guy.

Jim sat down in front of one of the computers and hit the space bar with his thumb. The monitor hummed and then burst into life. "Welcome aboard the *Arctic Flower*. What would you like to do? E-mail? Chat with someone on shore? Download your photos to disk? Send streaming videos back and forth with someone? Make a DVD of your—"

Jim stopped fiddling with the mouse and raised his eyes. The blank stare of the little TV camera met his gaze, and, for the first time in half a day, Jim smiled.

52

On the morning of the third day, a couple of moon-suited medics showed up to check Corso's medical condition. They took his pulse and blood pressure and checked his side, which was pronounced safe but sore. Apparently, the tip of the knife blade had only penetrated as far as the surface of the rib, which had been partially displaced by the force of the blow. They administered an antibiotic and recommended rest. Soon as they left, Corso went outside. He'd thought the matter over at some length and could not make a compelling case for spending what could be his final days walking around in a haz-mat suit and respirator. After the scene with Holmes, he was unable to imagine a scenario in which he remained uncontaminated. Might as well be comfortable.

The morning was steel wool gray. Everything . . . the sky, the city, the waters of Puget Sound, all of it so similar in hue it seemed as if the world could have been turned upside down and nothing much would have changed.

Holmes's body had been gone since early on the previous day. The area had been hosed down and then treated with some kind of bleach solution, so that when Corso strolled out onto the fantail promenade that morning the first sensation to reach his brain was once again the smell of a Laundromat.

The ship was anchored a mile south of Four Mile Rock. Just about smack in the middle of the bay, as far from land on all sides as they could be without infringing on the shipping channel. The *Arctic Flower* was now surrounded by a flotilla of barges. A nearly endless stream of boats ferried supplies and medical personnel to and from shore. Isolation was a very busy place indeed.

To the north and south, Coast Guard cutters stood sharp and ready, prepared to repel both media incursions and potential escapees, as Corso padded behind the bar and fixed himself a mimosa for breakfast.

"What do the numbers look like?" the mayor asked.

The CDC guy scoured his way through a computer printout until something caught his eye. "We've got a confirmed count of three hundred ninety people being held on board. Two hundred three crew members, six police officers, two civilians and a hundred seventy-nine maintenance personnel of one kind or another."

"What kind of . . ." Marty Morningway hesitated. "I mean of the three hundred ninety, how many can we expect to come down with the virus?"

"Nearly all of them." The guy looked around the room. "Allowing for a four percent incidence of people whose immune systems will successfully fight off the disease and another nine percent who will not become infected purely by chance, we can estimate that approximately three hundred thirty-nine people will likely become infected."

As a buzz began to circle the room, he held up a restraining hand. "If we factor in the fact that the wipe tests on the crew areas came back with only marginal signs of contamination and that the crew has been able to maintain a greater level of isolation than the passengers, the reasonable expectation would be that we will have somewhere in the immediate vicinity of a hundred and fifty infected people, of whom we can expect approximately a hundred thirty will die."

"You mean to tell me, what with modern medical science throwing everything it's got at these people—"

"There is no cure," the CDC doctor interrupted. "No serum. No vaccine. At present, the best we can do is keep their fluids up and make them as comfortable as possible. Untreated, Ebola Zaire has a ninety-two percent mortality rate. Treatment, regardless of the quality or quantity, can be expected to drop the number by no more than six percent."

A pall settled over the room, as everyone considered the numbers. Finally, Harry Dobson broke the spell. "So sometime in the next five or six days, we're going to get our first cases showing up. What then?"

Dr. Helen Stafford leaned forward and folded her hands on the table in front of her. "The period surrounding the onset of the disease is going to be critical." She took a deep breath and gathered herself. "Ebola damages the brain. It creates psychotic dementia. At Maridi, victims ran from their beds, out into the street, without knowing who they were or how they had gotten into their present situation."

"None of these poor souls will be running in the streets," the FBI agent threw in.

The doctor shook her head. "The point is, once we start to see victims, we're also going to see people who are simply terrified, and it's going to be very difficult to tell the frightened from the infected."

Harry Dobson checked his watch for the date. "Five days," he said, as much to himself as to the room.

Before anyone could respond, the conference room door snicked open. All eyes swiveled that way. A King County deputy pushed his two-tone brown uniform into the room. He walked quickly over to the sideboard which held the coffee pots and water and grabbed the remote control.

"I think you're gonna want to see this," he said.

The picture had a fun-house effect. The poor quality of the transmission allowed Jim's face to remain fluid, to move from thin to fat to square to round and back. Any hint of mirth, however, was immediately trampled by the grim expression on his face. "This is Jim Sexton reporting live from aboard the *Arctic Flower.*"

He spent five minutes relating the current state of affairs aboard the ship. Then, one by one, he introduced the other ten inhabitants of his area and allowed each to broadcast a greeting to whomever they chose. Some were long-winded. Some too overwrought to finish. Several were in Spanish. The cops went last. Everybody got their say. When the sounds of men shuffling in and out of the room finally subsided, Jim looked steadily at the camera and said, "I've noticed an interesting phenomenon since I've been aboard the *Arctic Flower.*" He tried to smile, only to have it wither on his lips. "I mean most of us spend our days glued to the tube watching CNN and the national news, hearing all this Ghost Ship stuff, listening to the figures about how many of us are going to die, and you know what?" He paused a beat. "Nobody thinks it's going to be them.

Everybody thinks they're the one who's going to survive." He shook his head. "I mean like . . . me too. There's just something inside us refuses to believe we're going to"—he stopped—"that we're going to end up being just another statistic. That we're going to be one of the ones they find melted down in their own beds." He looked away from the camera for a moment. "Maybe that's why we've survived for this long. Maybe that's the skill that's allowed us to . . ."—he waved a diffident hand—"what are we gonna call it? Maintain dominion over the planet? This absolutely unreasonable sense of hope . . . this kind of totally unwarranted optimism, that allows us to go on almost no matter what."

The tone of his own voice brought his monologue to a close. He ran a finger beneath his nose and looked at the camera. "This is Jim Sexton reporting for KING Five News."

53

Dr. Helen Stafford adjusted the microphone. "I think it would be safe to say that sometime in the next twenty-four to thirty-six hours, we should start seeing our first cases aboard the *Arctic Flower*. Yes."

She pointed at Wolf Blitzer, holding the CNN microphone in the front row.

"Sources tell us that, as of this morning, there have been two cases of Ebola found among shoreside personnel. Would you care to comment on that?"

"Actually three," she corrected. "A union electrician. A truck driver. And a security guard in the employ of the steamship line. All three were, at one time or another, aboard the *Arctic Flower* on the night of the terrorist attack. All three are presently in Level Four isolation at Harborview Hospital." She ignored the sea of waving hands. "As of an hour ago, we have identified fifty-six citizens who have had face-to-face contact with any of the three. Members of my staff and of the Centers for Disease Control are taking all the appropriate steps to minimize the spread of the virus."

She listened again. "No. Privacy laws prevent us from releasing the names."

The questions and answers went on for another fifteen minutes before Helen Stafford rose from her chair and pointed to her watch. "It's been a long day, ladies and gentlemen. The seventh in what I imagine will be many such days. If you'll excuse me."

They'd run the video feed through a bevy of electronic enhancement techniques in an attempt to stabilize the image. Despite their efforts, the results were, at best, sketchy. Jim's face no longer morphed as he talked, but the stabilization process had so flattened his features as to render him nearly unrecognizable to all but his closest relatives.

"Jim Sexton reporting live from aboard the *Arctic Flower.* Day Seven," he intoned. As he rambled on about the weather and the discovery of a cache of liquor in a forward locker, his voice once again began to rise and to take on a more stentorian tone. The change in his demeanor had been noticed by any number of national commentators. Some suggested that he was unsure of his equipment and thus felt a need to be more forceful; others lay the change in his demeanor to the fact that his live feeds had become a regular staple of every major news organization in the world, thus catapulting him from local also-ran to internationally recognized reporting icon.

"Tonight the decks are deserted." He paused. "As we near the end of the incubation period, people have begun to take our situation more seriously. In the past couple of days everyone seems to have taken to their rooms, venturing forth only when absolutely necessary. Tonight we truly are the Ghost Ship, the one you see on the television, our own little universe floating on the waves of Elliott Bay, waiting to face our fate, wishing each other well when we can and hoping like the devil that we'll be the one who survives, even if it means they won't." He shrugged at the camera. "So for tonight anyway, this is Jim Sexton reporting for KING Five News. Good night."

The presence came to him slowly. Like a finger gently lifting an eyelid or the soft arrival of dawn. He'd been dreaming he could fly. All the other kids in his elementary school stood openmouthed and dumbfounded as he soared above the playground with a dreamy expression etched on his face.

In the moments before he opened his eyes, he was overcome by the clarity of the images. The green of the grass. The deep red color of the earth and the fine gray gravel of the road. He opened an eye and it all disappeared.

The digital clock read twelve-fourteen A.M. The ship was motionless. Corso lay on his back staring at the ceiling. As the moments passed, he began to feel a tingling sensation run across his bare chest. Almost as if he could feel someone's eyes on him from across a crowded room. Although he wasn't cold, he had the sudden urge to pull the blanket over himself, but instead sat up in bed and stretched.

"You're a heavy sleeper," the voice said.

The sound pulled Corso out of bed in a single bound. He stood, quivering, sweeping the room with his eyes until he caught her outline seated in the armchair in the far corner of the stateroom. "You might want to put your trousers on," she said from the darkness. She smiled. "It's up to you of course," she added.

Realizing he was naked, Corso bent at the waist and felt around on the floor. He took his time, buttoning up his jeans before slipping the T-shirt over his head. When he was finished, he snapped on the light over his nightstand.

"How long have you been here?" he asked.

"Not long."

He took a deep breath, trying to quiet his pulse. "I don't suppose it would do any good to ask you how in hell you got in here."

"No," she said. "Probably not." Before he could speak, she rose from the chair. "Aren't you going to offer a lady a drink?" she said. "From what I can see, you've got a whole bar to yourself."

"What's your preference?"

She thought it over. "A martini. Bombay Sapphire. Olives."

"I can manage that," he said and headed for the door.

She followed him outside. Around the back of the ship to the bar, where Corso snapped on the bright lights and proceeded to put together a shaker of martinis. She watched in silence as he worked.

The persistent fog had cleared, leaving the lights of the city spread out across the dark water like fallen stars. Corso slid her drink across the bar at her and raised his own glass. "Salute."

"Salute."

He watched her throat move as she swallowed, waited until she put the glass back on the bar. "To what do I owe the honor of this visit?" he asked.

She took another sip. "I came to make you an offer," she said.

"One I can't refuse."

"Something like that."

"Why me?"

It was a question for which she was prepared. "Because you have a history of being where you're not supposed to be. You seem to have a knack for ending up in the middle of things, of making trouble, both for yourself and for others."

"Such as?"

"Such as your problems with *The New York Times*."

"Done our homework, eh?"

"Always."

"What do I get in return?"

"Your life."

Corso folded his arms across his chest. "You can't catch this, can you? This hemorrhagic fever, you're immune to it."

"Yes, I'm immune to it, and I can make you immune to it also."

"There's several hundred people on this boat and god knows how many others elsewhere who could use the same thing."

"That wouldn't do at all," she said.

Corso smirked. "Because then you'd have to admit you made the virus in the first place, wouldn't you? There wouldn't be any other credible explanation for having the antidote, unless you'd manufactured the original virus."

"If you say so," was all she said.

Corso opened his mouth to speak, but she waved him off. "Everyone makes it, Mr. Corso. How could they not? How could they be unsure what their enemies were doing and purposely not keep pace? How could that kind of largesse be explained away later? What could be said to a decimated people? 'We thought nobody was doing this kind of thing anymore'?" She made a disgusted noise with her mouth. "Everyone who can create germs is doing so. Some are merely more adept than others."

"Hundreds of people are going to die before this is over."

"Hundreds of people are going to starve to death in Africa while we're having this conversation." Her tone was flat. Her eyes unwavering.

"And you want me to do what?" Corso asked.

"I want you to deliver a package for me."

"In return for which you'll make me immune to the virus."

"Yes."

"This package . . . does it contain any type of—"

She read his mind. "No," she interrupted. "It's merely a photograph."

"Of?"

"Of the person you'll be delivering it to."

"Memento?"

"Loose end." She reached behind herself and pulled out a manila envelope which she had secreted under her belt and beneath her coat. She dropped it on the bar and picked up her martini glass. "Go ahead," she said.

Corso pulled the flap back and extracted the photo. Two men, passing something between them. Corso recognized one of them immediately. He'd seem him on TV.

"The other man's name is David Reubens. He used to be a genetic engineer for the Russians."

"Used to be?"

"The Russians went broke."

"So?"

"So he sold his product to the highest bidder."

Corso flicked the photograph with his fingernail. "The other gentleman here."

"Precisely."

Corso threw her a disgusted look. She made a rude noise. "What else was Reubens supposed to do. He had a wife . . . children. A nice apartment in Moscow." She waved a disgusted hand. "What was he supposed to do, when overnight everything he had worked for was gone? It's like you Americans are so fond of saying: 'A man's gotta do what a man's gotta do.' "

He studied the picture for another minute and then looked up. "I take it this . . ."—he shook the picture—"this explains how a bunch of pathetic East Indian terrorists get their hands on a high-tech bioengineered virus."

"This completes the circle." She checked her watch. "Time is short, Mr. Corso. What do you say? Do we have a deal or do we not?"

Corso found himself suddenly filled with voices, as if his solitary inner dialogue had suddenly become a heated debate. The call to refuse the antidote as a matter of principle. The call to die a noble death rather than profit from anything tawdry. The call to insist that everyone on board the *Arctic Flower* be given the antidote as well. Each righteous incantation he dreamed up more infeasible than its predecessor. They went on and on. It was all he could do not to burst out laughing. "Deal," he said.

She smiled. "Your room. You're going to need to lie down."

54

No dreams at all. No feeling. No moving. Just a sense of being suspended in warm water. And then the drums began. Deep and rhythmic. One two, one two, into infinity they thumped. He listened to the drumming for what seemed like days before he had an idea. He was asleep. He was dreaming. All he had to do was . . .

He couldn't. Muster a muscle. Open an eye. Raise his hand. He couldn't.

He began to rock, or at least to try. Rolling left and right, trying to move a little farther on each roll. The drums got louder. He rocked harder. Trying to use the momentum of his last effort to improve the next. Back and forth to the sound of the drumming. And then he teetered on the edge, experienced a moment of free fall and hit the floor face-first, driving the air from his lungs.

He gasped, fighting for breath, rolling over onto his back where he lay for what seemed an eternity, pulling air in and out of his chest in great whooshes.

With great effort, he levered himself into a sitting position. Unable to raise his eyelids, he used his fingers to peel the lids upward. The world swam in his vision. Tears ran down his cheeks. He removed his fingers. The lids stayed up.

Slowly, moving in stages, he gathered his strength and managed to raise himself to sit on the edge of the bed, where it all came back to him in a sudden rush. The stateroom. The woman. Lying on his back while she gave him the injection. The paralyzing heat of whatever was in the syringe as it coursed through his veins, and then the all-encompassing darkness settling over him like a velvet cape.

Must have been a dream. Some inner defense mechanism designed to provide some measure of relief from the looming specter of death. The body's way of keeping the stress level in check. Wishful thinking at its finest. He lowered his watery eyes. A small brown Band-Aid decorated the inside of his left elbow. Took him three tries to peel it off. A single spot of blood on the gauze made a serious dent in the dream theory. He moved his eyes across the room. The manila envelope on the nightstand dismissed the notion altogether.

Using the walls and furniture for balance, Corso crossed the room and pulled open the outside door. The blast of cold air sent a series of shudders through his body. He leaned heavily against the doorjamb until the shaking subsided.

It was daytime. The weather was clear. The sky a muted blue. The air was full of the smell of seawater and diesel fumes. Using the rail for support, he made his way aft. Pair of martini glasses on the bar. One nearly full. One empty. So much for dreaming.

He kept moving. Got to the starboard rail. Seemed like the whole bay was full of boats and barges. An armada coming and going from the *Arctic Flower*. More action than the past week combined. On his way back to his room, he put the martini glasses in the sink.

Five minutes in the head, running cold water over his face and then brushing his teeth, and he was a new man. A little shaky but otherwise okay.

He snapped on the TV. Peter Jennings. Nice clip of the *Arctic Flower* floating around in Elliott Bay. PLAGUE SHIP. "The inevitable has come to pass. Despite a complete news blackout, ABC News has confirmed an earlier report. Hemorrhagic fever is now rampant aboard the *Arctic Flower.* Medical teams from as far away as the Midwest have responded to this emergency and are now engaged in the process of trying to help those on board in any way they can. What we know for certain—"

Corso changed the channel. Jim Sexton, settling in for his morning broadcast. Corso smiled. Sexton finally had his big break. Probably not exactly what he had in mind, floating around on a seagoing isolation ward, doing his impression of the electronic grim reaper, but what the hell. He was having his fifteen minutes of fame. Should he, by some twist of fate, survive the experience, it was safe to say he would be in great demand within the industry. Amazing how one's moment comes around.

Jim Sexton was looking more disheveled than usual. Looking a little bit bleary. Probably been up all night. Lots of chaos on his deck maybe. He shuffled the papers in front of him on the desk and then finally looked up at the camera.

"Jim Sexton on board the *Arctic Flower* reporting for KING Five TV. Day nine and our worst fears have come to pass. Nearly everyone is sick." No doubt about it. Sexton was either ailing or drunk or both. "Not feeling very well myself," Jim slurred. "At least three people on my section of the ship have already melted down." He went on to describe the army of medical personnel who were on board trying to isolate the victims and console the terrified. Having come to what appeared to be the end of his report, Jim Sexton squared his shoulders and leaned closer to the camera. "You know," he said, "when you find yourself in a situation like this, where you're probably not going to make it through, it gives you pause to wonder just how in the name of God you managed to end up where you are." He waved a spastic hand at the camera. "I'm not talking about just bobbing around out here on this floating morgue. I'm talking about my whole goddamn life. About my dreams. About my fat-ass wife who doesn't give a rat's ass about me as long as I keep paying the damn bills. Who's gotta be the worst fuck in history. I mean like . . ." Corso sat straight up in the chair. Definitely both. Sick and drunk.

"A pair of daughters"—he waved the hand again— "don't care whether I live or die as long as they can shop at The Gap and talk on the friggin' phone." He shook his head. When he looked back at the camera, it took him a while to focus. "And you know, I'm doing this because . . . I don't know, I'm doing this because . . . I thought it might get me ahead. Maybe make those assholes I work for sit up and take notice of me. Just for once, maybe they'd finally notice me. Stop handing out jobs on the basis of a hair helmet or a big pair of tits . . . maybe look for a little depth . . . maybe . . ." The station pulled the plug on him. The screen went dark for a second, then came back with the Technical Difficulties screen. Segue to an antacid commercial. Corso couldn't help but smile. "Way to go, Jimbo," he said out loud.

55

First out were the dead. Or what was left of them. A hundred seventy-seven, if the news organizations could be believed. They came out on gurneys. Loose like jelly, inside thick black bags. Sealed metal boxes rolled with a solemn flourish over to hearses, where waiting families stood ready to take charge of their loved ones. Last bodies out were those of the four cops who had perished. A solid line of blue uniforms awaited their remains. Corso could make out Harry Dobson and the rest of the SPD brass at the far end of the gauntlet. The police band played "Amazing Grace" as the bodies were wheeled by.

Next came the sick. A baker's dozen of them. Those who had contracted the disease but who, for one reason or another, had managed to survive. These they rolled unceremoniously over to waiting ambulances, where they were immediately secured and driven away in a symphony of sirens.

The landward side of Pier Eighteen was a madhouse. Maybe a hundred TV remotes from all over the world. As many people as could possibly squeeze into the area between the pier and the solid line of Metro buses parked nose to tail to prevent the crowd from spilling out onto Alaskan Way.

Then . . . the rest of them . . . mostly the crew . . . those who, by the grace of God, had been spared the plague. Corso brought up the rear. Or at least he thought so. As he stood outside the elevator watching a multitude of tearful reunions, he heard the muted *ding* of another elevator arriving. He turned, expecting to see one of the army of security personnel. But no. Instead, out stepped Jim Sexton, looking hale and hardy.

"Glad to see you made it," Corso said.

"You too," Jim said.

"I thought . . . you know, that last broadcast . . . I thought you were—"

"Turned out to be the flu."

"Ah. What next?"

"No idea." Jim looked out over the crowd. "Guess I'll get a hotel room and take it from there."

"Good luck," Corso offered.

Jim Sexton nodded his thanks and stepped out onto the dock. Corso stood and watched as Jim made his way among the reunited, among the grieving, among the assembled multitude for whom this moment would forever be foremost in their memories. When he was no longer able to pick Jim Sexton from the throng, Corso followed suit, making his way through the crowd, toward the gate at the far end of the yard.

He was studying the gate, trying to figure out how he could get out without being deluged by the press, when he heard his name being called. He looked out over the crowd. Took him a minute, but there they were. Charly Hart, Harry Dobson and a woman he'd never seen before. They shook hands and clapped shoulders.

"My wife Kathleen," the chief said.

Corso acknowledged her with a bow and a stiff handshake.

"Glad to see you made it," the chief said, checking the immediate area. He turned to his wife. "I need to have a few words with Mr. Corso," he said. She nodded and stepped away, with Charly Hart at her elbow.

The chief moved to Corso's side. "Lotta static about the two guys in the freezer."

"Somebody musta jostled the switch," Corso said.

The chief smiled. "You been watching me on the tube."

"Wasn't a hell of a lot to do."

The chief looked Corso in the eye, liked what he saw and then nodded. "Good," he said. "We've got enough to do without that kind of shit."

"What's the final tally?"

The chief's face darkened. "A hundred seventy-seven so far from the ship. At least that many on land." He shook his head. "It'll be another three weeks or so before it all shakes out. Counting the people in the tunnel, they're estimating the final figure will be somewhere in the vicinity of six hundred dead."

"Imagine if they'd pulled it off."

"The fact that they didn't is in no small measure attributable to you."

"Aw, gosh and golly," Corso hemmed.

"I mean it."

"Me too."

Before the chief could speak again, Corso asked, "Can you get me out of here? I need to get to the airport."

"I'll have a unit take you wherever you need to go."

"I've got something I've got to do first," Corso said.

"I'll have the unit over by the gate."

The two men shook hands. Corso turned and walked away. Over to the section of chain-link fence where the media were crowded together like sardines in a can. "How'd you do it, Mr. Corso? How'd you survive?"

"I made a deal with the devil."

A laugh ran through the crowd. The questions went on for another ten minutes, until Corso held up a hand. "I'm really not a good source of what may or may not have happened. I was locked on a section of the ship by myself. If you want details, you'd be far better off asking somebody who was there."

"Mr. Corso, the two terrorists in the freezer. Could you—"

He raised both arms and quieted the crowd. "I do have something I want to say." Only the whirring of cameras could be heard. "There was a man. His name was Roderick Holmes." A buzz ran through the throng. "Yes, same guy," Corso said. "It's a long story, but suffice it to say, he had the opportunity to kill me and chose not to." Corso cleared his throat. "In return . . ."—he paused—"in return, I promised, if I survived, I would tell you what he had to say." Corso pulled a worn piece of paper from his pants pocket. He took a moment to scan it before he looked up at the sea of cameras again. "He wanted you to know that his name was Roderick Holmes and that he'd been a policeman in the Indian state of . . . I hope I'm pronouncing this right, . . . Madhya Pradesh. That all he ever wanted to do was to help his people. That he'd loved a girl since they were children. That they'd married and had two girls of their own." Corso paused and ran his eyes over the crowd. "When the Bhopal tragedy happened, he volunteered to be transferred to the area. He wanted to help his people. The government insisted

the danger was over. That decision cost him everything. His wife, his children, everything." The crowd
was still now, standing at rapt attention. "His wife died
giving birth to something that looked like a lump of
coal. His daughters died of breast cancer before they
even had breasts." Corso tried to make eye contact with
all of them. "He wanted me to tell you that his only regret"—he paused and took a deep breath—"his only
regret was that he wasn't able to kill every single one
of you."

Corso folded the paper, put it back into his pocket
and strode away amid a rush of shouted questions.

As promised, a police cruiser waited just inside the
gate. Corso opened the passenger door and slid into the
front seat next to the big African-American cop who
sat behind the wheel.

"Where to?" the cop wanted to know.

"The airport," Corso said.

56

"He's expecting me."

The pair of marine MPs manning the front desk looked Corso over like a duty roster. If their expressions were any indication, he had been found, in some way, seriously substandard. The one sitting down reached for the phone, then changed his mind. He nodded at the one standing at attention, who, without further prompting, did a clean left face and began to march down the hall.

"Have a seat," said the marine. The phone rang. "Yes sir . . . no sir."

Corso looked out through the glass doors, over the sidewalks toward the parking lot where he'd left the rented Chevy Malibu. He'd passed through three checkpoints, so they must have known he was coming, making him wonder what this final hoopla was all about.

Huge concrete planters, overflowing with fall flowers, were spread over the forty yards leading to the front doors. The sky was without clouds and azure blue. A perfect fall day on the East Coast. The smell of leaves floating in the air. Just a touch of winter on the tip of your nose when you walked.

"Sir."

Corso looked up.

"If you'll follow me, please."

Corso grabbed the briefcase he'd bought at the airport and followed the marine down the long polished hall, to the next to the last office on the right. The marine moved to the side but made no move to open the door.

Corso nodded his thanks and stepped inside. Government issue top-of-the-line office complete with flag set in the corner. Pictures of the guy behind the desk posing with an impressive array of dignitaries, including the head man, just down the road in D.C.

"I don't believe we've met," Colonel Hines said.

"I've seen you on TV."

"And I, you." He gestured toward a chair on the far side of the room, under the window. Corso shook his head.

"If you don't mind, I'll stand."

The decision seemed to force Hines to reevaluate. He looked Corso over like a used car. "Well then, you mentioned David Reubens."

"Yes," Corso said.

"I'm not sure I'm familiar with the name. I—"

Corso cut him off. "If you weren't familiar with the name I wouldn't be standing here." He set the edge of the briefcase on the desk, popped the latches and pulled out the manila envelope. When Hines made no move to take it from his hands, Corso dropped it on the desk. "I'm just the messenger boy, Colonel. All I volunteered to do was bring you that envelope." He snapped the briefcase closed. "My job is done."

Hines picked up the envelope, looked up at Corso. "Have you seen this?"

Corso said he had. "And I'm betting there's a lot more of those where that came from."

Hines slid the photo from the envelope. While the colonel's face never moved as he gazed at the image, Corso watched his blood drain into his neck. Hines threw a glance at the shredder on the far side of the room, then looked up. "And what am I supposed to make of this?"

Corso thought it over. "I hear your father-in-law's about to retire from the Joint Chiefs." Hines made a "so what" motion with his hand. "I think the idea is you do what's right here. That you don't embarrass anyone any more than necessary."

"And what would that be?"

"That's entirely up to you."

Blood had returned to his cheeks. He got to his feet. "You don't understand."

"I don't want to," Corso said quickly.

"These people we've put in charge of our safety . . . they're a . . . a . . . bunch of bureaucrats—joke . . . a bunch of idiots not prepared for anything." Hines's voice rose. "It's a joke . . . they're not ready for what's coming. They just play at it so the public feels better. Nothing short of a disaster is ever going to shake them out of their stupidity. You know why?"

Corso didn't answer. Hines didn't care.

"Because we're the most arrogant people on earth. Because it's never happened here. Wars happen other places. Devastations happen somewhere else, but never here. Closest they ever get is television." He waved a disgusted hand. "It's just the way it is. Nobody wants to be inconvenienced."

By that time, Corso was back in the hall. Backlit by the front doors, the floor was shiny as a mirror as he strode to the security desk. "Could you please open the briefcase, sir?" said the sitter. Corso complied. If the sight of the totally empty interior was unusual, he didn't let on. "Thank you, sir," was all he said.

Under different circumstances, the ride to the airport could have been pleasant. Fall foliage was in full swing. A thousand shades of red and brown and yellow covered the low hills, but Corso hardly noticed. He spent the drive wondering if the woman would be as accurate about the colonel's character as she'd been about his. If he'd known the answer was to be so shortly forthcoming, he might have looked at the trees.

An hour later, he was sitting in a cracked plastic chair waiting for his flight. CNN ran on the overhead tube. Closed captioned. "Reports from Fort Detrick tell CNN that Colonel David Hines, former director of the U.S. Army Medical Research Institute of Infectious Diseases, has apparently committed suicide by gunshot. Sources say . . ."

Corso got to his feet. First class was boarding. He fished the boarding pass from his pocket and walked over to the gate. The woman smiled. "And how are you today, sir?" she inquired.

Corso didn't answer.

57

C orso opened the damp envelope.

Dear Frank,

If you're reading this, I guess you must have survived, as I prayed so hard you would. Like you always said, "God protects fools and drunks, and only the good die young."

I've had a lot of time to think lately. Time to go back over my life and sort of take stock of where I've been and where I'm going, if you know what I mean. All I know for sure is that my dreams haven't come true. That everything I grew up wanting has somehow slipped away leaving me somewhere I never imagined being. It's hard to describe exactly what I'm saying. As a matter of fact, I'm not sure I know myself.

Anyway, I've decided to go away. Start over someplace new, maybe with a new set of dreams, hopefully with a new set of results. I don't know what I want. All I know is that this isn't it. I've sold the house, closed my studio and left without telling anyone but you. Wish me well. I'll think of you often.

Please, Frank, please honor my last request. I know how you are. How you can't stand things being out of your control. So I ask you. Please, if everything we've ever had together means anything to you at all, please don't look for me.

XXX
MEG

A renegade journalist, Frank Corso has been
known to get himself into sticky situations.
But this time . . . the trouble comes
knocking at his door. Dragged in.
Hauled across country. On the run.
Frank Corso finds himself in

NO MAN'S LAND

Available in hardcover
from William Morrow

And no one's going to get
Corso out of it—except himself.

Don't miss this latest thrill ride.

1

"As of this moment, we are holding one hundred sixty-three hostages. Starting at eighteen hundred tonight, I'm going to shoot one of them every six hours until Frank Corso is delivered to me." The hand-held camera shimmied, but the voice never lost its tone of command and the hooded black eyes never wavered.

The picture rolled once and then the screen went blank. Governor James Blaine looked back over his shoulder at Warden Elias Romero. An unasked question hung in the air like artillery smoke.

"His name is Timothy Driver," Elias Romero said. "He's a transfer from the State of Washington. Doing life without . . . for double aggravated murder."

A glimmer of recognition slid across the governor's pouchy face. "The navy guy? The captain?"

"Yes sir," said Romero. "Driver used to be a Navy captain." Romero cleared his throat. "Came home a little early from a cruise. Found his wife flying united with some local guy. Lost it. Got himself a gun and offed them both, right there in his own bed. Blinded another inmate and stabbed a guard during his first week in a Washington prison. The con was a big player in the Aryan Brotherhood. The guard was an old hand . . . popular with the staff. Washington figured it wasn't safe to keep Driver around their system any more . . . so they shipped him to us."

The governor jammed his hands into his suit pants pockets. "How the hell could something like this happen?" he demanded. "Meza Azul is supposed to be . . ." he stopped himself. "As I recall, the design was supposed to prevent something like this from ever taking place."

"Yes sir . . . it was." Romero pointed to the bank of surveillance monitors nearly covering the south wall of the security office. The screens were blank and black. Romero cleared his throat. "We've got the last minute and forty-five seconds of tape before Driver turned the security system off. It's quite . . ."

"Let me see it," the governor interrupted.

Romero crossed the room, jabbed at several buttons and then stood aside, allowing the governor to belly up to the monitor. White static filled the large central screen.

"It's quite graphic," Romero warned.

"I'm a big boy," the governor assured him.

The picture appeared. Shot from above. Somebody in a guard's uniform putting an electronic key into what appeared to be an elevator door. The figure pocketed the key and bounced his eyes around all four walls before removing something from his inside jacket pocket and turning his back on the camera for a full thirty seconds. "It's Driver in a guard's uniform," Romero said. On screen, Driver had straightened up and was poking his index finger at the keyboard on the wall as Romero narrated. "He just used a security key in the elevator to the control module, then . . ." he raised his hands in despair. "And then somehow or other he disabled the fingerprint recognition technology."

"Say again."

Romero reached around the governor and pushed the stop button.

"On any given day, only five men have access to the central elevator. "The pod operator, who you're about to see in a minute and the four senior duty officers." He dropped his hands to his sides. "He found some way around it." He moved quickly to the console. The figure started to move again. "Look. He's punching in the security code."

On screen, the door slid open. Driver stepped inside and momentarily disappeared.

Blaine's face was red now. "How in God's name did a prisoner get hold of any of that?" the governor sputtered. "A uniform . . ." He waved a large liver spotted hand. ". . . the security code. How could . . ."

Romero merely shook his head, refusing to speculate. He stuck to the facts.

The picture cut to the interior of the elevator where the man in blue stood calmly in the center of the car, hands folded in front of him, bored expression on his face.

"Driver had an appointment for a medical checkup. We're guessing he somehow overpowered the team we sent for him." Romero shrugged and swallowed hard. "Somehow or other, he must have . . ." Romero searched for a word. ". . . he must have *induced* the guard sergeant to part with the security code."

"And the fingerprint identification?"

"No idea."

The two men passed nervous glances as the picture

cut to the interior of the control module, where an African-American man in a starched white shirt swiveled his chair, turning to face the elevator door, just in time for the man in blue to step inside and point to the bank of security monitors. "Check sixty-three," he said in a command voice.

Without a word, the man in white turned his back on the closing elevator door and began running his fingers over his keyboard. Whatever was supposed to appear on monitor sixty-three would remain forever a mystery as Driver looped what appeared to be a length of thin wire around the other man's neck, made a sudden twist at the nape and began to pull with sufficient force to lift the man in white from the chair. His fingers clawed at his throat and his eyes tried to burst from their sockets, as rivulets of blood began to pour down over the white shirt with the Randall Corporation logo on the pocket, as he began to convulse, his legs beating time on the hard stone floor, his open mouth spewing . . .

James Blaine turned his face away. While the governor was busy retaining his lunch, Romero reached around him and pushed the stop button. Silence filled the room like dirty water.

"This wasn't supposed to be possible," James Blaine choked out.

Elias Romero kept his face as hard as stone. "Yes sir," was all he dared to say.

The governor was right. From day one, Meza Azul, Arizona, had been designed to hold the worst collection of criminals in the United States. Worse yet, the prison was the centerpiece of an entire community whose very existence owed itself to the twin notions that Meza Azul was one hundred percent escape-proof and that incarceration could be a highly profitable enterprise.

Unlike many of its predecessors, MA, as the residents liked to call it, had not started life as one of those quaint little mining communities, wedged high among the jagged sandstone and granite spires of the nearby San Cristobel Mountains or as one of those dust-covered stage stops masquerading as ghost towns down on the valley floor.

No . . . the privatization of the Arizona Department of Corrections had led to a complete rethinking regarding the placement and staffing of new prisons. While the state had preferred to use the opportunity to revitalize one of these long dead towns, private enterprise had quickly recognized the folly of this approach.

First and foremost, to take on an existing town was to take on its residents, many of whom, it was sad to say, were ill-suited to the rigors of employment in a modern maximum security prison. While the initial report to the state attorney general had used such terms as "trainability" and "technological recidivism" to describe the problem with the locals, it was generally understood that what they meant was that the kind of folks who chose to shrink from progress, the kind of iconoclasts who stay behind when the circus moves on were generally either too smart, too stupid or too lazy to be of any use to a dynamic new enterprise such as the Randall Corporation had in mind.

Of course they couldn't come right out and say something like that, so they couched their recommendations in more positive terms such as "family friendly" and "self containment," and thus Meza Azul, Arizona had been created.

Truckers along I 506 swore the facility had been

born overnight, cut from a single piece of cloth and dropped whole onto the desert floor, prison, houses, school, post office, golf course, movie theater, swimming pool, palm trees and all. Badda Bing. Gone today. Here tomorrow. Welcome to the twenty-first century.

For the past seven and a half years, the State of Arizona's cut from the Meza Azul Correctional Facility had been the difference between profit and loss, between surplus and deficit and was regularly mentioned by the governor as being emblematic of the imaginative fiscal policy with which he had brought the state back from the precipice of financial ruin.

James Blaine had no doubts. Spin doctors be damned. No way he could distance himself from Meza Azul. This was his baby, and the longer it went on, the worse it was going to be for his chances of re-election.

"What now?" the governor demanded.

"We've got FBI negotiators on the way." Romero checked his watch. "They should be here by six tonight." His big brown eyes rolled over the governor. Waiting. Not wanting to be the one who asked the question. Ten seconds passed before the question asked itself.

"You think we can handle this on our own?" Blaine asked.

Romero shrugged. "Probably not."

"We've got over eighty State Patrol officers on the scene right now."

"Driver's opened two-hundred forty of the cells. Mostly in Cellblock D. The bikers. Maybe some of the Mexican Mafia too. We had to put some of the Hispanic overflow in with the bikers."

The Bikers owned the south half of D Building. The

African American Congress had the north half. The Mexican Mafia and the skinhead Nazis shared B Building. The Bikers would have preferred to live with the Mexicans, but there was no way you could put the Nazis and the Africans in together. The Mexicans hated the Nazis, thought they were the biggest scum-sucking maggots on the planet. They'd have rather lived with either the Africans or the Bikers, but there was no way you could put the Nazis in with the Bikers. In addition to seeing the Nazis as mutants and as a disgrace to the white race, the Bikers also hated them for horning in on the meth-amphetamine business, both inside and outside the walls, and, most of all, they hated the skinheads for besmirching their much beloved Nazi insignia.

The governor winced and ran a hand over his face. Before he could speak, Romero went on. "They've got hold of the armory," he said.

"Which means what?"

Romero had to force the words out of his mouth. "Which means they've got access to every kind of automatic weapon available on the planet." He hesitated. Took a deep breath. "And about three million rounds of ammunition."

James Blaine ran a hand through his hair and turned away. He could feel how thin his hair had become in recent years. He'd once had "presidential hair." That's what they'd called it, "presidential hair."

A knock sounded on the door. Neither man spoke. The door opened a crack.

Romero's executive assistant Iris Cruz looked from the warden to the governor and back. She was thirty, twelve years his junior, her once hour-glass figure turning into something more like a time clock. They'd been sleeping together for the past nineteen months. Ever since Iris's husband Estoban had tired of his life in America and returned to Mexico. Estoban's shadow was still in the yard when Romero made his intentions clear. He'd wanted to for a long time, but had resisted. Iris had known from the beginning. Women knew these kinds of things. Just like they knew when a man was never going to leave his big fat wife like he'd been claiming he was going to do all these months. Sometimes women would block it out for a while, but they knew. They always knew.

"I got that book you wanted," she said, without making eye contact.

Romero crossed the room in four quick strides, plucked the book from Cruz's manicured fingers and closed the door. He stood for a moment looking down at the book's cover, then flipped it over and perused the picture on the back before opening the back cover and reading the flap copy.

"What have we got?" the governor wanted to know.

"It's a book by Frank Corso." He held up the cover so Blaine could see. *Red Tide. A Novel of Passion by Frank Corso.* "It's the book he wrote about Driver." The governor started his way. "Says Corso lives on a boat somewhere in the Seattle area," Romero said.

"Call Seattle," Blaine said. "Get this Corso guy on the way." He blew out a huge breath. "I'm calling out the National Guard."